NEWMARKET

A YEAR AT THE HOME OF HORSERACING

NEWMARKET

A YEAR AT THE HOME OF HORSERACING

John Carter

Published in Great Britain by
SportsBooks Limited
PO Box 422
Cheltenham
GL50 2YN
Tel: 01242 256755
email: info@sportsbooks.ltd.uk
www.sportsbooks.ltd.uk

All photographs by Trevor Jones, Thoroughbred Photography,
except for those on pages 3, 10 and 11 which are courtesy of the National Horseracing Museum.

Cover design by Alan Hunns, alan@hunnsgraphics.demon.co.uk

A catalogue record for this book is available from
the British Library.

ISBN 978 1899807 62 8

Printed and bound in China by 1010 Printing International Limited

DEDICATION

To Dad and my girls; Mum, Paula and Elisha

ACKNOWLEDGEMENTS

So much help, so many people to thank.

Firstly I must thank all the subjects in this book upon whom the chapters are based. They all shared their time, knowledge and views with unfailing patience and good grace. To them all, thanks. It was a pleasure to work with each of you. My enjoyment of the 2007 season – and all the future ones – has been enriched because I have a vicarious interest in your fortunes. Good luck.

In addition there were others in the racing industry who helped: David Bradley, Paul and Sue D'Arcy, Laura Green, Colin Harris, Gill Jones, Kim Leet, Sally Noseda, Jonathan Powell, Kate Turner. Above all thanks to Alistair Haggis, the Public Relations Director at Newmarket Racecourses, who met all my 'just one more favour' requests with unfailing enthusiasm and efficiency.

To sports-writers, Frank Keating and Dudley Doust, thanks for your inspiration. Thanks to my publisher, Randall Northam, for supporting the concept and resisting any urge to "cull" my manuscript – and to Trevor Jones for the photographs which illuminate it.

Finally, and most importantly, heartfelt thanks for the unfailing love and support of my family. Particularly my Mum and Dad, my wife, Paula, and my little daughter, Elisha ("come on the red one"). They make it all worthwhile.

CONTENTS

FOREWORD

When my father sent me to Newmarket in July 1985 it was like landing on another planet. I couldn't speak English, I was just 14 and around my neck was an identification tag so that someone from Luca Cumani's stables could recognise me at Luton Airport.

I was straight to work, and riding out the next morning the vast size of the place and the amazing amount of horses we could see on the heath was overwhelming.

I was incredibly lonely in this strange racing town, so different from the bright lights of Milan where I was brought up. Most nights for the first few months in my digs in the Bury road I would cry myself to sleep in a room hardly bigger than a broom cupboard. In those early weeks it felt more like a prison than a refuge.

I was so homesick that given half a chance I would have run away and caught the first plane back to Italy but for the certain knowledge that my dad would send me straight back again to Newmarket.

Luca has said I was pretty wild in those early days. He is on record as stating I was badly in need of a firm hand to straighten me out. I don't remember it that way. I'll admit that might have been the case a few years later but until I found my feet in Newmarket I was naive and so quiet nobody would believe it now. I reckon for the first six months I was the best, most hard-working apprentice in his yard.

In the early days I used to cycle to work on a bike that cost me £80. It was a tough start in an alien environment so far from my family. I used to be so hard up at the end of the week I'd help out in Cuthie Suttle's little betting shop in the afternoons to supplement my wages.

I've now lived in or near the town for more than half my life. Eventually I came to love the rhythms of the place, the early season rituals as we tried out the best horses on the gallops, the long journeys by car day after day to distant racecourses and arriving back in the middle of the night before starting the same old routine on the heath a few hours later.

Newmarket's two racecourses have provided me with a lot of my best days in the saddle. One I shall always remember was in May 1989 in the Coral Bookmakers handicap shown live on TV. I was a mad keen apprentice and I was riding a horse called *Didicoy*. My horse was well backed and I produced him fast and late to catch *Hafir* on the line. I felt that was a massive moment for me. Half an hour later I managed a second winner on *Khaydara*. I was on my way.

My links with Godolphin have brought me dozens of Group 1 winners. *Mark of Esteem*'s hard-earned success in the 1996 2000 Guineas was one I treasure. Because the finish was so tight three of us had to wait out on the course, circling round and round, until the result was announced. When *Mark of Esteem*'s number was called first I leaped excitedly into the air, landing in the arms of our travelling head lad John Davis.

It was just a natural expression of enthusiasm that I'd won the same famous race which my father had twice captured in the seventies but that moment of instinctive delight cost me a £500 fine for making illegal contact with John before I weighed in!

The punishment didn't end there. The three jockeys involved in the finish picked up bans for whip offences. Jason Weaver got two days, Philip Robinson four and I was stunned to be suspended for eight days. I felt it ridiculous but a sign of the times. I was censured for doing my job though eight days would have felt much longer if we'd been beaten.

Each year jockeys enjoy the bonus of racing on the July course during the summer. Like most regulars I welcomed the big improvements to the facilities introduced in 2007. Sometimes as I canter down to the start on the July course I look across to the point near the Devil's Dyke where my life almost ended in a plane crash on a bleak summer's day seven years ago.

And I count my blessings that I managed to scramble away from the blazing wreckage with the help of Ray Cochrane who is now my agent.

Frankie Dettori

PREFACE

In order to explain why this book has been written I need to strike a personal note. I took to horseracing as a child and have had an affection for it ever since. At six feet tall, nature had clearly decided emulating Lester Piggott would be impossible so my sports became cricket, football and golf. However, when driving through the outskirts of Newmarket towards business meetings in London I enjoyed glimpsing horses on the gallops. The town just had something: atmosphere, history, a certain feel that was attractive and alluring.

I got a similar buzz each time I went racing there as the carousel of colour raced past towards the winning post with the blur of the racing silks, the thunder of the horses' hooves and the urging of the punters.

In 2005, I shadowed Newmarket's clerk of the course at the spring meeting for a magazine article. It was then I decided to try and enter their world for a longer period.

The poet Francis Hope once wrote of his eagerness to travel:

Then, forehead against the pane, I suddenly feel
The longing open-armed behind the bone,
To drown myself in other worlds, to steal
All lives, all times, all countries not my own.

My "longing" was to "drown myself" in the community of Newmarket and to get to know some of the characters – the jockeys, the trainers, the owners, the stable lads – to learn more about what they do, how they do it and what it is about this town and the sport that attracts them.

With Newmarket Racecourses' support that is exactly what happened and what a fascinating experience it has been. The people who inhabit Newmarket are a remarkable bunch. When first discussing the potential for this book with the public relations director at Newmarket, Alistair Haggis, I asked whether he thought there were sufficient characters to make it an interesting read. His response was to smile. Now I know why. The town has "characters" aplenty – but as well as character there is also professionalism and graft, talent and ambition. It was an education to follow them.

Finally, some words on structure. After picking who to follow through the 2007 season I resisted any temptation to gravitate towards others who were enjoying greater success. I wanted to give a true flavour of racing's ups and downs and if that involved more downs than ups then I would take the hit in the name of authenticity.

Each chapter has an introduction, the main text – usually against a backcloth of a key day in the subject's calendar – and, at the end of the book, "End of Term", the story of Champions' Day, documents how the season panned out for each of them. It ties up the loose ends.

Of course one hundred thousand words does not tell the entire story. I'm sure there are other people in Newmarket and the racing industry who have equally fascinating stories to tell. In addition there are organisations located within the town – Tattersalls, The Jockey Club, The British Racing School and The National Stud to name but four – which warrant books on their own, but receive little mention in this particular one.

Nevertheless I have no doubts my objective has been met. It was a year, an experience, I shall never forget – there are few better "worlds" to "drown" in than the home of the horse.

John Carter

The Pre-parade at
the July course.

ONE

HQ'S HERITAGE

"PIGGOTT RODE THE HORSE TO WHAT TURNED OUT TO BE HIS LAST
WINNER IN A CLASSIC. THE NOISE OF THE CROWD WAS
AMAZING. SOME DAYS LATER I WAS WALKING DOWN
NEWMARKET HIGH STREET, STILL ON AN ADRENALIN
HIGH, AND WHO SHOULD I BUMP INTO BUT PIGGOTT
HIMSELF. OF COURSE I WAS MUCH TOO MUCH IN AWE
TO SPEAK TO HIM BUT THAT'S ALL PART OF
NEWMARKET – THAT THESE LEGENDS LIVE IN THE COMMUNITY."

THE NATIONAL HORSERACING MUSEUM has been located on Newmarket high street since 1983. It provides an informative and fascinating insight into the history and spirit of horseracing and is well worth a visit. In addition to the type of features found at most museums, they have temporary exhibitions, a shop and a café as well the practical gallery, where you can have a hands-on experience of horseracing. You can, for instance, ride a race on "Legless", the resident riding simulator, which will increase your respect for the fitness of professional jockeys.

However, the premises are limited and when we first spoke the curator Graham Snelling was keen to be on the move. He may specialise in delving into the past but he is also an ambitious man who recognises the need to look to the future. He wants the museum to be invigorated by a smarter appearance, room to grow, new exhibits and experiences and a greater use of modern technology.

This is much-needed because the museum loses money each year even though it is gifted the current premises on a peppercorn rent from next-door neighbours, the Jockey Club. The museum generates funds by charging admission and from the on-site shop and café but it is an independent museum with charitable status and little in the way of sponsorship.

When we spoke hope was on the horizon. There was a possibility that they might be able to re-house the collections in the Palace House stables where there would be scope for expansion. Certainly Snelling wanted to keep the museum in the town on the basis that, "if it was somewhere else you wouldn't get the unique history of Newmarket as a backdrop. The town and all that goes on with regard to horses and racing is also an exhibit."

The museum, for instance, organises guided tours to nearby stud farms, trainers and the gallops.

Graham Snelling *The Curator*

So in December 2006 that was Snelling's primary aim for the following year: to seek clarity on the museum's future and hopefully begin the move from one building to another. I sensed that from his point of view the sooner progress was made the better. It would lift a weight from his shoulders.

Anyway, if that was his challenge, then mine was to try to get a feel for the history and tradition of the town and its community. There needed to be a bridge in my mind between past and present because it is impossible to appreciate one without the other.

Snelling turned out to be an excellent man to help.

Newmarket sits on the Suffolk/Cambridgeshire border, sixty-five miles north of London and encircled by Ely, Cambridge and Bury St Edmunds. Its high street was bombed during the Second World War and has never really recovered its former glory. To the untrained eye Newmarket could be viewed with disinterest; an unremarkable East Anglian market town, unworthy of a detour off the A14.

However, there is one feature that gives it status and vibrancy: its role as the headquarters of horseracing. First and foremost it boasts the two racecourses: the Nat West Rowley Mile (for spring and autumn meetings) and the July Courses (for the summer). They are among British racing's elite venues along with courses such as Epsom, Ascot, Cheltenham and Aintree. They host more than fifty group and listed races each year, more than at any other British racecourse, including two of the five "classic" flat races. Of course that alone is not enough to justify the "home of horseracing" billing. There are fifty-nine other racecourses in Britain, from Perth in the north to Newton Abbot in the south. But nowhere else can claim that title.

It is primarily the community that inhabits Newmarket that makes it so special. In addition to the race venues it is home to seventy trainers – not to mention the stable lads and lasses who work there – sixty stud farms and the undoubted stars: three thousand thoroughbred racehorses. And there is quality as well as quantity. The top racehorses, the top trainers, the top stud farms. Newmarket is the best place to find them.

It also houses several of racing's governing bodies, authorities and organisations which, in addition to the National Horseracing Museum include:

Tattersalls Park Paddocks, the world's most famous bloodstock auctioneers. Some of the greatest thoroughbreds in racing have been sold here for thousands of guineas.

The Jockey Club, which arrived in Newmarket in 1752 and was able to regulate racing because it gradually bought up the land in the area. Their rules became adopted throughout the country and emulated worldwide.

And the British Racing School – a purpose-built training facility for the development of jockeys.

In total, seventy per cent of the town's working population works directly or indirectly in the racing industry. There are saddlers, vets, blacksmiths, racecourse officials, groundsmen and administrators. Others work in the opulent breeding studs and more still in the stables dotted around the town centre. Certainly the dynamics of Newmarket are unique. Many members of the racing community socialise, share a love of horses and the sporting spectacle of race days – and would defend each other to the hilt to outsiders. As a result the town lives and breathes horseracing. It smells of horseracing.

However, as in a university town, most are not natives. They moved here to pursue their chosen profession and many are in competition with each other: trainers guard secrets and court prospective owners; jockeys try to get the best rides; stable lads move around for a better wage. So although bonds and friendships do blossom it can also be highly competitive.

In addition the town contains a wide range of wealth and status. There are some – a number of trainers and breeders for instance – who are prosperous and influential, often coming from privileged backgrounds; whilst stable lads and lasses are comparatively poorly paid. It has been this way for nearly four centuries.

Another unique feature of the town are the two thousand eight hundred acres of training grounds on the easily accessible heath. Every morning the horses wend their way from stable to gallops, helped by special routes, their own traffic lights and right of way ahead of cars. Morning rush hour in the town is unlike any other. The pecking order is clear and the thoroughbreds are at the top of it.

The training grounds are split into two sides. Along the

Fred Archer, one of Graham Snelling's top three jockeys of all time.

Cambridge Road is the flat and sweeping racecourse side while the Bury side is prettier with its trees and hills. There is a gallop available for all types, regardless of the stage of the race-day preparation, whether it be Warren Hill, Bury Hill, Side Hill, Long Hill or the Limekilns which features a left-handed turn that simulates Epsom Downs. In total there are fifty-seven miles of turf gallops and canters as well as all-weather alternatives; all paid for by owners who contribute around £1.25 million a year by paying a Heath Tax for each horse. They do so because it provides unparalleled sprinting ground and second-to-none facilities.

Aesthetically, too, there can be no doubt that it is money well spent. Whoever you speak to in Newmarket acknowledges the feel-good factor that accompanies a trip to the gallops. Photographer, Trevor Jones, who certainly knows a decent picture when he sees it, says: "Newmarket in the early morning with the horses on the gallops is terrific". Michael Prosser, clerk of the course at the racecourses, considers Warren Hill one of his favourite places on earth. He says: "When the season is just kicking off and you get an early spring morning with the horses galloping down Warren Hill then that is just wonderful".

And so on. Truth is, whoever you speak to says much the same. If there is one picture postcard of Newmarket to store in the mind then this is it. Milky, misty dawns where the colours on the flat East Anglian heathland gradually grow richer, illuminating strings of thoroughbreds being put through their paces by their work riders. There are colts and fillies; bays and chestnuts; all finely tuned, haughty looking and purposeful, with little to identify them other than the rugs that bear their trainer's initials. Newmarket is essentially a working town that just happens to have the racehorse as its core industry. But for those who search for romance – and indeed a heart and soul – then the heath is where to find it.

It has always been thus. As far back as the seventeenth century the reigning monarch, Charles II – of whom much more later – used to sit perched at the top of Warren Hill in a little wooden kiosk known as "The King's Chair" to observe the horses at exercise. And to fully understand and appreciate Newmarket it is important to look back even before Charles II; to appreciate the town not just as it is in the twenty-first century but how it has evolved over the past four hundred years.

To obtain that historical perspective there is no one better to speak to than Graham Snelling. Snelling is tall, slim, in his forties, with a full head of grey hair. He is a pleasant, mild-mannered man with a stronger sense of humour and more opinions than you might expect of your common or garden museum curator.

That said he is, by nature, a bookworm. He loves history, studied it at A level and has made a career out of it ever since, working at the Imperial War Museum at Duxford, the British Museum in London and the Art Gallery and

Museum in Cheltenham before coming to Newmarket.

Born in Cambridge, he grew up supporting the local football team, but though he often visited Newmarket there was no early enthusiasm for racing. Indeed he still suffers an allergic reaction to horses and the only claim to racing pedigree in his family is that his great-grandfather was a policeman at Epsom Downs on the day in 1913 when suffragette Emily Davison threw herself under George Vs horse, *Anmer*, during the Derby and was killed.

But Snelling always had a desire to twin his interests of sport and history and he first became interested in racing twenty years ago when he took over as display officer at the Art Gallery and Museum in Cheltenham.

He says: "Cheltenham is a racing town and during Gold Cup week it had a wonderful atmosphere. There was a massive influx of genuine racing fans, many of them Irish, who enjoyed themselves so much that I remember that some pubs often ran out of Guinness. I began to go horseracing, gambled a bit and, above all, became hooked on the atmosphere of it all. And I became inspired when the museum ran an exhibition of the famous Victorian jockey, Fred Archer."

Since moving back to East Anglia and the National Horseracing Museum fourteen years ago he has become responsible for creating collections that inform and capture the imagination of visitors. To that end he has spent countless hours in the library above the museum swotting up on the history, doing the hard yards of research, building knowledge and answering nearly four hundred racing enquiries a year. It was up there, above the museum, in one of several small, dimly lit, book-filled offices that Snelling patiently explained over several cups of coffee how it was in Newmarket in the early days and how it has come to be. Occasionally he scuttled off to find the relevant book to check his facts and figures – because inaccuracies can never be countenanced – but in truth it was more out of modesty than need. He demonstrated an impressive knowledge of his subject.

He started his tour de force: "Newmarket didn't invent horse-racing. That dates back elsewhere in Britain to the Romans and probably back to the Bronze Age. There are records of horseracing in the twelfth century, when it's known to have taken place on public holidays in London and at Chester on Shrove Tuesday. The history of organised racing in Britain goes back to the seventeenth century and Newmarket's involvement is largely thanks to three generations of royalty: James I, Charles I and Charles II.

"It began with James I's arrival from Scotland in 1603; a fortuitous meeting of place, person and circumstance. He was forced to stay overnight by heavy fog and recognised that the landscape and heath suited his equestrian interests. Although those interests centred mainly on hunting and hawking, he also owned racehorses and attended races here in 1619. From this time the destiny of Newmarket moved along a different path.

When his normal watering hole, the Griffin pub, proved inadequate he had a house built for his greater comfort. Indeed so 'comfortable' was he that the House of Commons petitioned him to concentrate more of his time in running the country.

"By now public races had begun to be set up all over England. Many of the events were held at 'Bell Courses' which got the name because the prize was usually a silver bell. James' successor Charles I inherited his father's enthusiasm for racing and hunting and was also an excellent horseman. He competed himself and started a series of races known as 'Royal Plates'. During the Civil War he became a prisoner in his palace in Newmarket and in 1649 Parliament ordered his execution. For eleven years Britain was a Republican Commonwealth and during that time all horseracing was banned by Oliver Cromwell.

"However, in 1660, Britain returned to a monarchy and Charles II took to the throne. He travelled to Newmarket each spring and autumn and stayed for weeks at a time, along with a large entourage intent on riotous fun. Lord Macaulay noted that 'it was not uncommon for the whole court and cabinet to go down there, posting in a single day. The streets were alive with colour. Jewellers, Milliners, Players and Fiddlers, venal wits and venal beauties'.

"The first official race to be run under written rules, 'The Town Plate', took place at Newmarket in 1664. Charles II actually rode to victory in the race in 1671 and 1674.

"His connection with Newmarket survives to this day, because the name of the Rowley Mile course comes from his nickname of 'Old Rowley', which in turn came from the name of his favourite horse. The Rowley Mile was one of three courses at Newmarket, the others being the July Course and the Beacon Course, which to this day connects the other two. Had he spent less time in Newmarket – and less time with his famous mistress Nell Gwyn – and more attending to matters of state, Charles II might have enjoyed a longer life. Nevertheless the enthusiasm of royalty for horseracing did wonders for the sport's popularity".

These links remain in the modern era and Snelling digresses to share that he has met aristocracy and members of the royal family. He says: "The Queen has owned horses that have won both the 1000 and 2000 Guineas and is a frequent visitor to both the gallops and the races here at Newmarket. And nine years ago I had the pleasure of taking Princess Anne around the museum. She was very interested, keen to go where she wanted to go and asked lots of detailed questions. She went forty-five minutes over her schedule. It was clear that she shared her mother's passion for racing. It would appear that Prince Charles doesn't quite share this passion. I'd like royalty to retain the interest in horseracing which has been such a tradition in the sport."

Returning to the past, Snelling adds that there were three significant developments through the eighteenth century.

Graham Snelling at the
National Horseracing
Museum

Firstly, Arabian stallions were imported and bred with British mares, resulting in the forefathers of the thoroughbreds racing today. All modern racehorses descend in the male line from three foundation stallions: the *Darley Arabian*, the *Godolphin Arabian* and the *Byerly Turk*. This was first evidenced in awesome physical form when a horse called *Flying Childers* – foaled in 1715 and fathered by the *Darley Arabian* – was brought to Newmarket. Legend seems to suggest that he was not so much a horse as an equine thunderbolt with dynamite in his hooves and wings on his back. He was described as the "fleetest horse that ever ran at Newmarket, or, as generally believed, that was ever bred in the world".

Secondly, in the middle of the century, horseracing became the first regulated sport in Britain with the formation of a governing body, The Jockey Club.

And, thirdly, the end of the century saw the establishment of three of the classic races which are still run today. The St Leger, run over one mile six furlongs and 127 yards in Doncaster, was first run in 1776 and the Oaks and the Derby, both run over one mile and four furlongs in Epsom, began in 1779 and 1780 respectively.

Although Newmarket did not host any of those classics (except during the Second World War when it hosted pretty much all of them with vast crowds in attendance) by now the foundation had been laid and it was establishing itself as the home of the racehorse, filled with trainers and their staff; saddlers, blacksmiths and jockeys.

So, twenty-nine years after the first Derby, Newmarket was well placed to host what was to become the fourth classic. There were twenty-three entries, all contributing one hundred guineas each. This was rounded down and led to the name of the race – the 2000 Guineas, a thoroughbred race for three-year-old colts and fillies run over a distance of one mile on the Rowley Mile.

Five years later, in 1814, a race was run between ten fillies that were entered at a subscription of one hundred guineas each, leading to the name of the 1000 Guineas. It became the fifth and final "classic". Originally the race was run over the Ditch Mile, flatter and easier terrain than the Rowley Mile. It was not until the 1870s that it was moved to its current home.

The early years of both races saw small fields. In 1829 and 1830 the 2000 Guineas was a two-horse race and the 1000 Guineas in 1825 saw the only walkover in classics history. But gradually the fashion moved from head to head two-horse marathons to larger fields, younger horses and shorter distances. And, year by year, the legend of the Guineas has evolved. They are the first classics of each new flat season; springtime curtain raisers and nowadays always contested over the Rowley Mile.

This mile is one of the more famous stretches of racing territory, though it is not universally treated with the reverence to which it may be entitled. A comparison with the seaside golfing links of the Old Course at St Andrews in Scotland is pertinent. Both have attracted criticism as well as praise. Often enthusiasts travel vast distances to play St Andrews but leave disappointed, irritated by all the bad bounces and sideways lies; unable to quite fathom what the fuss is all about. In the same way the Rowley Mile leaves some cold – quite literally. Unchecked winds that seem to blow in from Siberia can make it feel chilly and lacking in atmosphere.

The trick, of course, with both locations, is to appreciate the importance of the past. They are not modern constructions; they are living antiques and all the better for it. St Andrews represents golf as it was played in its infancy. Same stretch of turf, same inclines and slopes, same challenge. And so it is with the Rowley Mile.

Certainly, it does not have the "Pimm's and panama" ambience of its attractive sister, the July Course, a couple of miles away. But bloodstock agent Tom Goff is just one who recognises its place in the history books. He says: "When you stand at the top you can look across the heath and apart from the odd car driving down Cambridge Road the scene with the trees on the far side near the Dyke has been the same for the last three to four hundred years. That's what makes it a remarkable place. It's steeped in history."

It was in Shakespeare's time that the green plot of the Rowley Mile first became a stage for sporting drama and theatre. Little has changed since. The longest straight in racing poses the same challenge to today's horses and riders as it has down the years. So visitors with imagination and a sense of history and tradition can appreciate that the latest batch of thoroughbreds are, almost literally, running in the hoof prints of champions past.

Champions such as:

Sceptre, who in 1902 became the most recent of four fillies to have completed the 1000 and 2000 Guineas double. She also won the Oaks and St Leger.

Hypericum, George VI's filly, won in 1946, the first race back on the Rowley Course after it had been run on the July course during the Second World War.

The great *Nijinsky*, who became the most recent of fifteen winners to complete the classic Triple Crown of 2000 Guineas, Epsom Derby and St Leger in 1970.

Oh So Sharp, who also won three classics by taking the 1000 Guineas, the Oaks and the St Leger in 1985.

And *Brigadier Gerard*, who stormed to 2000 Guineas success in 1971 in an epic finish with *Mill Reef*.

Nor is the strength of Newmarket's racecard reliant on just the two Classic races. There is, for instance, the "Autumn Double" to consider: "The Cambridgeshire" and "The Cesarewitch". The first is a handicap over one mile, one furlong which provides one of the heftiest betting events of the year. It was first run in 1839 along with "The Cesarewitch", which took its name from the heir to the throne of Russia.

The twenty-one-year-old Tsarevich, destined to become Alexander II, paid a visit

Graham Snelling The Curator

to Newmarket and donated £300 to the Jockey Club, which used the gift as prize money for the new race. The contest is a gruelling marathon over two and a quarter miles, starting in one county and finishing in another. Strangely, due to the set-up of the Rowley Mile, almost half of it is run outside of the sight of spectators. It is only in the last ten furlongs that the field emerges into the straight and general visibility.

If the Cesarewitch is one for the out and out stayers then the July Cup is over in the blink of an eye. Run over just six furlongs, it has been contested since 1876 and has remained the centrepiece of Newmarket's July Meeting as well as one of Europe three main sprints. Finally the Dewhurst Stakes deserves a mention. This is the race for the precocious two-year-olds who are likely to really put their names in lights the following season. To illustrate the point, the first winner of "The Dewhurst" was *Kisber* in 1875 and he went on to win the Derby the next year.

These prestigious races have been cornerstones of the racing calendar at Newmarket for more than a century. But if these cornerstones and those of the Rowley Mile and July Courses are unchanged then everything that surrounds them has certainly altered – and early racing differed greatly from its modern equivalent.

Firstly, says Snelling, "the horses would have been exercised and fed differently. Few of the sophisticated modern-day training techniques would have been used. For instance the trainers of the nineteenth century tended

to make their horses gallop in heavy clothing. They were kept heavily rugged in heated, non-ventilated stables and carefully kept out of draughts.

"By the start of the nineteenth century proper bookmakers were beginning to evolve and have their influence. This played a part in an increase in skulduggery with poisoning of

The Rowley Mile in the 1890s.

horses by rival owners, trainers, bookmakers and gamblers. Of course there was no testing."

Snelling has evidence to support his words: between 1809 and 1811 four racehorses died and others became very sick after drinking water poisoned with arsenic from a trough on Newmarket heath. Daniel Dawson, a tout who hid in bushes on the heath watching trials and reporting back to bookmakers, was found guilty and hanged in front of fifteen thousand spectators. The bookmakers behind the plots got away scot free.

Another difference was in the size and nature of the crowds. "They would have been larger than today," Snelling says. "They would have included the aristocrats and the wealthy from London who dodged the highwaymen to travel to Newmarket by horse, carriage or train. And also a camp of 'hangers-on' who fed upon their crumbs so to speak. There would also have been pickpocketing and many people would be selling their wares, different foods and drinks, as well as cockerel fighting and other sideshows.

"Facilities for those spectators were primitive. There was a stand constructed in the time of Charles II but obviously nothing like the Millennium Grandstand. Partly because of these limited viewing facilities, when a race was begun by the starter's shout of 'go!', spectators were able to ride chaotically down the racetrack after the horses and there were sometimes as many as a thousand people on horseback pursuing the field towards the finish. Little wonder that in 1802 a spectator fell, was trampled on and brought down the horse behind him which died. It was chaos.

"Towards the middle of the century a starting flag was introduced and the wholesale cavalry charge of spectators was banned.

"In those days, of course, what we would now call 'media coverage' would have been limited. Photographs were not invented at that stage, so any images of the race would have been painted. At that stage television coverage was a long way distant.

"And the jockeys would have weighed less. A fourteen-year-old called Kitchener rode in the Chester Cup in 1844 and weighed just two stones twelve pounds. I saw his racing silks and they were like baby clothes. Jockeys were so indebted to the trainers that they would 'waste' in what we would now see as a dangerous way. Equally dangerous was the lack of protection – no helmets and none of the chest guards that modern jockeys wear."

Snelling becomes most animated when he starts talking about jockeys. Whilst doffing a historical cap in the direction of Francis Buckle and Sir Gordon Richards he rates Fred Archer, Lester Piggott and Frankie Dettori as his top three during those two hundred years of Guineas action. And of these three he has a particular soft spot for the man who sparked his interest in horseracing when he constructed an exhibition in his name.

Fred Archer was born near the site of the Cheltenham racecourse in 1857 and became the most successful jockey of the Victorian era. He was champion for thirteen consecutive years until 1886, riding 2,748 winners from 8,084 starts. He won a total of twenty-one classic races, including the Epsom Derby five times. At Newmarket he won the 1000 Guineas in 1875 and 1879 and the 2000 Guineas in 1874, 1879, 1883 and 1885. Though pencil slim, pallid in complexion and buck-toothed, Archer was adored and admired by the English public and gained an almost iconic, David Beckham-like status.

Snelling confirms: "Archer was one of the first sporting heroes. He became an apprentice jockey with the trainer Matthew Dawson at the age of eleven and soon gained respect from Dawson and all involved at the yard for his ability to fearlessly ride the more difficult horses. He was stable jockey between 1874 and 1886 and they made a winning partnership. He had an obsessive desire to win, and if he failed he was very hard on himself. He once put his brother over the rails in a race. He would also go up to the winning owner and ask whether he could ride the horse in the future. So he could be ruthless."

Archer's success was unprecedented and there was a phrase used by London taxi-drivers, "Archer's up and all is well", which meant that as long as Archer was the jockey the horse was certain to be successful. The phrase was the Victorian equivalent of raising a thumb to show that everything is OK.

When Archer won his first race at the age of twelve he weighed just four stone eleven pounds, but by adulthood he stood five foot eight and a half inches tall, very tall for a jockey, particularly in those times. As a result his career became an ongoing, irreconcilable conflict between his talent and the length of his frame. He had to diet far more than other jockeys. To help he drank a purgative known as "Archer's Mixture" that was so strong that a friend was unable to go racing the next day after he had sampled a spoonful.

This wasting had an effect on his health and, after suffering from depression and delirium following the death of his wife in childbirth, he committed suicide by shooting himself. He was just twenty-nine. The news triggered a remarkable outpouring of public grief. On the day it broke, buses in London stopped every few yards so that people could buy an evening paper. The Prince of Wales sent a wreath to the funeral. Newmarket came to a standstill on the day that he was buried alongside his wife and the son, William, who had also died prematurely. Their combined ages totalled just fifty-two years.

Since that sad day there have been many reported sightings of Archer on a ghostly white horse at the Pegasus Stables which he built. Snelling says that it is also said that his ghost haunts Newmarket Heath, that he knows people who state they have had a "ghostly experience" and adds, "many visitors to the horseracing museum say that they feel something eerie about the place".

Perhaps that is little wonder because at the time of writing there is a feature on Archer in the museum which contains the pistol with which he shot himself. Indeed Snelling has taken part in a television programme that sought to establish whether there are genuine psychic phenomena involved. It was unproven but the legend remains…

On the subject of phenomena, even eleven years after his last ride, images of Lester Piggott in the saddle remain easily in the mind: the familiar tight-cheeked, waxwork face, a tall figure riding incredibly short so that his backside sticks high in the air, a style that was subsequently widely adopted.

Piggott had racing in the genes. His father was a jockey and trainer and his grandfather rode the winners of two Grand Nationals. The young Lester won his first race at the age of twelve, standing just four foot six inches and weighing five stone four pounds. He soon became a teenage sensation. He rode to a Derby victory aged eighteen and went on to win eight more. He was also successful at Newmarket, winning the 1000 Guineas twice and the 2000 Guineas five times. Amazingly the first and last victories were forty-six years apart.

Quite apart from the high achievement, Snelling spots other common threads in the careers and psychological make-up of Piggott and Archer.

"They were both tall for jockeys and

Piggott also struggled to keep his weight down to eight stone. Like Archer, Piggott also hated losing and there is a story that in one race Piggott dropped his whip, but snatched one from another jockey. Equally they were both ruthless in trying to get the best rides".

They were less forthcoming in entering the public eye. Piggott lives in Newmarket, has visited the museum and as a result Snelling has met him several times. He says: "He seemed to me to be a modest, shy and self-conscious man. We once persuaded him to open a fete for us but it was clear that he was not keen to speak into the microphone".

Lester Piggott and Tony Hirschfield, the owner of Cheval Court Stud, after *Mont Etoile*, which they co-own, had won at Royal Ascot.

Of course Piggott had long been known in the game for his – shall we say – inclination to look after the pennies. There is a story that when he was a youngster in digs in Newmarket he won a good race and brought home a bunch of flowers for his landlady. She was delighted. At the next rent day Lester's contribution was five shillings short. You're five bob out luv' said his landlady. 'No that was the price of the flowers' said Lester.

Snelling defends him. "We must remember his roots. He was born into a very modest family, just before the Second World War. Even now I believe he makes sure he signs every autograph to a specific person so that the autograph can't be sold on eBay".

Unfortunately the character trait led, in 1987, to a conviction for tax irregularities, three hundred and sixty-six days of imprisonment and the removal of his OBE, an act that caused Piggott great sadness and distress. But he resumed his career as a jockey following his release, leading to victory in Snelling's favourite race at Newmarket.

"It was 1992, the 2000 Guineas, and I was in the stands on a spring afternoon for my first big race since I'd moved to the town. The previous week I'd been listening to BBC Radio Two and Jimmy Young had been encouraging all the housewives to back Piggott on a horse called *Rodrigo de Triano*. Just by his sheer excellence Piggott had done much to expand the popularity of horseracing and he had become known as the housewives' favourite. He had thousands of followers.

"Sure enough Piggott rode the horse to what turned out to be his last winner in a classic. The noise of the crowd was amazing. Some days later I was walking down Newmarket High Street, still on an adrenalin high, and who should I bump into but Piggott himself. Of course I was much too much in awe to speak to him but that's all part of Newmarket – that these legends live in the community".

Another legend who lives near the community – in Stetchworth – is the last man in Snelling's top three – Frankie Dettori. Unlike Archer and Piggott he does not struggle with the public eye. In fact the Italian embraces fame.

Snelling says, "Dettori is selected for his talent and the way that he has promoted the sport. He has marketed his talent very cleverly and has been great for the sport. He has charisma, pizzazz and a touch of the theatrical and has become popular for his outgoing personality as much as his talent. I don't think Archer or Piggott would have appeared on *A Question of Sport*."

He has also visited the museum. "Because Frankie has been financially successful I'm not sure he has quite the same drive as an Archer or Piggott. I think that near-fatal plane crash when the pilot died and he miraculously escaped relatively unscathed, has changed his outlook on life. And of course he's got five children so I am sure he is keen to spend as much time with them as possible."

Frankie Dettori, with that media savvy and globetrotting existence, neatly completes the time travel. It began in the days of William Shakespeare and Sir Walter Raleigh when James I of Scotland made his overnight stop in foggy Newmarket and discovered the heathland.

Four centuries on, horseracing is big-money, big-time sport, fighting for its niche in the entertainment industry. There is wall to wall media coverage, global television audiences and six million visitors to British racecourses each year. So horseracing has developed and evolved. One constant has been the integral role of Newmarket as the spiritual home of the sport; a role that looks assured for a while longer.

TWO

AMBITION AND APPLICATION

"My wife nags me to take Sundays off but I have to be in the yard on a Sunday and I have to be in the yard on Christmas Day and Boxing Day. It means a huge amount to me. Every day if I can have any bearing on our success then it's worth me being here."

MANY PEOPLE WERE GENEROUS in giving their time for this book, none more so than the London-born professional trainer, Jeremy Noseda.

Our association began at the start of the year as he mused over prospects for the season ahead with what I came to recognise as a characteristic enthusiasm and commitment to high achievement.

During a sun-blessed spring, when the flat racing season was moving from trot to canter, I witnessed the training regime as the star thoroughbreds continued their preparation to contest the big prizes.

Then I shadowed him through Sunday 6th May when one of those big prizes, the 1000 Guineas, was contested in front of a global audience of millions.

The day turned out to be a bittersweet experience. During the winter Noseda had been optimistic about the race but warned that racing is nothing if not unpredictable. How right he was. Alas, this knowledge offered him little solace against gross misfortune. In these circumstances shadowing him at close quarters felt uncomfortable – but he is a professional so he got on with the job and devoted his energy and focus into making the best of a bad day. It was an education to witness.

The story of Jeremy Noseda's build-up to the 1000 Guineas was a drama in three parts.

January 2007. An unusually cold day in an unusually mild winter. Office of Jeremy Noseda, Shalfleet Stables, Bury Road, Newmarket.

Ambition. Ambition. Ambition. Read any newspaper or magazine article on Jeremy Noseda and that is the word that keeps featuring. It is clear this is a man of serious intent who has no problem deciding what appears on his wish list.

Ambition: How, at the age of just thirteen,

17

he decided that above all else he wanted to be a professional racehorse trainer.

Ambition: How the brainy teenager turned down five universities, including Cambridge, to pursue that dream.

Ambition: How he declined to move to France to train for Sheikh Mohammed al Maktoum because he wanted to set up a yard in England under his own name.

Ambition: How he gave himself five years to become established in the industry and – once that was achieved – set his sights on an English classic and to begin to emulate the record of his hero, Vincent O'Brien.

So far Noseda has consistently turned ambition into reality. Two thousand and six, his ninth year as a trainer, saw *Sixties Icon* deliver that first classic win in the St Leger and the trainer also enjoyed victory in the Irish 2000 Guineas and two other British group one races.

The table below, based on prize money won in 2006, gives confirmation of Noseda's position in the pecking order of trainers. It shows an outstanding strike rate. His horses were successful in nearly one in five of the races in which they competed.

For most, finishing eighth of the English-based trainers licensed by the Jockey Club (of which around seventy are located in Newmarket) would be cause for serious champagne-flavoured celebration.

Certainly many can only aspire to such riches and be confident of their future. For most the needs are at a more basic level and they live uneasily on the precipice of financial oblivion. If they get the rub of the green each season they can stay afloat; with misfortune they could well go under.

For Noseda, though, eighth is not enough. He wants to be in the top three and slugging it out on equal terms with the likes of Sir Michael Stoute, down the road at Freemason Lodge. At present he is not quite there, kept buoyant by a mixture of graft, acumen, backing and the odd headline-making thoroughbred.

The killer question is: how can he make that quantum leap?

It is a thought that occupies him – not for the first time – as he sits in his office in the middle of the 2006/7 winter and turns his attention to the summer ahead.

The stables themselves are neat and well kept. They smell like stables and look like a place of work; not as plush or glossy as those of Godolphin but businesslike and functional. One of the stable lads described it as "a proper racing yard with old-fashioned values", which, you suspect, is as its owner would want.

Pos	Trainer	Wins	Runners	Success %	Prize Money
1	Sir Michael Stoute	107	487	22	£3,027,295
2	M Johnston	158	1,005	16	£1,868,198
3	B W Hills	103	734	15	£1,741,362
4	R Hannon	127	1,067	12	£1,753,310
5	Saeed bin Suroor	70	247	28	£1,610,204
6	M R Channon	127	1,027	12	£1,548,626
7	B J Meehan	74	532	14	£1,472,261
8	J Noseda	46	249	18	£1,264,719

Jeremy Noseda in
trademark hat.

Jeremy Noseda The Trainer

Noseda's office is situated in the heart of Shalfleet and is the hub of the operation. There are two adjoining rooms. Through French doors he can walk from his office straight into the living room of his house; the other door leads to the work area of his racing secretary (upon whom he is hugely dependent for administrative support) and his bookkeeper.

This arrangement works well because it allows Noseda's work to merge seamlessly with his home life (which is the way he likes it) and not waste commuting time – which is clearly a blessing when the morning alarm rings before dawn breaks.

On the office walls and shelves there are books and handbooks (mainly about racing but some about football), pictures and trophies. There are a small portable television and a vast mirror behind an antique desk upon which there is a large amount of neatly piled paperwork, all of which will need to be reviewed shortly. The thought leaves him cold. He much prefers to be outside with the horses.

He sits behind the desk on a leather chair, again an antique. Despite having grey hair and a demanding job he certainly looks no more than his forty-three years, thanks, perhaps, to plenty of fresh air and a disciplined lifestyle. What is most noticeable in his demeanour is the drive and focus. When he looks at you, his brown eyes are unwavering whether he is listening or talking. He is straightforward and you sense he does not waste time wallowing in self-doubt or dealing with fools.

So he does not agonise too much on why he is not yet at Stoute's level. For him it is about simple mathematics: he just does not train enough horses. "The number of runners in the prize-money table equates to firepower," he explains. "I want a bigger yard and more horses but I haven't found the right place. When I do I'll hopefully move to the next level. But at the moment I can't match Sir Michael Stoute and I can't match Godolphin. If you look at the table everyone that finished above me and the five below all train significantly more horses than I train."

So that is an aim for 2007, to complete his long-running search for new premises – as long as it fits the strict criteria that he has set himself – and so create the potential to increase his firepower.

His sights are also set on the 1000 Guineas, the first classic of the English flat season. "I'm an Englishman and I love England," says the patriot who will not even buy a foreign car. "I trained in America and I could have stayed in America but I came back because I love England. I missed it intensely. To me I'm driven by the desire to win English classics and the Guineas is an English classic."

He certainly has cause for optimism. "*Sander Camillo* is my big hope for the early part of the season," he says, "my big hope for the 1000 Guineas.

"If I arrive there in good nick and it doesn't rain then I think we have got a good chance. One of my biggest dangers is the weather because she loves fast ground. But I'm more than hopeful.

"I may have another two fillies in the race, *Simply Perfect* and *Rahiyah*, but I just feel that *Sander Camillo* has always struck me as being hugely naturally talented. The initial signs are good and I think there's so much more to come. I hope I'm right. The season will tell us.

"Already my mind is focused on when I feel I need to start picking up the tempo with her. Y'know I have a maintenance level now and I've already got dates in my mind – as long as she gives me the right signs – when I want to take her to another level in her training and then the next level, the next level after that and then pieces of 'work'. It's in my mind at this moment, so there's a framework already there. The filly will then tell me if it's right to take those opportunities but if need be I'll change things around because she's a living creature."

Noseda's third ambition underpins his entire philosophy and methodology: simply to coax the maximum from each horse of which it is capable. In some way these words come as a surprise. You might expect a statistical seasonal target such as entering the top five prize-money earners or achieving a certain number of winners but, as he explains, horseracing has too many variables to make predictions with any confidence.

"I would be disappointed not to repeat the five group one victories of 2006," he says, "but it's not an exact science. I could get a virus in the yard and be wiped out for three months. It's a precarious thing and there has to be an element of realism."

Equally he does not want targets to influence the way that he treats the horses.

There is a season-long provisional itinerary for each one that sets out the most appropriate races for them to contest – but always with a constant awareness of the danger of burnout. As he says, "You can only go to the well so many times."

He also feels that the nature of racing had changed. "In racing now with the advent of Godolphin and Coolmore the quality horses are in fewer hands than in a long while. Unless you can tap into that and have a supply from these larger owners – whether Godolphin, Coolmore or Aga Khan – there's only a limited amount of quality horses to get your hands on. I think I live in an era where it's possibly harder than it was twenty-five years ago to have good horses. It's become concentrated."

The list of champion trainers over the past ten years confirms this. Sir Michael Stoute was champion in 1997, 2000, 2003, 2005 and 2006; Saaed bin Suroor in 1996, 1998, 1999 and 2004 and Aidan O'Brien in 2001 and 2002. Just three different champion trainers in ten years – and all with strong links to the elite, dominant owners.

So instead of aiming for the title of champion trainer, Noseda, at least for the moment, sits down in his office around March time and lists out what he thinks is achievable for each of his horses if each one stays sound and accomplishes all it is capable of. It is purely for personal reference and it gathers dust in an office drawer, unseen by others, until the end of the season when he returns to it to muse over how the season actually panned out.

So ambitions aplenty; however, articles that shine a spotlight only on this part of Noseda's personality do him a disservice. His success should not just be attributed to ambition. Ambition as an individual trait can be overrated. Ambitions are two a penny. Almost everyone has them. The point is that people do not achieve just because they want to. It is when ambition links up with genuine commitment, drive, single-mindedness and self-belief that success and excellence really begin to beckon.

Certainly he is animated on the subject: "It's amazing what you can do if you really want to and you are single-minded enough to say 'I want this, I want to do it' and you are prepared to commit to it and make sacrifices along the way. It's an ethic. That's what makes the difference, people applying themselves to the maximum. It frustrates me when people don't work harder, but that's the way of the world."

He sees this drive in many of the owners that he deals with – many of whom are successful businessmen – and also spots it in the sporting world. "If someone with great talent doesn't have that ethic they'll never achieve what they should achieve," he says. "You see it in sportsmen. There are golfers out there as talented as Tiger Woods, but they don't work as hard as Tiger and they haven't got his mental approach. What separates him is his mindset – he's just totally focused. Pressure doesn't seem to affect him."

The themes of ambition and application feature through Noseda's life so far. As you might expect it was in his DNA. "My parents are self-made people," he says, "and they've done well for themselves through hard work and achieving the most they could with what they had available to them. Hard though I've worked, I've never worked as hard as they did."

His parents had no connections with racing. His father's favourite sport was football and Jeremy was taken to watch Chelsea. Later he "naturally rebelled" and became a season ticket holder at Tottenham Hotspur. In view of that interest in football his parents may have been surprised to find that the youngster's primary sporting passion became horseracing. He can remember being "really sad when *Nijinsky* was beaten in the Arc, which was in 1971 when I would have been eight years old". He watched the ITV Seven on television, following form, trying to pick winners and getting his father to lay out his pocket money at the age of nine or ten.

The ambition and application traits were also evident at the age of fourteen when Noseda decided that he wanted to emulate Vincent O'Brien, and become a racehorse trainer. Since then he has "concentrated all of my powers to try to achieve that and get there – it was a determination to do what you wanted to do".

A year later he learned how to ride under the patronage of David Mould, who gave him his first hands-on insight into horses and taught him the nitty-gritty of riding. Part-time jobs in the stables of Brian Swift and Jeremy Tree during school holidays whetted his appetite and at the end of his schooling he rejected

Jeremy Noseda, Frankie
Dettori and the great
Lammtarra when Noseda
worked for Godolphin.

those university offers to move into full-time employment as an assistant to John Dunlop.

Noseda speaks fondly of Dunlop's influence. "Working for him was the steepest learning curve. Without the help and employment he gave me over five or six years I don't think I would be where I am now. He's the man I owe the most to because the foundation he gave me left me in a position where I was experienced enough and good enough at what I did to be assistant to John Gosden in California and then in Newmarket. John Dunlop is the foundation for all that. He set me up to get good jobs later on in my apprenticeship before becoming a trainer in my own right."

In 1993, Sheikh Mohammed asked him to join Godolphin, where he stayed for two years at the beginning of what has become an immensely powerful outfit. Noseda was low profile but influential in preparing top quality horses to achieve great success. His two years there coincided with wins in both the Epsom Derby and the Prix de l'Arc de Triomphe, not to mention numerous triumphs worldwide in major races.

But then came a parting of the ways. Sheikh Mohammed wanted Noseda to train in France. "It was a very generous gesture," says Noseda, "but I am English through and through and this country is where I always wanted to train."

Instead he went briefly to Hollywood Park in California with fifteen horses in his care before, after eighteen months, jumping at the chance to return to England to buy the renowned Shalfleet Stables from the retiring Paul Kelleway.

There were the traits again: ambition and the application to make the big decision and then make it work. He felt that by now he had served his apprenticeship and gave himself five years to make it as a trainer. He did not want to be an also-ran and if he did not "cut it" then at least he knew he had put heart and soul into fifteen years' preparation. He recalls: "In all the years I worked for people I only went on holiday once and in the first eight years that I had a licence – two in America and six here – I never went on holiday. I worked seven days a week. I was prepared to make the sacrifice and commit totally to get to where I wanted to be."

Even now you sense that he takes holidays almost grudgingly and it is not long after he has enjoyed the first rays of foreign sunshine that thoughts of home begin to creep into the active Noseda mind. He confirms: "I go on my holidays in November each year – which is the quietest time of the year for me. And once I come back I want to be in the yard. I don't want to be away from these horses. I want to train them each day." And when he says "each day" he really means it. "Maybe I'm not a great delegator. So it's hard for me to remove myself from the day-to-day running. My wife nags me to take Sundays off but I have to be in the yard on a Sunday and I have to be in the yard on Christmas Day and Boxing Day. It means a huge amount to me. Every day if I can have any bearing on our success then it's worth me being here."

So when Noseda was invited to the 2006 World Cup final he accepted the offer but made sure that he caught the earliest available flight back from Berlin – at an unearthly hour the next morning – so that he was back on Newmarket Heath for second lot.

Just a few hours in the company of Jeremy Noseda immediately puts to bed any misconceptions that the people who inhabit the horseracing industry are amateurish. If prize money and wins were allocated based on the professionalism and commitment of each horse's trainer then he could be confident of a highly successful season. However, racing is a much more fickle friend than that – and it would be fascinating to witness how the summer would pan out for him.

Heading towards the finish of the Nat West Rowley Mile, a track steeped in history.

THREE

GIRL POWER

"I NEEDED TO RIDE LIGHT AND THE TRAINER SAID 'GET IN THE SAUNA'. OF COURSE THE LADS WERE ALL THERE WITH NOTHING ON AND I'M SIXTEEN, WITH A TOWEL WRAPPED ROUND ME. AND THEY WERE THE WORST LADS YOU COULD HAVE IN THERE, Y'KNOW, WITH ALL THE BANTER. AND I WAS SO EMBARRASSED AND THEY WERE JUST WINDING ME UP. THAT WAS THE START OF A REALLY BAD DAY. I WAS NERVOUS WHEN I GOT CHANGED – THAT'S ALWAYS WHEN THE NERVES ARE AT THEIR WORST – BUT THEN I GOT ON THE HORSE AND THE NERVES WENT."

Trainer and former jockey Paul D'Arcy's description of what it was like to ride in a race – "put on silk pyjamas and boots, get on a motorbike, rev it up to forty miles per hour, exchange the handlebars for reins and then get twenty other motorbikes to manoeuvre for position around you" – should rapidly disabuse any notions that riding a horse in competition is easy.

With an expert on board it may look that way to the untrained eye, but a one thousand, five hundred pound thoroughbred at peak fitness is incredibly strong and travels at high speed. The jockey is perched precariously on short stirrups and with no support so that when the horse is in full stride the only parts of their anatomy in contact are the inside of feet and ankles. This demands coordination, reflexes, balance and strength. If they were to lean forward, back or to the side more than a few inches then a fall would be likely. In addition, they have to think like a horse, sensing his mood, gauging his fitness and courage, cajoling him into giving his best.

Those who excel in this task are to be admired – and when females prosper in what has generally been the sole preserve of men then that admiration is all the stronger. In fact twenty-four-year-old Hayley Turner could claim that her achievements so far match any character featured in this book.

When asked "Is she good? Do you rate her?" several people in the horseracing world who know their onions gave similar answers, their words containing the normal understated praise that is typical of the racing community. They considered for a moment and then picked their words carefully: "Yes. She has a chance. She could be the one."

Hayley Turner The Jockey

By "the one" the experts meant that they felt that Turner has half a chance of carving out a long-term professional career. Think of sports that require a mix of technique and physique. Sports like golf, tennis, swimming and badminton. They are all contested based on gender because so few women are able to compete with the men.

In the world of horseracing, women have managed such a feat only in North America. Most notable was Turner's inspiration, Julie Krone, a four foot ten inch, seven stone, pocket dynamo, who retired in 1999 after riding three thousand five hundred winners in the United States and amassing £46 million in prize money. The Canadian Emma-Jayne Wilson has also become established. However, the racetracks and attitudes to female jockeys in North America make it an easier environment in which to make a living.

As Turner explains: "Over here one of the hardest things is getting used to the tracks. If you try to get someone to push a big gangly colt around Epsom over a mile and a half, you've got to go up and down and left and right. But in the United States and New Zealand the tracks are round and that's why females do a lot better over there – because it's more about balance and getting the horse to go for you."

If Turner manages to emulate the success of Krone and Wilson and inch into, say, the top twenty of the two hundred and fifty professional flat race jockeys in Great Britain then that would be a remarkable achievement. Do not bet against it. Turner may specialise in riding on the flat but so far in her young life she has successfully cleared every hurdle put in front of her. Cynics and, it has to be said, historical evidence, have doubted the likelihood of her clearing each one but so far she just keeps sailing over them.

In February 2007, she sits in the Rutland Arms Hotel on Newmarket High Street, sips a soft drink, and speaks of her progress from sitting on a pony at the age of three through to the life she now leads as a professional jockey. As she does, she cuts an attractive figure with brown eyes, brown shoulder-length hair (more usually found tied up under a protective helmet) and an athlete's physique around a diminutive frame.

Her accent reflects her Nottinghamshire upbringing and her manner is direct yet warm. Discussions confirm that she possesses an unusually high work ethic, self-assurance and drive, albeit camouflaged under a smiley and bubbly nature that has helped her to become popular and accepted in the changing room where cutting banter is the mother language.

As she details her progress it is as if each new hurdle that she describes might have been specifically erected to test her resolve so that when she eventually became a professional she possessed the necessary deep reserves of mental toughness.

For the first hurdle she needs to dredge the memory banks to uncover early days at riding schools. Turner's mother, Kate, is a freelance riding instructor based near Southwell racecourse and the horse-mad youngster followed her around, helping,

Hayley Turner,
a woman in a
man's world.

mucking out and seizing ad-hoc opportunities to ride. Hayley says that this was a critical part of her early development: "I was taught to ride on lots of different, tricky ponies. If you have the same horse, after a while you don't learn anything. But if you ride different and complicated horses you seem to ride better."

This, allied to tuition, helped develop horse sense and riding skills. By the age of ten she was, according to her mother, "getting a tune out of a horse", an ability later put to the test when she owned her first horse, a two-year-old with a teenager's temperament called *Wallace*. He was named after the children's animation, Wallace and Gromit, and was certainly a character. He was hell to ride. By the time that *Wallace* was bought at Newark Sales the fifteen-year-old Turner had won cups and trophies in local shows but to coax him over even a couple of jumps was an achievement. She recalls, "*Wallace* was so naughty. I fell off him every day. But I wasn't fazed and just got put back on. It was a challenge."

Before *Wallace* retired to graze at the age of four, Turner used to muck him out every morning before school. It confirmed to her that she loved being around horses – and if she could handle one as rebellious as *Wallace* without losing the will to progress then she clearly had some steel in her. She recalls: "I loved it so much and being a jockey appealed big-time. I was always into it, and I wanted to do something a bit more exciting than eventing and show jumping. I wanted to go a bit faster."

After revelling in a "taster day" for prospective jockeys at Doncaster she spent summer holidays with local trainer Mark Polglase before furthering her career at the Northern Racing College in Doncaster. This ten-week course provided a qualification, lots of laughter and confirmation that she wanted to "give it a go", although that appeal waned temporarily when she moved from the college to work for a yard. Even now she is unwilling to name the stable but shudders at the memory. "I was sent to a yard in Buckinghamshire – Mum and Dad dropped me off – and it was awful. I was in the middle of nowhere with no car and no one to help me get anywhere. I was sixteen and really unhappy and then a rat ran across my bedroom floor and I just thought 'I don't want to be here.'"

Alarmed, she moved back to home to work for Polglase, though she did also take a course in Newmarket which enabled her to become a formal 'apprentice' – a young jockey tied by contract to a licensed trainer while learning the business of flat race-riding. Again her resolution was tested on her debut, a memory that will never leave her. "The first day I ever had a ride was at Southwell," she recalls. "I needed to ride light and the trainer said 'get in the sauna'. Of course the lads were all there with nothing on and I'm sixteen, with a towel wrapped round me. And they were the worst lads you could have in there, y'know, with all the banter. And I was so embarrassed and they were just winding me up. That was the start of a really bad day. I was nervous when I got changed – that's always when the nerves are at their worst – but then I got on the horse and the nerves went.

"Mum and Dad were there watching me make my first ride. I got around the first bit and then my horse broke its leg. The horse looked after me and it didn't fall and I jumped straight off. They had to shoot it and I had to hold the horse. The adrenalin was rushing through me; it was such a shock. I didn't cry even though I wanted to. I just thought there's no way I'm going to cry. I had to untack the horse when it was dead and then I was trundling back down the course with my saddle and my mum and dad are asking 'where is she? What's happened?'"

In fact, they had watched the rest of the field breeze past minus their sixteen-year-old daughter and her debut mount. There was an anxious and confused pause before ambulances hurried to the incident and, of course, they feared for Hayley, her mother "running up and down the rails like a headless chicken, wondering where her daughter was".

Turner recalls: "It didn't put me off, and if that didn't put me off then nothing was going to." She had eighteen rides in her first season (2000) and the eighth one was a maiden winner in an apprentice race at Pontefract. But the rookie was green. "I wasn't very good," she says. "My dad puts on DVDs of my winners and I was so bad. I just look at myself and cringe, thinking how did that horse win with me on its back? I rode a horse at Epsom. It was a big meeting on Channel

4, and Epsom is a course where you have to move over rails. I was all over the place and people who see the DVD just laugh. I lacked strength and also I was learning. I was thrown in at the deep end a little bit. But the horse was strong and I didn't know where I was going. I'd walked the course but I was just a bit overwhelmed by everything."

Fortunately help was at hand and she says that the senior jockeys have always been helpful. She remembers one race when she was at the back of the field alongside Kieren Fallon. Even in a lost cause, Turner was still pushing her mount forwards but with no effect. At the end of the race, after the two had pulled up, Fallon said, "Hayley, you don't need to be hitting it. Save your energy when you're beat. Once your horse starts dropping back, put your stick down." Turner adds, "That was a lesson quickly learnt. It's just common sense but as an apprentice, you do need to be told."

And you do need to listen. Turner cites the twin qualities of self-awareness and self-criticism as significant in her development because she recognises the constant need to prove herself or risk going out of fashion. "I think one of the best things about me is that I'm self-critical," she says. "Even if I'm doing well I still strive to do better and I think that's the key to improving. If you think you've arrived then you're never going to get better. I know things can change quickly in racing. I'm also aware that plenty of top apprentices have become 'where are they now?' subjects."

Girl Power: Turner in action

She continues, "After that first season I realised I was way short of standard. I decided I need to strengthen up and went to a pre-training centre in Thomasville, South Georgia, in the United States for three months. I rode out and learned a lot of timing, because pace over each furlong is timed. I strengthened up. I was like a backward two-year-old that needed putting away for the winter. When I came back I felt like I'd clicked. It felt comfortable. And when I came back I thought I ought to go to Newmarket."

And so she moved from her family, Polglase and the Midlands to racing HQ.

She says, "I thought, 'If I'm going to make a go of it, I want to go to a big yard, with a trainer who has a good strike-rate with apprentices.'"

She began what remains a prosperous relationship with Derby-winning trainer Michael Bell. Bell has been a mentor as well as an employer to Turner and can take credit for the way that he gradually increased her opportunities, out of the spotlight and with few fanfares. She recognises this contribution: "I thank him for most of my success. Working for him has been a big stepping-stone. He has always been big on taking weight off horses with a big handicap – so that's always been an advantage for me. He's been very good to me."

Bell also encouraged the trust of owners. "It was the owners that questioned me," she explains, "because they're paying so much money that they always want the best jockeys. So getting owners to allow a female apprentice on their horse was difficult. But he worked hard to get me rides with them." And with each ride Turner developed her knowledge, credibility and experience (she rates the latter as the most significant attribute in a successful jockey) until she was able to achieve her breakthrough season.

Two thousand and five put her name in lights and there remains tangible evidence of this in her Newmarket house. By her own admission it's a terrible, corny joke but one that she enjoys telling:
Question: What's on the telly tonight?
Answer: The Apprentice Champion Trophy.

And sure enough, that is where it sits, quietly gathering dust on top of the television: a trophy that was presented to Turner – and the joint winner, fellow Newmarket rider, Saleem Golam – at the 'Lesters', the horse-racing equivalent of the 'Oscars'.

Turner became the first woman to hold the title and joined an illustrious roll call of champions that includes Lester Piggott, Pat Eddery and Frankie Dettori.

"At the start of the season," she recalls, "I never gave the championship a thought but I had a good run and asked my agent to look up the stats because I knew it must be close. Towards the end of the season it stressed me out and I didn't handle it well. I don't think it affected my riding but the title was such a topic of conversation for everyone. I just wanted to put it to the back of my mind but, every day, the car park attendant would say something and then the man on the ticket gate and so it went on. They were all being supportive but I was glad when it was over."

She was feted with further garlands when Channel Four viewers voted emphatically for her as their racing personality of the year. She polled no less than forty-three per cent of the vote to top a shortlist that included Tony McCoy and Jamie Spencer. These awards and the resultant publicity were welcome but Turner was fully aware that the harsh, icy wind of reality would be blowing the following season and it would be make or break for her career.

A fully licensed apprentice jockey can claim a weight advantage conceded by professional jockeys on account of their inexperience. Apprentices are also known as 'claimers' because they 'claim' this allowance, which amounts to seven pounds, until they have won twenty races, five pounds until they have won fifty races and three pounds until their ninety-fifth win. Of course

Hayley Turner The Jockey

this makes them a more attractive option for trainers and owners. But once the ninety-fifth winner is notched they lose the automatic right to take weight off a horse's back and they are then fending for themselves in a success-driven marketplace, touting for work and being judged at equal weights against the hardened professionals who inhabit the weighing room.

Losing the allowance is undoubtedly the pivotal moment in a rider's career and plenty of gifted young riders vanish without trace along with their weight advantage. For females this is a particularly demanding challenge and a hurdle that many felt Hayley Turner would fail to clear. Previously the only women to have ridden out their claim in Britain were Alex Greaves, Emma O'Gorman and Lisa Jones. And of those only Greaves achieved longevity, partnering three hundred winners in a fifteen-year career and becoming the first woman to ride in the Derby in 1996.

Turner was acutely aware of the magnitude of the task ahead. She cancelled her annual skiing holiday at the start of 2006, eager to "get her head down" and fight for her living – and to the surprise of many observers she did indeed manage to establish herself. Business remained brisk. She was booked for six hundred and seventy three rides during the year and notched up thirty-six winners. She remained regularly employed by Michael Bell and Mark Usher and other trainers were also happy to call upon her services.

Turner's confidence improved and she felt that she became established and accepted as a bona fide professional flat race jockey. By the end of the season her statistics were becoming increasingly impressive.

Year	Rides (GB & I)	Winners	Prize Money
2002 (apprentice)	94	9	£35,296
2003 (apprentice)	228	14	£88,087
2004 (apprentice)	354	34	£271,330
2005 (apprentice)	605	53	£341,548
2006 (professional)	673	36	£262,898

Turner finishes the last drops of her drink in Newmarket's Rutland Arms at the same time as she finishes the story of her progress so far – and one wonders what new hurdles will test her during 2007. At this stage, like Jeremy Noseda and many others within the racing industry, she is bursting with optimism and ambition as she surveys the season ahead. The challenge will be to retain those qualities through to August and peak season (see The Shergar Cup – Chapter 15)...

FOUR
SHALFLEET

"A PROPER TRAINING YARD WITH OLD-FASHIONED VALUES."

Tuesday 15th April, early morning, Shalfleet Stables, Newmarket

The orderly ritual of stable life is repeated most days and it begins this morning when the first stable lads clock in at the dark and unearthly hour of 4.30am to health-check and feed the horses. If they were not so busy they would be able to observe the gradual transformation from night to day, heralded by an orange and salmon-pink sunrise that slowly reveals a cloudless sky.

Jeremy Noseda says that he struggles to get out of bed but despite the hour he appears immediately purposeful by the time he has walked from his house into the yard. By then the remainder of the stable lads have arrived and "first lot" have been groomed, tacked up (saddled and bridled) and are beginning to make their way from stables to the "indoor ride" (which has the look of a mini-aircraft hangar) where they circle, ridden by their work riders. The indoor ride is an undercover area often used for this pre-exercise warm-up. It also offers respite against poor weather and a safe, enclosed environment for breaking in yearlings.

There are thirty horses in this first "lot", three-year-olds and older, a talented crop featuring some outstanding fillies and all fit and healthy enough to undertake vigorous exercise.

Noseda stands in the middle of the circle and orchestrates activity. He wears brown boots, jeans, a designer shirt, covered by a windproof, waterproof jacket bearing his initials (JJN) and a trademark wide-brimmed hat. He buys one hat a year in London and they keep him warm on chilly early mornings. Though he never raises his voice or waves his arms around there is no doubt who the "guvnor" is. The atmosphere is businesslike, quietly efficient, focused. Indeed, that typifies Noseda's style and the stable's whole modus operandi: businesslike, quietly efficient, focused.

Noseda wants bigger stables so that he can increase the number of horses he trains. However, what Shalfleet lacks in size it makes up for in facilities. In addition to the standard stables, offices and exercise areas it has, for instance, a horse-walker which can be used for the warm-down period and also for gentle exercise for injured or unfit horses.

The newest innovation is an equine spa. Noseda is pleased with the addition and says,

"It's an aid in dealing with horses that have issues with ankles, shins and knees." To maximise the benefits of the treatment, the water is regulated at a temperature of between two and four degrees with a concentration of salt to intensify the healing effects. A typical spa session lasts ten to fifteen minutes and works the horses' muscles and cardiovascular systems without putting excessive strain on their legs.

However, as with most properties, the chief selling point is not the facilities – it is all about location, location, location. There are trainers' yards dotted all over Great Britain yet there are certain places such as Newmarket where there is a concentration near top-quality gallops.

Few are better sited than Shalfleet. It is on the historic Bury Road – just minutes away from the turf gallops and all-weather surfaces. On the doorstep are the renowned Long Hill and Warren Hill (which tend to be the ones most used by Noseda) while just a couple of hundred yards up the road are the Limekilns and the Al Bahathri polytrack.

Including the training-grounds on the racecourse side of town, there are fifty miles of turf gallops which have been maintained, year in year out, for more than three hundred years. This extensive choice ensures that every horse can be catered for no matter what its needs and it is the primary reason why Noseda chose Newmarket as his base when he returned from America.

Jeremy Noseda oversees
first "lot" at the indoor ring at Shalfleet.

The two-year-old *Sander Camillo*
winning the Albany Stakes at Royal Ascot in 2006.

6.25am – first lot moves from the indoor ride to an adjacent larger outdoor ring which is part of those communal facilities available in Newmarket. The movements of the thoroughbreds remain leisurely as they ease into the day. This loosening up (scheduled to take around thirty minutes) before and after training is important to warm their muscles and avoid pulls, stretches and tears to their muscles and tendons. The horses are finely tuned athletes and Noseda would no more permit them to come straight out of their stable and gallop than a Premier League football manager would allow his team to walk straight from the team bus and contest a big match. Throughout, Noseda oversees all activity.

Eventually, muscles suitably relaxed, the group moves in an orderly single file from the trotting ring across the Bury Road. Although cars are required to stop and let them pass some of the work riders acknowledge the courtesy. They look calm and relaxed, handling with ease any skittish behaviour. It is just a routine day for the riders; this is the first lot of the day, two more to come. Some are veterans, most young and fresh-faced. Just occasionally the silence is spiced with banter and laughter as they share in-jokes and as the day progresses noise levels rise. Most accents are English but there are some from overseas as well. The gender split is even.

If it sounds workaday and mundane that is because it is. Newmarket does not exist as a tourist attraction. Its appeal is that it is still, after all these centuries, a genuine working town.

Is this something that Noseda appreciates? "I only live here because of the job that I do," he explains. "Neither of the tracks here are my favourites. I have more affection for York and Ascot. However, I do have a great affection for English racing; it's the greatest in the world. There is a definite affection for the history and the tradition and that what we have here is safeguarded, so that it remains the centre it is."

Of course, Noseda's string is not alone is using the Newmarket training facilities. Because this is a town of some three thousand thoroughbreds, there is always a group from the stables of trainers like Sir Michael Stoute, Sir Mark Prescott or Peter Chapple-Hyam easing up Warren Hill or one of the other gallops. The only way you can tell the difference is to look at the rugs that the horses wear. This morning Noseda's string carry the initials 'JJN' – just like the number plate on his jeep and the logo on his jacket – in red writing on a black background.

As the first lot of 'JJNs' cross the Bury Road and move onto the gallops the group splits up. Most head to Warren Hill where they will twice canter up the incline. A smaller group heads for one canter up Long Hill which provides an easier workout. Among the smaller group are two who run tomorrow: *Shevchenko* and *Sander Camillo*, the latter easily identified by her white face and the pink cap and body-warmer worn by Jeremy's wife, Sally, who has ridden her out each morning for the last two years.

At this stage "Sander", as she is known, is favourite for the 1000 Guineas. She has her first outing for two hundred and eighty days tomorrow in the Nell Gwyn Stakes on the first day of Newmarket's Craven Meeting. She had her last "work" three days ago so today's exercise is gentle and undemanding, just six furlongs in length. Like a hothouse plant, the idea is that she blossoms on schedule, somewhere around 3.15pm on 6th May for the 1000 Guineas.

Noseda thinks she is currently at ninety per cent – or within two grass gallops – of her peak, which is perfect at this stage of the season. Yet he is concerned by tomorrow even though he expects her to run well and win comfortably. He describes it as a "horrid race". He recognises that the filly needs the workout – indeed has been "screaming" to run since February and has "grown stale" with the training regime that she has been following since last summer – but knows that if she wins and wins well, that's only to be expected. If she runs badly, loses, or sustains an injury then the whole preparation for the Guineas, now just eighteen days away, will be thrown into the air.

Noseda climbs into his jeep and makes the short drive to the parking area halfway up Warren Hill. He has one eye across the heath land in the distance to track "Sander" as she moves gently through the gears up Long Hill. The other is focused on the main contingent of the group as they canter, generally one by one, up Warren Hill on the all-weather surface.

Although the string moves with the fluency of athletes this morning they are nowhere near top speed. The effort could be described as third gear: brisk and demanding and sufficient to develop their cardiovascular fitness, which, in turn, helps the heart and vascular system to transport oxygen from the lungs to the work muscle cells. Yet it is not what racing folk call "work". Work tends to take place on Saturdays and Wednesdays.

It moves the intensity up a gear and helps to define a horse's ability and racing fitness; the nearest a horse gets to showing its true colours other than race days. Yet even at work they do not gallop at the same fifth gear, gut-wrenching pace of race-day.

Noseda watches ten yards away as each one passes, lit by soft, early morning sunlight, and instantly recognises each of the horses. He provides an impromptu commentary: "That's *Red Blooded Woman. Sweet Gale.* A filly called *Luck Be a Lady.* Her ankles were immature last season, so hasn't run much. But she's quite good. Runs at Newmarket on Thursday. That's *DemiSemiQuaver.* And there's *Simply Perfect.*"

Noseda considers the grey *Simply Perfect* to be "a tough filly, battle-hardened if you like, and a group one winner. I think there're only two horses with a better chance in the Guineas (*Sander Camillo* and the Irish contender, *Finsceal Beo*)."

And so on. He knows them all; their names, their pedigree, their conformation, their current physical condition, their personalities, their intended schedule of racing, exercise, rest and nutrition. It is this attention to detail that allows Noseda and his team to create specific training programmes. Each horse has a unique tolerance to exercise. Some thrive on regular work and others prefer less intense training with long periods of recuperation. And all are trained in cycles, building to a peak that can only be maintained for a relatively short period of time. Certainly if horses galloped every day even the strongest of them would burn out.

He eleborates: "On the training side there's a whole process to follow for each horse from breaking it in – and then it's for me to judge how much preparation a horse needs. I might work him twice a week doing hard work – and as they are building up you look at each horse, the ways he blows after working. You're starting to get a picture in your mind of when he will be ready to run. There are horses here that could be ready to run in six fast gallops and others that might need twelve to get to the

Jeremy Noseda
orchestrates activity.

43

same level. My job is to look at each horse and establish which level they're at.

"There's a basic regime, but within that regime you need to look at each horse and that's where any trainer's skill comes in – where he adjusts it to suit different horses. Most horses will comply with the regime but some won't. It can be subtle, a gut feeling. If I see a horse run brilliantly a week before it's due to run I curse. I'm thinking 'Am I just a week too late?' I'd rather be one gallop short than one too many. It always worries me."

After they canter up Warren Hill, the horses ease round in an oval and walk back down it. Noseda is waiting. As each one passes he asks the work rider. "OK? OK folks? OK? OK there?" Most report no problems but one states that *Red Blooded Woman* coughed four or five times after her canter. This is not unusual, just something to watch. In addition word comes that *Shevchenko* has lost a plate when cantering up Long Hill. So Noseda issues suitable instructions to ensure the horse is walked back to the stable as quickly and safely as possible.

The trainer's nightmare is for some form of virus to spread through the yard. That can wreck a season. Coughing, loss of appetite and general lethargy can be warning signs, as is a high temperature. Ideally it is between 99° and 101° Fahrenheit. Anything over 101.5° is a problem. In Noseda's yard each horse's temperature is taken before exercise then again after 6pm each evening. Going around the whole stable can take up to an hour.

The breeding of these finely tuned equine athletes means they are susceptible to everything going: muscle tears, pulls and strains, viruses, inflammations, infections, abscesses and internal bleeding to name just a few from a depressingly long list. If they are just one per cent from their physical peak then that can be the difference between a race won and a race lost. As a result the vet is a frequent visitor to Shalfleet and every other yard in Newmarket.

After a second canter up Warren Hill, the larger group of first lot walks back to the stables and the indoor ride where they warm down. Again Noseda is constantly checking with the riders to make sure that all is OK: "OK? No coughing? OK folks?"

Then the horses are washed down, rugged up and left to rest in their stables. The slopes of the stables become awash with suds and the redolent aroma of horses, hay, saddle soap and liniment. Each horse has its own stable with its name on the front, the date it was born and the name of its dam and sire. As first lot are tucked away some of Noseda's owners make an impromptu visit and he pays them due attention.

7.40am – Between "lots" the work riders grab some breakfast and Noseda goes to his house, eats toast, skims the papers (the *Daily Mail* and the *Racing Post*) and catches up with the news on breakfast TV with his wife Sally. This particular morning he also muses on the key skills he needs to do his job well. "The main thing is to get your horses happy, healthy and fit," he says. "Those are the things that you're driving for. You need a huge help from staff, that's critical – but the primary objective is to have horses with talent. Then you're ninety per cent of the way there to doing a good job. A lot of it is common sense – how you feed the horse, a routine.

"You have to spot the odd ones that need something different. Down the years people have created a shroud of mystique around it but I don't think that there is a mystique to it. It is your knowledge of pedigree, what you see and input from your staff that will tell you over what distance to run them and how you progress from there. There's a huge element of common sense and a gut feel for when you might, at a certain point, do something a bit different. And then you just go with your gut."

Does he ever become emotionally attached to the horses? "Not really, though there's one, *Soldier's Tale*, that I'm attached to because we've been through so much together. I just love the horse. He is my favourite of all time. He's just so tough and brave all his life, always a fighter. He's had part of his stomach removed and has to have a special diet and we live in daily fear of another colic attack. One night after he'd had surgery I was woken at three in the morning by the vets who said they thought the time had come to put him down. But we gave him another forty-five minutes and he came through. Ninety-nine horses out of a hundred would have given up.

"But, other than *Soldier's Tale*, although I do everything I can to treat them well and give them the best chance of success I don't get emotionally attached."

By contrast his wife Sally – who, by the way, thinks her husband is a bit more compassionate than he will admit – says she gets "sick with nerves" every time *Sander Camillo* runs.

The training cycle begins again with second lot at 8.10am. This time it is mainly the younger horses – some three-year-olds, several two-year-olds and those who might be backward or have recently raced. Unusually, Noseda departs to attend the Newmarket "breeze-ups" (see A Breed Apart – Chapter Six) so he passes operational responsibility to his vastly experienced right-hand man, David Bradley.

Bradley, a Yorkshireman, has been in racing for thirty years. He has worked for Michael Bell, Luca Cumani and Godolphin before meeting Noseda while working as head lad for Maktoum's family racing operation in Dubai. He has lived in Newmarket since 1981 and been employed by Noseda here since 1998. He is a loyal lieutenant who nowadays cannot imagine working for anyone else.

He understands and appreciates "the guvnor's" way of working: his endless attention to minutiae and need to be practically involved at every stage. Even when Noseda is away at sales around the globe he phones Bradley so they can jointly create the training "board" for the next day. Bradley calls it a "proper racing yard with old-fashioned values" and there are several like Bradley at Shalfleet: long-serving men loyal to their employer because they believe he runs it the way it should be.

Jeremy Noseda The Trainer

Bradley rides out most days on an older mare, *Fantastic View*, but not on Wednesdays and Saturdays when the faster "work" is undertaken. In the last couple of years he has ridden horses which have broken legs when galloping. On both occasions he survived unscathed but thinks third time may be unlucky.

Under Bradley's supervision the second and then the third lots stretch their limbs in the usual way: warm up, canter twice up Warren Hill and then warm down and wash down before being settled in their stables.

After each horse completes its morning

exercise it refuels. The type of nutrition varies depending on whether the horse has just raced, or is preparing to race, recuperating, ill or injured. Traditionally the stable diet has been hay and oats but the feed of modern horses is higher in fat content and highly digestible fibres which are an essential ingredient for digestive health. In the lead-up to a race or when full galloping work is being undertaken the food is a more complex mixture that provides high energy.

Hydration is equally important. Each horse is provided with two buckets of water in the morning, at lunch and in the evening. During routine checks Noseda and his stable staff will check hydration levels. If there are

On the heath

any doubts then a pinch of the neck gives more clues. If the skin flops straight down it is a good sign; if it does not it suggests dehydration. After races electrolytes may be added to the water and stable lads are fully aware that horse-box travelling is inclined to lead to dehydration.

"I have a nutritionist," Noseda explains, "and we are constantly looking at each horse's diet and how we can maximise that diet to create a healthy horse that has access to as much energy as it can get. There's a few things that we change nearer to a race, though of course it depends on the horse. With most we lighten the weight of the feed and increase the energy level. For some, like 'bleeders' (horses who are inclined to bleed after heavy exercise) we might even try to dehydrate them a little because horses that carry less body fluid are less likely to bleed."

By midday the "lots" have finished and the work riders leave the premises – that is unless it's Friday when Noseda performs a "stand by your beds" review of each stable to ensure it is spick and span. Some riders return for evening stables between 4.30 and 6pm but they work – unusually for Newmarket – a one week on, one week off rota for that. However, that does not mean the stables are deserted. The work riders are just part of the team. There are also mucker-outers, a full-time blacksmith, a travelling head lad, a maintenance man, as well the bookkeeper and racing secretary in the office. They are the behind the scenes backbone of the yard.

Midday is the time of day when trainers often leave for the races. Noseda, though, tends to remain at Shalfleet. "I don't go racing a huge amount, not as much as you might expect," he explains. "I feel that when a horse gets in the horse box to go racing I've done my job. What I would do at the races is not going to make any difference to how the horse is going to perform. So out of preference I'd rather be here amongst the horses, because it's in the yard where I can make a difference."

Indeed, he also declines some trips abroad – such as to Dubai in January – to remain at the hub. "I need to be here," he says. "I have horses which I need to be getting sorted out for April, May, June, July and August. We're laying down foundations now for what will happen in the summer."

Instead Noseda seizes the opportunity for a lunchtime break. Occasionally he lunches alone and snatches a brief doze. More often it is a working lunch with owners. In his office he keeps a list close by of all the owners who have placed horses with him. It contains names, addresses, telephone numbers, email addresses and the names of the horses. He makes a point of keeping close to each of them.

"Owners are investing a lot of money and they need feedback," he says. "It's about being straightforward and honest with people. They might send you a horse because they think you can do the best for the horse and then you have to build up that trust between you. All my owners are also my friends. I trust them and they trust me. It's a different relationship to a strictly business association."

If owners chose to move elsewhere then Noseda's reputation and business prosperity would suffer – but whilst he creates and nurtures these relationships he is noticeably more reluctant to actively promote his stable and try to woo prospective new clients. Truth is, it is something with which he is just not comfortable.

"Maybe I should push harder; write to people, go to the sales and hustle," he says. "But I don't feel that I want to go and hustle people. I'm not a great social person. I don't write letters to people asking to train their horses like some. I do my job – the results publicise me and my owners may recommend others to me – and to me the only way to promote myself is through what I do on the racecourse.

"Maybe I should be more forceful – but I feel that I can do the job, my owners trust me and if others see that then they'll ring me. I feel I should let them decide 'Let's invest our horses in that man' – and that's the way I deal with it."

2.15pm to 3.45pm. Office work. Even the spoken words leave Noseda cold. He finds the horsey part of his role the easiest and the most pleasurable. Alas, there is endless paperwork to be dealt with as well. This is where his racing secretary, Kim Leet, is crucial. She coordinates vaccinations, transportation, declarations and entries, staff registration and health and safety issues. Often she needs Noseda's deci-

sion-making and signature so it is important that she uses the time she has with him efficiently. As a busy man his time cannot be wasted. To help they share a daily "to do" list which is kept on her desk.

In addition, Noseda deals with people – usually on the phone. In addition to the owners there is his form man, vet and nutritionist, the on-site staff at Shalfleet and – whisper the words – the media. This is not a group to which Noseda will ever be accused of pandering. You sense he has little respect for some of their number. He tends to have the afternoon racing on the television in his office as he works through the paperwork but mutes the sounds until the actual race commentary begins – and when he reads the *Racing Post* it is no more than a cursory scan. His wife is encouraging a more media-friendly approach but he has little interest in the copy that fills many of the pages.

He explains: "Racing journalists mainly experience me at the racecourse and at that time I'm very focused. In addition I hate people criticising my horses. If people do it I can have no time for them at all." In addition, superstitiously, he won't be interviewed before a race on the TV about how his horse will run: "I don't want to talk about it before a race and it's only worth talking about afterwards if you've won."

4pm – It is, you feel, with relief that Noseda escapes from the paperwork and the ever-ringing phone into the late afternoon sunlight of the yard for "evening stables".

He performs a tour of the yard, stopping at

each stable to check the health of the inhabitant; observing them at rest, assessing their general demeanour and running a hand down their legs to check for heat or swelling. He is looking for tell-tale signs and usually the stable lad or lass is also present – having prepared their charge for inspection by cleaning, brushing and grooming – to provide their opinion. Those signs might be in the shine of their horse's coat, the brightness of the eyes or in their appetite. Certainly the trainer has an obsessive interest in his horses' feeding as it gives such a strong indication of their health.

Noseda remarks that it would be so much easier if horses could communicate. Then they could direct him to the source of the niggle or tell him how sharp they feel – and he, in turn, could motivate them with an inspiring pep-talk.

Noseda may be talented but he is no Doctor Doolittle so he is forced to use more conventional methods. "You have to spend enough time around the horses to see what suits to make them tick," he explains. "In the evening I will wander and especially in the summer when we train and race them hard I just look at horses in boxes. Even when they are in rest I feel you can pick up clues if you know what their normal is, and the normal way they react to me.

"If you observe them enough you can see differences in the way they look, act and behave; if they look tired, if they look sulky, whether they look like they've had enough. There's enough there to create a picture in your mind of where it is and where you want it to be."

This is where he really comes into his own because Noseda really, really needs to know horses – and specifically the horses in his care – to pick up those nuances that can make a difference. As with humans each has its own personality and individual quirks and foibles. Some are calm and placid; others are highly strung and bite, and kick. Equally some are able to run several races during a short period of time whilst others might need lots of time between races to recover. Knowing each one is one of the great arts of the business: with ninety-three horses under his supervision this takes some doing.

Even if Noseda misses evening stables due to racing commitments he aims to return by 6pm so that can prepare "the board" for the next day. This lists who rides which horse for each lot next day, which horses need special tack, what clothing is required, which horses are going racing and which will just go on the horse walker or in the equine spa. His observations will help him to define his itinerary for each animal.

He can also refer to his comprehensive paperwork records. "I document what every horse in my yard does every day," he says. "It helps me to confirm my thinking. I can go back to records from my time with Godolphin and, for instance, look at the exact programme for *Lammtarra* prior to winning the Derby first time out." Again, it is all about attention to detail as well as an awareness of the big picture.

By 8pm Noseda's packed work day is

largely complete, though work-related thoughts continue to buzz around his head. He does have hobbies. He likes art and wine and regular trips to White Hart Lane, home of Tottenham Hotspur, provide a welcome diversion. However, even when he is physically off duty he finds it difficult to switch off entirely, particularly when the mobile phone interrupts so regularly.

He recognises that he will need to lower the current tempo if he is to keep going as a trainer beyond the age of sixty. So perhaps it is fortunate that he finds no attraction in Newmarket's social life. He admits "I prefer cola to champagne and ten o'clock is a late night by my standards."

After dinner and maybe some television it is off to bed. Little wonder he always sleeps well. No sooner has his head hit the pillow than the early morning alarm begins this ritual again.

FIVE

MAN FOR ALL SEASONS

"BEFORE A FIXTURE YOU DON'T LEAVE ANYTHING TO CHANCE.
YOU CHECK AND DOUBLE CHECK."

MICHAEL PROSSER WAS THE FIRST of the characters featured in this book I met. I shadowed him for a day in 2005 and produced a small article published in the East Anglian Daily Times. *It gave me the idea for this book.*

Over our meetings I have grown to admire and like him. Partially, I think, because we have some similarities: a passion for cricket, a young family and, I was later to find out, a period where we had to endure a serious illness to our partner. Fortunately in both cases there was a complete recovery.

However, there the similarities end. Before the birth of his first child and his introduction to the delights of dirty nappies and Thomas the Tank Engine, Prosser was close to being a workaholic. He is a pea from the same pod as his boss Lisa Hancock, and the trainer, Jeremy Noseda.

I used to subscribe to the view that the people who administered racing were amateurish old fogies and part of an old boys' network. Michael Prosser changed this opinion. He often referred to himself as a "grafter" and I suspect in his mind there are few higher praises than to be described in this way.

When he left Newcastle University, in 1988, he was undecided what to do and applied for a range of jobs outside of the racing industry. Deep down he knew they were not for him. The genetic, gravitational pull to horses led to him choosing the less lucrative but perhaps more emotionally fulfilling role as a stable lad in Cornwall. Yet if he had chosen the alternative path he would probably have become a successful businessman, as his father was. He has all the necessary attributes. Anyway, the city's loss is Newmarket's gain as he is integral to the operation at racing headquarters.

Wednesday 16th April, 6.10am, the mile post on Newmarket's Rowley Mile racecourse.

The first day of the season at racing HQ is precisely six hours and ten minutes old – and the new dawn reveals blue skies and high cloud, some of it dark, most of it light and harmless. The turf is dewy but already beginning to dry.

The temperature is four degrees Celsius and there is a chill to the air, but there has been no overnight frost. Nor has there been any rain. Twenty-five days have passed since the last significant downpour.

The course is almost deserted; just a few industrious early morning ground staff and a slim, fresh-faced man of forty with neatly

Michael Prosser
on the Rowley Mile.

cropped blond hair, Barbour jacket, and wellington boots. He frequently pokes a heel or stick in the turf or bends to pick up a divot and deposit it at the side of the racetrack as he zigzags down the Rowley Mile towards the imposing Millennium Grandstand dominating the skyline ahead.

The man – Michael Prosser – will walk the course at dawn on each of Newmarket's thirty-seven race days during the coming season to gauge the official "going". It is one of a very long list of tasks he oversees on race days. "Before a fixture you don't leave anything to chance. You check and double check," he says in the distinctive clipped tones of racing professionals.

This morning he has ample reason to be dog-tired after a night of little sleep. "My two-year-old has a cold so he needed some attention," he explains. "That's fine. When you have children you take sleepless nights on the chin. And to be brutally honest with you I'm not the greatest sleeper in the world anyway. The night before a big fixture like the Craven Meeting, the first of the year, there are plenty of things running through your mind."

Yet, despite the sleep deprivation, he gives no indication of sluggishness. Quite the reverse. He moves at speed and with a veritable spring in his step, fuelled by a naturally high metabolism, the adrenalin of a big race day and several reasons to be abnormally cheerful.

Firstly it is the start of a new season, which for anyone who loves the sport as much as Prosser provides an eager sense of anticipation.

Secondly, he is pleased by what he sees before him. Prosser admits that he loves the smell, look and texture of racing turf. "My wife says I'm weird," he laughs. Certainly he is fully aware that Newmarket's topsoil is composed primarily of a silt loam or silty clay loam, overlying chalk brash. He can also recite, without a moment of hesitation, that the top surface consists of perennial ryegrass with elements of fescue, cocksfoot, bentgrass and crested hairgrass and that part of Newmarket's heathland is officially protected as a "site of special scientific interest".

This enthusiasm and knowledge, along with the degree that he holds in agriculture, denotes him as an expert, bordering on an anorak. It is just as well because he has the weighty responsibility of being custodian of the racetracks at both the Rowley Mile and the July Course – and failure to deliver top-quality conditions is not an option. It always has to be spot on. Whether it is Wembley, Wimbledon, Lord's or Newmarket, the playing surface is the stage for the theatre that unfolds above. The better the stage, the greater the theatre.

Those twenty-five rainless days (since before National Hunt's Cheltenham Festival) could have caused a problem but Prosser is upbeat. "The turf is as good as it's been since 2001 which was a very wet and advanced spring in terms of growth of the grass," he says. "This year we've had more rain in the first nineteen days of January than we'd had in the first two months of 2006 so the moisture is in the ground. The grass has been growing vigorously and it's healthy.

"Funnily enough it isn't so much the drought or the dryness that has caused us headaches – because we can water for that. It's more the night-time frosts that we were getting. Night-time temperatures were hovering around zero and that put the grass back. Then, in the last week the frosts have disappeared, temperatures have risen, we've watered and the track has taken off and the sward thickened up. For an April fixture it's in good condition."

With the forecast set fair there is no need for up-to-the-minute weather updates as he walks the course. This morning he can enjoy a rare few moments of tranquillity accompanied by just the optimism of a new season, a panorama of green, green Newmarket turf and a vast East Anglian sky. He agrees: "It's a particularly pleasurable experience, walking down the Rowley Mile at six o'clock in the morning, just admiring what is in front of you."

Another reason for his buoyant mood is the birth, five days before, of a daughter, Alice.

Alice had been born at the West Suffolk Hospital in Bury St Edmunds the previous Thursday, weighing in at six pounds, twelve ounces. Alice's birth, like that of her brother, Tom, had become – in racing parlance – longer odds after Prosser's wife, Kit, was unwell in 2003.

With furrowed brow, Prosser recalls this difficult period: "I was very angry – angry that someone aged just twenty-seven should have to go through this; angry for the impact on my own life. It was a very difficult time of our lives."

Thankfully Kit's recovery was full and complete and Alice's birth has been the icing on the cake; the ultimate reason to be cheerful as he makes his way down the Rowley Mile and comes to a definitive view on today's going. Prosser provides advance assessments (published in the racing press) in the days leading up to each meeting. Throughout he has been predicting "good to firm" and "good to firm" is what he delivers.

With turf there are seven official states of the going: hard, firm, good to firm, good, good to soft, soft, and heavy. Normally one category will cover the whole course, though, just occasionally, Prosser's statement will allow for variations on different parts of the track: for example "good, good to soft in places".

This morning Prosser is particularly pleased that astute watering has balanced the dry spell. He clarifies: "You don't want the ground to be too quick at this time of year. The Craven Meeting is built around three-year-olds and a few nice two-year-old races so the one thing that you don't want is jarring ground. We were mindful of that so I was aiming for ground on the good side of good to firm – and we've provided it."

But why is the creation of the racing ground so important? "It's because we're judged on the quality and competitiveness of the horseracing and the ground dictates this because it is so fundamental to the horse," he explains. "As a result the going is also fundamental to the decision of any owner or trainer to run a horse.

We have some amazing horseracing here – the first classics of the season, Champions' Day, the July festival – and that turf is key. Top-quality horseracing is what draws the race-goers and it is their support that makes Newmarket so successful."

Of course, the weather affects the going and, given the traditional English preoccupation with its erratic climate, Prosser should surely be due a mention in the Queen's honours list. He talks about the going all the time because a trainer or member of the media is always keen for an update. There is just no escape within the town.

Even when he is out with his family he will get a tap on the shoulder and the perennial enquiry. He says that in the week leading up to the Guineas weekend he is inundated with questions. "I get phone calls all day," he says, "and then at home in the evening. It's just the nature of the job."

This thirst for information is because the going provides a useful indicator of a horse's prospects. How each one copes with conditions depends on a variety of factors: their galloping actions, bodyweight, stride pattern, muscularity, strength, flexibility, bone structure and neurology. But each one has its own preference; some are mud-lovers, some act on a drier surface. Either way the going is critical to their chances.

The ideal surface for flat racing which suits most horses is a lush covering of grass on moist soil that provides both "give" and "spring". There is always pressure on Prosser and his team to deliver and the ground staff try to work with the weather to retain and maintain that ideal; cutting, watering, nourishing and manicuring with the same diligence as green keepers at an Open Championship golf course.

This morning some were in as early as 6am and all ten have been here since 7am, so that when Prosser links up with the head groundsman at 7.10am it is clear that preparations are ongoing and organised. It has not always been quite so slick. When Prosser first came to Newmarket the twenty-eight hectares of racing surface needed attention and they were not the only problem. "Things needed to improve and within a couple of weeks it was apparent that some people wouldn't appreciate my style," he recalls. "Some left and that allowed us to bring in some fresh blood which was important."

In addition, he invited agronomists to review the turf, machinery and irrigation and give "warts 'n' all" feedback. All parties agreed – investment was needed and he went to the board, requesting finance. They supported the proposals and the transformation began. He focused his staff on day-to-day maintenance and brought in expert contractors where they were most needed. This change paid rich dividends and is reflected in the quality of this morning's surface.

Prosser summarises: "I'm seriously proud of this team and seriously proud of what we have achieved here with the ground staff. I consider them all to be friends and I will bend over backwards to help them. I want them to work with me – and they do. We've reduced the number of ground staff and focused on creating a team that can diversify."

7.20am – once Prosser is happy with the state of the racetrack and preparations of the ground staff he drives to the Links Stable Yard where horses and stable lads who are long-distance travellers stay on the night before a race day. He makes sure that the stable manager is happy and the facilities – the hostel where the stable lads sleep and the stable yard itself – are in good order. He is delighted. All looks fine.

Next he returns to his main office in Westfield House about a mile away from the Rowley Mile. There are numerous emails to deal with, documentation for future racing to pass on to the veterinary officer and phone calls to take. His direct line and mobile are constantly ringing, often at the same time, with trainers or the media asking about the forecast and the going. With this in mind Prosser makes one call of his own, just making sure that the weather is still set fair. There is no change, no prospect of rain.

Prosser also handwrites a timetable that will be posted on the noticeboard in the weighing room. The timetable lists when horses should enter the parade ring, when they should be mounted by the jockeys, their departure from the parade ring, arrival at the start, and, finally, the moment that the starting stalls are released for the race to begin. With Racing UK covering the racing this afternoon, it is essential that races start on time. The importance of television coverage

for major sponsors, who play such an important role in helping to fund prize money, cannot be underestimated.

Prosser lives close to Westfield House. This morning, unusually, he takes the opportunity to pop home briefly for coffee, toast, a check on his wife's recovery from labour, Thomas's streaming cold and little Alice's progress. He manages to fend off the phone calls for fifteen minutes then returns to Westfield House for more paperwork and, at 10am, a live interview over the phone with Racing UK. During the discussion he provides clear and articulate information about conditions before promoting the quality of the racing and the delights of Newmarket.

It is becoming clear that the clerk of the course has a much wider range of duties than just turf maintenance and the going. He is not just a man of the track. His responsibilities are wide and varied, including other areas on the course such as the stewards' room, the stables, the winners' enclosure, saddling boxes, parade ring and pre-parade ring. And then there are the veterinary surgeons and the medical team.

Nor does it end there. He needs to help frame each season's racing programme so that the racing is consistently world class and then promote that product by talking fluently to the media.

"In life," he says, "you need to be able to communicate and get on with people. That's one attribute that is required of the clerk of the course. You need to be capable of portraying an image and able to tell people what's going on in a confident and positive manner."

Michael Prosser
in the parade ring.

Michael Prosser The Clerk of the Course

However, that is by no means all that is required. His job description is as long as the Rowley Mile and needs a multi-skilled high performer. Communication skills are important as are media polish, diplomacy, an encyclopaedic horseracing knowledge, groundsmanship, management and administration skills.

Prosser ticks all those boxes. During his first thirty-four years – through his childhood, education and early career – he acquired the mindset, expertise, knowledge and experience to become a successful clerk of the course at Newmarket. Yet he freely admits that he spent much of his early life uncertain about his future. So even though he was travelling the journey, he was not entirely sure of his destination.

It helped, like many others who now inhabit the Newmarket racing community, that he had horses in his blood. His grandmother, Stella Carver, owned racehorses, many trained by Fred Rimell. One of those horses, *ESB*, won arguably the most famous Grand National of all when *Devon Loch*, ridden by Dick Francis, slipped on the run in to the finishing post. *ESB* galloped past the distraught figures to victory. Stella was also an international show jumper who, according to Prosser, "took on the men and beat them. At one stage she was one of the top show jumpers in the world". A sepia photograph of his grandmother in show-jumping action hangs in his home and his affection and admiration is palpable.

The young Michael lived just two miles away and was often at her stables or at the races at Stratford, Warwick, Towcester or Cheltenham with his two brothers and sister. There was also some land opposite where he had his first pony, *Sovereign*, chosen for him by his grandmother at the age of eight.

With his mother at the helm, the family developed ponies until at one stage they had as many as six or seven in the field. "We were good at what we did," recalls Prosser. His father was a successful businessman who found a niche in DIY stores in the early 1970s and was a talented cricketer in the Warwickshire leagues.

They were a hardworking, tough and competitive family; lovers of the outdoors who set high standards both for themselves and others. Prosser identifies his parents as positive and powerful role models and people he admires greatly. The youngster enjoyed an idyllic and simple childhood. Each day was much the same: wake up, feed the horses, muck out, ride, school, ride, homework, eat, go to bed. At weekends Michael also demonstrated that he was a talented horseman, representing the England junior team riding working hunter ponies. So he was gaining a strong understanding and appreciation of horses.

At the age of seventeen, with A levels under his belt, he studied agricultural economics at university but with no clear idea of where it might lead. He recalls: "Up till then I had lived a protected life – no partying, just a focus on sport. But I saw the light at university! I partied, perhaps too much, and built up some confidence. That said, I always did enough academically to get through."

Nor did he forget the horses. Each Sunday he would travel to Darlington to ride out six or seven of them in the morning in return for a splendid Sunday lunch and a couple of cans of lager. "It was my idea of heaven and great fun," he recalls.

After he finished university in 1988 he went to Australia, where he worked on a farm and taught horse riding before travelling for five months. If university brought him out of his shell then Australia toughened him. "Australians call a spade a spade," he says. "I like that. There's not too much grey in my world either. When you are a Pom in Australia, particularly one who plays cricket, you are going to get stick. And you have to deal with it."

When he returned home, he half-heartedly applied for corporate jobs in London before jumping at the chance to become a stable lad in Cornwall, where the man with a university degree earned no more than £9,000 a year. He spent another five blissful years as travelling head lad and subsequently assistant trainer with Paul Nicholls. Eventually the cold reality struck that he was now twenty-seven years old and still earning only £11,000 a year. He accepted that he needed to channel his skills and experience into a longer lasting and more profitable line of business.

He made tentative moves to become a trainer before taking over as estates manager at Wolverhampton, where it soon became clear that the ground team needed reviewing. Hard decisions were made (that toughening time in Australia proving essential preparation) and the team was duly reorganised. After a few months significant progress had been made and he became clerk of the course at both Wolverhampton and Southwell, later adding Worcester to his responsibilities. He undertook the necessary training in just six months and was soon clerking more than one hundred fixtures a year and working dawn to dusk hours.

This completed his grounding. He had "collected" the work ethic, high standards and love of horseracing gifted to him by his family; the confidence and knowledge of agriculture from university and an Australian toughness. In addition he now had practical experience in the industry – working in yards and, critically, as a clerk of a course. Little wonder that in October 2000 he was head-hunted by Lisa Hancock, newly installed as managing director, to take over as clerk of the course at horseracing HQ.

He endured a torrid first year – the biggest challenge of his professional life – not least because of the foot and mouth epidemic. He recalls: "There was no crossover period with the previous clerk of the course and I found that I had a huge amount to learn. Looking back, I underestimated the intensity and challenges of the job. At this magnificent place everything is so important. However, I met it head-on as normal and worked long, hard hours. I didn't feel out of my depth but certainly knew that I had to learn a lot and fast."

Michael Prosser The Clerk of the Course

Over the subsequent years Hancock and Prosser have worked closely and in the winter of 2006/7 she formally recognised his contribution by making him Director of Racing of Newmarket Racecourses. This means he has a place on the Board, a rare and prestigious achievement for a clerk of the course – and he also serves on the race planning committees of the British Horseracing Authority and Racecourse Association.

Prosser enjoys the opportunity this provides to develop: "I'm fortunate. Being on these boards and committees is instrumental to my personal development; I can offer an opinion and a view as well as learning from the vast experience of the other board members."

10.05am – Prosser is continuing to put all this knowledge into practice. After the interview with Racing UK in Westfield House he catches up with Hancock. During the season they undertake a clinical dissection of the coverage every time a Newmarket race meeting is videoed, looking for potential improvements, no matter how small. Prosser's office contains seven year's worth of tapes.

They're off. 2.04pm on 18th April 2007.
Newmarket's first race of the season is
won by *Arabian Gulf* ridden by Kerrin McEvoy.

Today, Hancock brings good news: advance sales for the Craven meeting are promising. This is another reason to be cheerful because during the winter Prosser worked with Hancock and others to change the fixture list. He explains: "One of the most frequent questions that I'm asked is 'What do you in the winter? The answer is that actually we develop – we put right what we think is wrong. For me it's largely about revisiting the whole of the racing programme."

Specifically, they reduced the Craven meeting from three days to two, largely because there had been small crowds on the first day in previous years and they had lost terrestrial television coverage. Instead they added another meeting in May. The early signs suggest that this might have been a smart commercial move – which is important because Newmarket Racecourses, like all businesses, always need to be aware of the bottom line.

Other changes include a Lester Piggott Day and a beefed-up July Festival; and in 2008 two new races, including the "Tattersalls Million", will take place at October's Cambridgeshire meeting.

By 10.30am Prosser is back at the Rowley Mile, inspecting the stewards' and weighing rooms. Half an hour later, three hours before the first race, he walks the course again, from the mile post back to the magnificent but currently empty Millennium Grandstand. He is accompanied by the senior steward and they ensure that the starting stalls are in place, the rails intact and there is no last-minute change in ground condition. On this occasion it remains "good to firm" though drying in a brisk breeze. Both are satisfied that all is in order.

The mid-morning walk is less tranquil than its 6am equivalent. The mobile rings regularly and there are trainers, jockeys and other "connections" also assessing the racing surface, picking and poking with heels and sticks. Prosser constantly confirms that the weather and going are set fair. His comments are factual and neutral. It is easy to find himself on the receiving end of an ear-bashing, particularly if the conditions do not match expectations. "Of course," he says, "I don't enjoy getting shouted at but I recognise that the trainers and jockeys are professionals under intense pressure to perform."

After walking the course Prosser goes to his office in the weighing room and rapidly changes into a grey suit, white shirt and yellow tie. Minutes later, at 12.15pm, he is in the winners' enclosure to deliver an interactive demonstration to the press with Turftrax's Mike Maher. They explain the use of a going stick that became mandatory for all turf courses from 31st March, though Newmarket has been using one for the past four years. The going stick is plunged into the turf and provides a statistical reading that can range from 15 (hard) to 0 (heavy). Today the racetrack measures 9.6.

There is no respite. Once the demonstration is complete Prosser rushes off to oversee Peter Chapple-Hyam's *Authorized* and Jeremy Noseda's *Sixties Icon* and *Simply Perfect* using the track for a training workout. He says "We provide a service for world-class horses and we have a policy that if a group one horse wants to work on our track we encourage it, provided we are able to make the media fully aware of what is going on. Of course we get good press from this. It helps everybody. My role is to make sure everything goes smoothly."

By 1pm the first horses are arriving and Prosser performs last-minute inspections of the pre-parade ring, parade ring, saddling boxes, winners' enclosure, stables and stewards' room. He also checks that all is in order with the veterinary surgeons and medical team. From now on he always has a walkie-talkie in hand, communicating to his team wherever they are located on the course.

Prosser describes the Craven Meeting, which has been a cornerstone of the Newmarket calendar for more than one hundred and thirty years, as "one for the purists," – and this afternoon they are arriving early and in good numbers. These days, thanks to all-weather tracks, flat racing takes place all year round. But now that the Grand National meeting is over (three days ago) the racegoers' focus begins to change from National Hunt to the flat and the Craven Meeting is always the first significant meeting of the new year.

That sense of renewal and freshness this afternoon is reinforced by blissful springtime weather. There is a slight chill in a brisk breeze that flutters the flags but skies are blue and temperatures touch 18° Celsius. On early-season days like this at racing HQ the manicured lawns around the parade ring are vivid criss-cross shades of emerald green and

there is an invigorating feel-good factor in the air. A chance for those flat racing purists to get stuck into the new season and eye up some of the potential stars.

And so it is that at 1.37pm, horse number seven, *Putra Square*, is silently led into the parade ring, closely followed by number fifteen, *Rose Row*. Their arrival signifies that the preparation is largely complete and the action is about to begin.

The wheels are easing into motion on a new season at Newmarket. Soon the rest of the field are circling and trainers and owners – in their suits and tweeds and trilbies – move into the middle of the parade ring. Sir Michael Stoute can be spotted talking to Manchester United manager Sir Alex Ferguson.

At 1.43pm Prosser enters the parade ring, talking on his mobile, and exchanging pleasantries with various "connections". His body language is passive, his hands deferentially behind his back. In them he holds a pen, the race card and a walkie-talkie. Although his role is to ensure that the pre-race timetable is rigorously followed there is no sense of any ego shouting "I'm in charge here". The casual observer would not even notice his presence.

Three minutes later he slips off to a place he loves: the weighing room. It is here that the true flavour of professional horseracing can be found. The smells, the colours, the energy, the banter: it is all here. The jockeys' room is particularly chaotic but the Newmarket tea-boy is on hand with grazing snacks such as fruit to replace lost energy. There is even a sauna for last-minute weight loss and ice cubes to suck on to aid re-hydration.

No sooner has Prosser entered the room than the jockeys are on their way, their racing silks adding more colour to the occasion. Another minute passes and Prosser is back in the parade ring. The bell rings and jockeys mount their horses. At 1.50pm they are on their way to the start.

As Prosser explains it is critical that they leave the parade ring ten minutes before the starting time. "The time can evaporate very quickly," he says. "It's a long walk from the parade ring to the track and then if you've got a ten furlong race – which can be the circumference of some smaller tracks – they've got to canter to post. You need to get your timings right."

By the time the field is nearing the starting stalls Prosser has moved up to the stewards' room in the main stand to see if anything unexpected happens during the race which relates to the course's facilities. It is from there he watches the horses enter the stalls. At 2.02pm they open, "they're off" and precisely two minutes and six seconds later the one mile and two furlongs have been covered and *Arabian Gulf*, trained by Sir Michael Stoute and ridden by Kerrin McEvoy, has won the Xplor Maiden Stakes (Class 4) by a neck from *Putra Square*.

Prosser's there, of course, when the winner is led into its enclosure.

This cycle repeats with each of the seven races. As the horses enter the parade ring he quietly orchestrates the movements onto the racecourse in line with the timetable. Weighing room, parade ring, stewards' room, winners' enclosure and then back to the weighing room – the cycle continues through the card. Prosser remains a blur of activity, fuelled by just the early morning toast and the buzz of the season's opener at the home of racing – at least until mid-afternoon when he seizes upon a slab of cheddar cheese.

The last race of the day is completed at 5.30pm. As the crowd disperses Prosser turns his attention to irrigation, overseeing watering of the track so it is in good shape for tomorrow's racing. He says: "The sun's been out, the wind's been blowing and it's been a particularly warm day for April. So I knew the ground was going to dry out. We've already made the decision that we'd water tonight so everything is already in position to do so as the last thing of the day."

Once the watering is mobilised and operational and the last spectator has left the track, Prosser can sign off the racing team. On the last day of a meeting, the Newmarket Racecourse Management team meet to take stock. This evening, however, he is able to leave comparatively early – at 7.30pm – back to the rather different demands of family life.

He does with another reason to be cheerful: a blip-free first day of the season. A healthy-sized crowd, great weather and top-quality racing. This is what Prosser is aiming for and he is never happier than when it has been achieved. "What gives me the buzz are days like the Champions' Day in 2006 when everything comes together," he says. "The racetrack was in great condition, the ground staff did all that was asked of them and more, the restaurants, bars and corporate boxes were packed, the atmosphere was superb and the quality of the racing was superb. That gives me a real buzz. At the end of such a day, I am a tired, but happy man. What more can you ask for in life?"

SIX

A BREED APART

"You've got to have an eye for what a successful, attractive horse should look like. I've always been a firm believer that with yearlings or two-year-olds in training that have never run, you normally know within five seconds of a horse walking out of a box whether you like it or not."

THE BREEDING, SELLING AND PURCHASING of thoroughbreds is arguably the most complex part of horseracing. As a result a vast industry has developed in the quest to create excellence in a racehorse – and then sell it for a handsome profit.

Only experts feel truly comfortable in this environment. To prosper you need a deep and genuine understanding of horses: their pedigree, their physique and the way they move.

Tom Goff is a specialist in this area and one morning he was patiently talking me through what his job entails. For my benefit he spoke largely in words of one syllable. Even this was quite an achievement as Goff, a sports addict, had been up much of the previous night watching his beloved England cricket team snatch defeat from the jaws of a certain draw, and, in turn, hand back the Ashes wrapped in green and gold ribbons.

For a while I was inwardly preening myself on how much sense it made. I was feeling pretty smart. Then the phone rang – and Goff began to speak to one of his clients in a language with which I was not remotely familiar. It might as well have been Japanese or Russian.

Horseracing – like most communities and certainly all sports – has its own language and vocabulary, crammed with phrases, anachronisms, jargon and terminology. The language of "racing" is particularly complex and on this occasion, Goff was talking in its most unfathomable dialect: bloodstock. He was talking of conformations, coverings, broodmares, gestation periods, pinhooking and stallions that "stamp their stock". To those in the know these are everyday phrases. For me, just listening sent my brain into meltdown.

Thanks to Goff I eventually learned what these phrases mean. So, for the avoidance of doubt and the sake of clarity:

"Conformation" describes a horse's build, physique and musculature.

Tom Goff The Bloodstock Agent

"Covering" is the act of mating when a mare is paired with a stallion to conceive a foal. The "covering" season lasts between 15th February and 15th July each year.

A "broodmare" is a filly or mare kept at stud for breeding purposes and the "gestation period" is the length of her pregnancy, which is about eleven months.

"Pinhooking" is the business of buying foals and selling them on as yearlings – a potentially profitable business as it cuts out breeding costs and keeping the pregnant mare.

And stallions which "stamp their stock" have offspring that display similar physical characteristics to themselves.

The ability to understand this kind of terminology and speak the language – allied to a deep horse sense and knowledge – are the main areas that identify bona fide members of the racing clan. Thanks to the remarkable friendliness and helpfulness of the likes of Tom Goff I eventually became able to converse in pigdin "bloodstock" but faking it as a fully blown member of the community would have been impossible. You cannot blag your way through without being exposed as an outsider – and to acquire the necessary amount of knowledge takes years. That said, I was more than happy. Just being on the edge of the bloodstock industry was a fascinating education.

Wednesday 18th April, 5.45pm, Tattersalls Sales Ring, Newmarket.

It can seem to take an eternity for the winter months to crawl past and the flat racing season to begin, but when it does it is off and running at a pace. Just thirteen minutes after the last race on day one of the Craven Meeting the spotlight travels one mile from the finishing post of the Rowley Mile to the bell that rings repeatedly at Tattersalls' Park Paddocks. It announces that the first major thoroughbred sale of the year is about to get under way.

The indoor sales ring has a high domed roof under which the horses are led in a circle surrounded by rows of seating. With the evening sunshine streaming in through the roof's windows it feels like a church as lot one enters the sales ring.

By then lot two is ready and waiting at the door and lots three to twelve are being led around in the nearby parade ring. It is the start of a three-hour conveyor belt of thoroughbred talent, available for purchase to the highest bidder.

A public auction at "Tatts", as it is known to regulars, is part-business, part-theatre, part-ancient ritual and almost impossible for the uninitiated to follow without the help of a translator. The auctioneer speaks at high speed, an endless, rhythmical stream of verbiage. It is a struggle to pick out the words as they tumble out, one after another after another.

"I have 28, 28, 28, 28 is what I have, 30 now, at 30, 30 is what I have 32, 32 now. 32 is all I have. Selling this lovely filly by *Johannesburg* at 32. 35, 35, 38 now. I got 38. 40 now. It's to my right. 45 now. 45, 45, 45 is what I'm bid. Selling at 45, 48 now. At 48, 48, 48. Any more at 48? It's against you sir. I have 50. At 50 now. To my right. At 50, 52. I gotta 52. 52. Selling at 52. Make no mistake. Selling at 52. It's against

Tom Goff with daughter Lydia

you. Any more at 52? Every inch a runner this one. At 52 this beautifully filly is sold. 52, at 52 now. Last time. Going for the hammer this time, at 52. Any more? At 52. Going at 52. Last chance. At 52,000 guineas. Sold!"

The currency is guineas, each one equivalent to one pound and five pence. This is possibly the only modern usage of what was once a common British monetary unit. Above the auctioneer the ongoing sale price is also electronically presented in euros, US dollars, yen and dirhams.

The auctioneer has a team of eagle-eyed spotters who stand next to him and pick out those who lift a bidding finger or nod a bidding head. Just as well. Despite instructions to the contrary bidding takes place from anywhere around the sales ring. In fact, bidders make it their business to lurk in the most unobtrusive locations: on the stairs and in gangways. There is a business reason for this furtive behaviour. Well-known agents like Goff do not want to announce their involvement as it may stimulate the bidding.

Goff, though, is nowhere to be seen for the first twenty-nine lots. Clearly they have not made it onto the shortlist. But for lot thirty – an Irish bay colt out of *Danehill Dancer* – he materialises on the outskirts of the sales ring and becomes involved in the bidding.

This is the crunch time, the most stressful moments of his job. Goff, only half-jokingly, describes auctions as "ninety-eight per cent boredom and two per cent terror". This is the "terror" element, as he communicates with his client – at the other end of a mobile phone

– whilst bidding on his behalf. He secures the colt at 57,000 guineas, the auctioneer's hammer confirming that his first purchase of the evening is complete. Goff mysteriously melts back into the shadows from whence he came, which is no mean feat when you are six foot two inches tall and solidly built. It is a strange business.

Auctions like these are when Goff's work comes to fruition in the purchase of racing and breeding stock. To understand why clients employ him we need to take a step back – to learn more about the importance of the genes and "conformation" of a young thoroughbred and discover how Goff gained knowledge in this area and then used it to create his business.

Any explanation of flat racing's cycle has to begin with the stud farms. These are the factories of the breeding industry, with some three hundred in Britain producing more than five thousand thoroughbred foals each year. Most retain stallions whose sole purpose is to cover mares. These stallions have usually had successful racing careers and it is hoped that they will "stamp their stock", producing offspring that have inherited their qualities along with those of the mare. Like humans, the genes of a thoroughbred are influenced by those of its parents and its wider family so owners choose a stallion – usually after much research, advice and pondering – whose characteristics best complement the mare and whose fee they can afford.

Breeders are trying to create a kind of genetic

harmony of temperament and physique that includes speed, stamina, power, conformation and mental toughness. This is the first occasion where Tom Goff offers his services. He provides guidance on this dating service to stud farms and mare owners based in England, Ireland, France and the United States so that the most compatible mating options are chosen for his clients' breeding stock.

Once the choice is made the owners of the mare pay an amount to the owners of the stallion at the stud farm and the covering takes place. The result is a little, gawky, uncoordinated, pop-eyed and spindle-legged foal. By the time of its first birthday it is referred to as a "yearling" and begins to be prepared for sale, still untamed and unridden – and certainly still unproven as a potential racehorse.

Breeding can be as unreliable and unpredictable in racing as it is in humans and acquisitions at this stage have an inherent and glorious uncertainty to them – all the more glorious if it is not your money that might go down the pan. Any purchase, from the cheapest to the most expensive, could be a heart-breaking, money-losing dud. Equally, some bargains will fulfil the dreams of their owners and become the headline-makers of the next two or three seasons.

How can you spot the difference?

Well, for the first-time investor with a layman's knowledge, the words needle and haystack come to mind. To the uninitiated all these horses look fit, healthy and primed to run fast; which is why they enlist the help of a man like Tom Goff.

Assessing the potential of a thoroughbred – like any athlete – is partly a matter of subjective judgement. But Goff can analyse the conformation and movement with an educated eye and then factor in his encyclopaedic knowledge of its pedigree. This leads to an informed judgement that gives the buyer the best possible chance of purchasing a horse with invisible wings rather than four left hooves.

Sometimes Goff's guidance takes the form of a professional valuation, sometimes he coordinates private sales but most of his work is at public auctions. Although he is a devoted family man with three children, he and his business partner, Richard Brown, are frequently abroad, attending every major thoroughbred auction in the northern hemisphere trying to unearth suitable horses. In addition to Tattersalls – with its venues in Newmarket and Fairyhouse in Ireland – this international circuit involves trips to the USA for the Keeneland sales in Lexington, Kentucky as well as sales at Saratoga, Fasig-Tipton and Ocala; the sale at Deauville on the Normandy coast in France and Goff's (no connection with Tom) based at County Kildare in Ireland and Doncaster in Yorkshire.

And for a cost of five per cent of the purchase price the client receives the benefit of Goff's experience, diligence and knowledge in this area. He says that his job at the auctions is always about balancing three components – conformation, pedigree and budget. That is where he adds value. Because he knows how the sales work and he knows horses.

The reason behind it all –
thoroughbred talent.

70

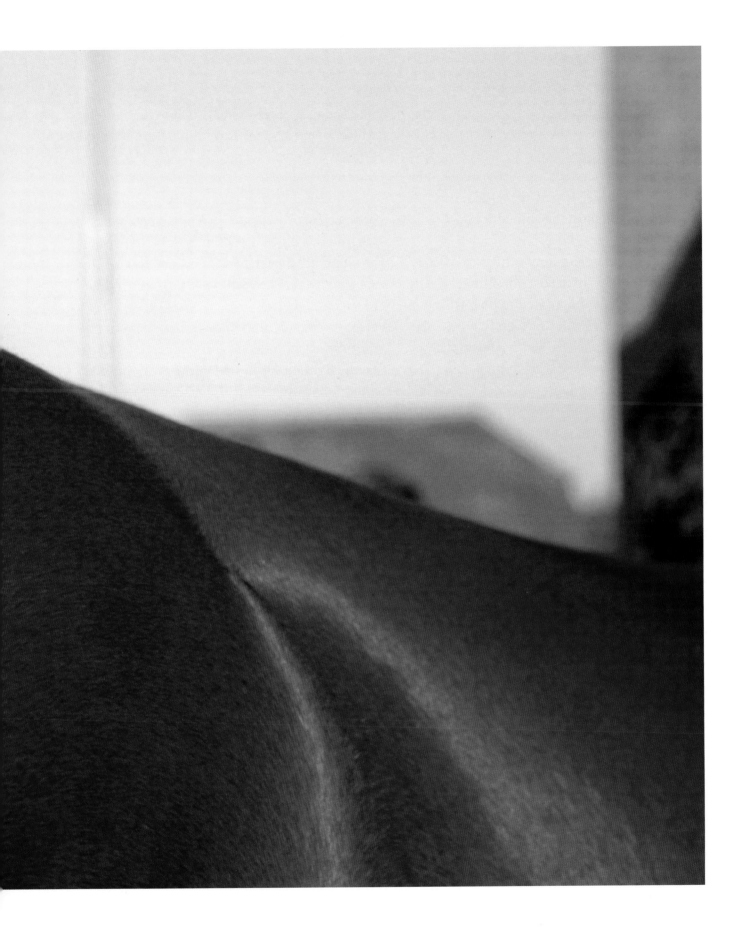

However, he was not born with that knowledge. Nor was there a manual or university degree available to help him spot the difference between the classic contender and the no-hoper. It had to be acquired the hard way, through a long apprenticeship.

Goff is remarkably similar to Michael Prosser, in that he knew from an early age that he wanted to be involved in horseracing but was not sure quite how – and, like Prosser, as much by luck as judgement, he actually followed a textbook preparation for the job that he now performs.

It helped that, like many of the horses that he inspects, he had decent genes. His parents were interested in racing and his uncle, Peter Scott, was a prominent sports journalist universally known as Hotspur of the *Telegraph*. Young Tom often visited Hotspur's house or a racecourse with him and found his enthusiasm "infectious". Scott took him to see the famous three-time Grand National winner, *Red Rum*, a horse which remains one of Goff's heroes.

Goff went to Eton and then Buckingham university before working in the property boom at the end of the 1980s. The 1989 crash put paid to that and he vacated his job in London's west end to work on a farm with a view to moving into the horseracing industry. By then he had the bug and it is a bug that he has never lost. Even now he speaks with a youngster's, misty-eyed enthusiasm: "The animal is a wonderful thing to be around. Sir Winston Churchill said that 'the best thing for the inside of a man is the outside of a horse'.

Just being around animals is a thrill and the whole racing game is a thrill. It's been referred to as the 'great triviality'. There are so many different angles to it, so many ways to enjoy, whether from a training, breeding or punting perspective. You name it. The big racing days, whether it's Ascot or Epsom or York or Aintree or Churchill Downs are fantastic days in the sporting calendar. I still look forward to them like a child really."

So it was a fillip for Goff to be offered the role as number two to the trainer Dick Hern. By then Hern was in the twilight of an illustrious career. He had overseen a procession of big race winners, including *Brigadier Gerard*. In all, between 1971 and 1995 he won seventeen classics, including three Epsom Derbys with *Troy, Henbit* and *Nashwan* before he retired in 1997. This success was all the more remarkable because in 1984 he was badly injured in a hunting accident that left him partly paralysed and wheelchair bound – and four years later he was diagnosed with a serious heart condition.

Goff speaks with great affection for his ex-boss: "Dick Hern was an enormously knowledgeable horseman who'd been in the game for decades and he was a remarkable human being. He'd not only triumphed in the game as a healthy person, he'd then had to re-learn how to train again and do it from a wheelchair or in the back of a car. That was a very different discipline for him. He had triumphed over adversity in a remarkable way and not lost any of his enthusiasm."

Of course the apprentice was bound to

absorb knowledge from the maestro, whether it be about the construction of the racing calendar, thoroughbred sales, studs or selections of yearlings. This gave Goff a solid foundation of horseracing expertise but if those three years with Hern were educational they were also challenging. The stables suffered debilitating viruses and respiratory problems and wins became scarce. Goff was uncertain of his next step; he had toyed with the idea of becoming a trainer but did not want to be an also-ran; and his time with Hern emphasised to him that significant funds would be required to set up a scale of operation that would be successful. Funds that, despite a privileged upbringing, Goff just did not possess.

"Having seen how it could be at the very top," he says, "if I was going to chip away with ten to fourteen horses I knew I would be miserable." He also grew to understand that whilst some people are born trainers, he was not one of them.

"Temperamentally I wasn't going to be suited to being a trainer," he muses. "In horse parlance I'm a 'box walker', a horse that walks round and round his box the whole time. I'm not a worrier but in training you can train a horse brilliantly and in a race everything could go wrong. Some people are temperamentally better suited. Like my mate Ed Dunlop, who on the outside always appears very relaxed and languid. But inside, when things go wrong, it's not fun."

So it was a choice of two options: journalist or bloodstock agent. Initially his inclination was with bloodstock, but he got married in 1996 to Catherine, and they were keen to move out of London. So when the opportunity arose to become the eyes and ears of the *Racing Post* in Newmarket he took up the offer. As with his time with Dick Hern, Goff learnt a great deal whilst becoming increasingly aware that this was not where his future lay.

He recalls: "It was a bastard of a job, constantly treading a tightrope between meeting the desires of the newspaper and the editor and the trainers. You need a good relationship with the trainers because you're constantly talking to them about horses, usually when there's bad news. But I also had to write stories to sell the newspaper."

The job did not pay well either and so Goff made the decision to move into bloodstock, which he felt had the potential to provide a reasonable living whilst allowing him to remain in racing. Besides, he says, "the whole selection process of choosing yearlings to be successful racehorses is something that always fascinated me and was something I wanted to be involved with".

In 1999 he joined the British Bloodstock Agency, working with Joss Collins. Collins had thirty-five years of experience and a wide circle of clients and friends. He was hugely respected and influential and Goff was delighted that they "hit it off". Two years later the British Bloodstock Agency was taken over in acrimonious fashion and Goff and Collins set up Blandford Bloodstock from scratch in July 2001. The business was just becoming established when tragedy struck.

Goff recalls with the pain still evident in each word: "It was February 2004 and the business was going from strength to strength. Then Joss got cancer and died within three weeks. It was just like that (clicks his fingers). From a business point of view it was potentially devastating to the company because Joss was the largest earner of fees at that particular time and earned sixty per cent of the company earnings.

"Few people gave us a chance of making a go of it and certainly there was a large element of flying by the seat of our pants. We just had to put the band back together. Our backs were against the wall. Inwardly I was devastated but I had to bury my emotions because we had to spend so much time working and trying to hold onto our client base, our market share in the bloodstock industry. There wasn't much room for sentiment quite honestly. It wasn't until later that it really hit me.

"Joss was such an inspirational character and such a knowledgeable person in the bloodstock business that his death had a massive effect on us. Y'know I'm very fortunate to have worked for two remarkable people in Dick Hern and Joss Collins – and a lot of what I've learned from them has hopefully rubbed off in some shape or form."

Since Collins's death the band has indeed been reconstructed and played on. Blandford Bloodstock, with Goff in tandem with Richard Brown, has become a profitable business with an international reputation for service founded on integrity, expertise and professionalism.

It can boast some outstanding successes down the years. Pictures of most appear on the walls of Goff's office situated in Newmarket town centre. But one recent bargain yet to appear – because Goff believes it would be bad luck for it to be hung up before the end of its racing career – is the chestnut colt *Dutch Art* (see Chapter Seven). Goff purchased him at Doncaster's St Leger Yearling sale for just 16,000 guineas. He became the outstanding two-year-old of 2006, winning all four of his outings including two group one races, and a contender for the 2000 Guineas when he became a three-year-old.

Incongruously, there is also the famous picture of English cricketer Andrew Flintoff consoling his Australian counterpart Brett Lee after England's two-run victory during the 2005 Ashes series; further evidence of Goff's love of cricket and old-Etonian appreciation of manners and chivalry.

Indeed it is those principles ("I want to be able to sleep at night") that ensure that Goff does not poach clients from other bloodstock agents. He hopes that Blandford's record will be sufficient to sell the company and attract new business – but he also nurtures relationships with his existing clients and keeps his specialist knowledge sharp and up to date to lessen the risk of being overtaken by his competitors.

"Our big challenge is holding onto our client base in what is an incredibly competitive market," he explains. "It's a bit like being a trainer. There are far too many trainers out there and far too many people who want to be bloodstock agents. We need to be buying

Tom Goff on his mobile while bidding at Tattersalls.
Next to him is Peter Chapple-Hyam.

group one winners every year just to maintain our market position and that's not easy because there's a lot of horses out there and a lot of able people."

That constant need to retain client base and market position is why, in the third week of April 2007, Goff finds himself spending several hours, split over several days, at Tattersalls undertaking the donkey work of inspecting horse after horse in preparation for the "breeze-up" auction that is to begin on the same day as the Craven Meeting.

Each year there are seven sales in Newmarket attended by buyers from more than fifty countries and every continent. It is recognised as the leading bloodstock auctioneer in Europe, selling ten thousand horses a year both here and at its Irish offshoot in Fairyhouse. Of those the most high-profile occasion is the yearling sale in October where the cream of the one-year-old, unraced horses are auctioned. Bidding for the classic winners of the future can be fierce and Goff describes it as his "most important week of the year".

There are also "horses in training" sales as well as the springtime "breeze-up sales" where the focus is on two-year-olds which did not get sold as yearlings or are being re-sold by "pinhookers", who buy horses, nurture them and then sell them on for profit. The sale is known as a "breeze-up" because each horse canters two or three furlongs before potential purchasers in the days leading up to sale and "breeze" is racing jargon for going at an easy pace.

"Tatts" has been located at Park Paddocks since 1965 (when it was first founded in 1766 by Richard Tattersall it was based at Hyde Park Corner) and the grounds are spacious and opulent. It is only two minutes from the modern-day Newmarket town centre, with its instantly forgettable fast food outlets and cut-price shops, but walking up the hill to Tattersalls is like going back in time.

Within the grounds there is a colonial feel, with immaculately maintained lawns, newly painted white fencing, raked gravel, numerous trees and well-constructed stables, paddocks, examination and sales rings.

This April the mood is accentuated by a series of cloudless, sun-blessed springtime days, birdsong and the early blooming of the cherry blossoms. When you add the noble, haughty and aristocratic bearing of the horses being led around then romantics may feel like they have stepped into the pages of a Henry James novel; at least they might if Range Rovers, Jeeps and open-topped BMWs did not populate the car parks.

This ambience is entirely lost on Goff. He has been here, and to sales like this all around the world, more times than he would care to remember – and now it is time for some bread-and-butter groundwork. There are two hundred and thirteen lots at this particular sale and Goff has to swot up on each one. This may seem an arduous task but at the Keeneland sales in Kentucky he views one hundred and fifty horses a day for two weeks, so it presents no great test of his stamina.

"You've got to be bloody hard-working," he explains. "You get out of it what you put into it. I'm a great believer in that. You've got to be able to work thoroughly. We can't look at every horse but we'll do our damnedest to. A lot of owners who know the game are not familiar with the sales process or they haven't got the time to spare. Some owners will take a much greater interest and look at horses with me. But the majority are busy, successful men or women and haven't got time to waste wandering around Tattersalls. A lot of what we're doing at sales is providing a filtration process if you like."

His technique for horse inspection has become as well grooved as the pre-shot routine of a professional golfer. He tours the stables and asks the "consignors" who prepare and present the horses at the sale to "get them out please", specifying the lot number. They do so at speed, treating Goff with respect and friendliness. It is not just that he is a potential buyer with a reputation in bloodstock. It is also that racing is a small world where most people know each other. Indeed, as Goff moves around the stables assessing potential purchases he constantly greets friends, colleagues and even the odd competitor. In addition the day is regularly punctuated by the ring of his mobile phone. He is always making arrangements, brokering new deals, managing relationships.

He begins his assessment by looking at the stationary horse side-on, gauging the conformation and general outlook. He then asks for it to be walked. A horse that walks well often gallops well and he is looking for a fluid gait which covers a good deal of ground with every stride. As the horse walks away he gets behind it, then scrutinises it as it returns, making sure it does not "paddle" in or out, that its toes do not turn in and that the legs are neither too flexed nor too straight which would put stress on the tendons and increase the risk of injury.

Goff has the bearing and solemnity of a cricket umpire adjudicating on a close run-out decision. He is absorbed and lost in concentration even though he has performed the ritual thousands of times. He knows that a well-built conformation is critical to help the horse to meet the ground evenly with every stride – and that this, in turn, increases the potential for athletic performance and minimises the risk of injury.

He often asks for this walk to happen twice or more. Throughout he is poker-faced and emotionless behind impenetrable dark glasses. Experienced Goff-watchers, though, can spot telltale signs that should encourage a prospective vendor. For horses he likes he will remove his sunglasses momentarily, get close to its neck, whisper sweet nothings and give it a pat.

After each mini-beauty parade he makes notes – meaningful to him, less so to others – in a catalogue provided by Tattersalls that details four generations of pedigree in the minutest detail, one page per horse. These notes will help him filter two hundred and thirteen potentials down to around twenty to thirty possible targets for his clients. His notes might state something like "straight through the hind leg", "pigeon-toed" or "too small". Equally there are some horses which warrant closer inspection and encourage him to remove the sunglasses.

"Now that's a nice horse," he confides of lot twenty-one, a bay colt by *Storming Home*; "a quality horse and no great pedigree, so a possible bargain." Lot fifty-three – another bay colt, this time by *Aldebaran* – also grabs his attention. He remarks that lot thirty-seven – a bay colt by *Montjeu* – is "elegant and a good walker", and thinks lot sixty-two – a bay filly by *Royal Applause* – has "presence".

"You've got to have an eye for what a successful, attractive horse should look like," he says. "I've always been a firm believer that with yearlings or two-year-olds in training that have never run you normally know within five seconds of a horse walking out of a box whether you like it or not. It's a bit like meeting a person for the first time. You either warm to someone or not – whether that's a kind of chemistry I don't know.

"I suppose you're looking for a horse that's robust, very correct, good scope and with class and quality that shines out, wherever you are. But when you're trying to spot future talent in

The sales ring
at Tattersalls

a future racehorse I think one can get carried away in searching for a perfect specimen."

Goff's scrutiny of the horses begins on the Sunday and continues right up to the beginning of the sale on Wednesday evening. Often he will return to a horse for a second and third look as he begins to narrow down his selections. Entwined within that is the breeze-up, undertaken a mile away at the Rowley Mile, where Goff watches them in action. Over three hours on Tuesday morning the two hundred and thirteen horses gallop for two or three furlongs, sometimes alone, sometimes with a stable-mate. Progress can also be followed on Newmarket's big screen and commentary is provided over the tannoy. They are watched by around one hundred and fifty agents, trainers, potential owners and press, dotted around in groups of twos and threes. Many have stopwatches in hand. All have pens and the Tattersalls catalogue.

This type of sale has its advantages compared to yearling sales. "The main thing is that you get to see a horse on the move," says Goff. "When we are at the yearling sales we've got to make up our minds whether a horse looks athletic or not just by seeing him walk. It's a good guide but nothing like the real thing and seeing a horse on the move cantering. Secondly, even though the horse might cost a purchaser a little bit more, the fact is that you are saving on about six months training fees. To many people, that will be a big advertisement."

Goff watches the breeze-up with trainer,

Peter Chapple-Hyam, which is no surprise as the two often "work" the sales together. In addition to owners, Goff will liaise with trainers who like to have a pool of horses available for sale when contacted by prospective owners. "Peter is a good mate of mine and an exceptionally talented trainer," he explains. "He came back from Hong Kong and we bought a few horses together at the Doncaster Yearling Sales and I'm also fortunate that he also uses me for some of his other purchases. Some of those are to order and some are speculative because a trainer needs to have something in the yard so that if someone rings him up and says 'have you got anything for sale?' he has got something available."

Goff continues to make notes in his catalogue. Some whose conformation and pedigree seemed interesting at the first look do not move so well and so the filtering process continues. By Wednesday he has completed his review of each horse, formed an opinion and speaks to his clients to firm up their needs – which can range from, say, a "sharp two-year-old to an Ascot Gold Cup Winner" – and their budget, which might be from £25,000 up to £350,000. That requires clear communication so that at the critical moment, when bidding is taking place, there is no confusion. Clerk of the course, Michael Prosser, had also picked this out as a prime requirement and Goff agrees: "My primary skill is to get on with people, because if you can't get on with people then you're not going to have any clients. You have to understand what they want and only by good communication can you do that."

In between the phone calls he has lunch with owners at the first day of Newmarket's Craven Meeting, watches the racing and then, at 5.45pm, he is back at Tattersalls, immaculately dressed in blue suit and white open-necked shirt. It is sale time; a six-hour marathon spread over two evenings.

On Wednesday evening – after that successful purchase of lot thirty – Blandford Bloodstock is outbid for the star turn of the evening, a grey filly, ultimately sold for 370,000 guineas. Undeterred, Goff acknowledges that it is a simple fact of bloodstock life that buyers with bigger budgets will, at times, wield superior purchasing power.

However, he was more successful in a dash of frenetic activity towards the end of the evening, making purchases at 55,000, 60,000 and 60,000 guineas, one in liaison with Peter Chapple-Hyam. On the second evening Sheikh Mohammed's agent secured the three most expensive offerings, outbidding Blandford Bloodstock on one occasion.

In total, one hundred and twenty horses were sold at the sale at a total cost of more than eight and a half million guineas and an average of 72,000 guineas. In 2006 Blandford Bloodstock spent more money than any other purchaser at the equivalent sale. In 2007 they made six more modest purchases (though still about "par for the course") on behalf of their clients.

Given Goff's track record it is likely that one or more of these two-year-olds will put their name in lights over the coming seasons – and that will always be the ultimate in job satisfaction.

He sums up: "My main aim is to be an honest broker and do a good job for our clients. Winning a Stakes race for anyone is a mega-thrill and the more the merrier really. Buying any horse cheaply who then does very well is as big a kick as you can get as a yearling buyer, really. A happy day at the office is seeing a horse that we have been involved with doing well and seeing yearlings bred by our commercial breeder clients selling for plenty of money."

SEVEN

FOUR-LEGGED FRIEND

LIKE DOCTORS AND THEIR PATIENTS, it is probably not advisable for writers to become emotionally involved with their subjects. Respect them, like them even, but keep a healthy distance so that objectivity and perspective can be retained.

I found this most difficult to achieve for this chapter, even though the subject contributed not a single decent quote. Pretty much everyone featured in the book professed their affection and adoration for the thoroughbred horse. They are stunning animals and the chestnut colt, Dutch Art, is as handsome as they come.

Little wonder that his connections seemed unusually smitten. Not only does he look good but he has a pleasant disposition and moves like a speeding arrow. Certainly four consecutive high-profile victories through the summer of 2006 did nothing to dampen their optimism that here was a horse with the potential to really put his name in lights as a three-year-old. Successful colts can be hard and bolshy, but Dutch Art was living proof that nice guys can come first.

Following his life and times over the winter of 2006 and the 2007 season helped me understand that there are three main filters through which thoroughbreds and the flat racing industry can be viewed.

Firstly, it was clear that Dutch Art represents a moneymaking, business commodity: both as a racehorse, with the potential to win significant amounts of prize money, and a stallion that could command mega-fees at stud. From his first outing he had been earmarked for the 2000 Guineas with its purse of £350,000. If he could give a good account of himself there then his reputation and stud value would be enhanced and a luxurious life as a stallion with Cheveley Park Stud would be assured.

Secondly, Dutch Art (and every other racehorse) exists as a means for gambling. His fitness, form, potential, physique, temperament and pedigree were the subject of close attention by prospective punters, suitably encouraged by the daily media speculation that precedes big race days. "Experts" employed various techniques and complicated statistical systems to judge his chances of winning the 2000 Guineas. It reinforced for me that if gambling was ever banned then the sport's popularity would immediately plummet – indeed horseracing and gambling have long been mutually dependent.

Finally, I am heartened to report, Dutch Art was the subject of great affection – from his owners, his trainer, the bloodstock agent who purchased him, and, above all, from the stable lass who looked after him. I do not think I met anybody at Newmarket who was cold or indifferent to the horse as a species. However, the adoration – indeed love would not be too strong a description – shown to Dutch Art by his stable lass was a pleasure to witness. Tracking the horse's build-up to the 2000 Guineas largely through that stable lass, little Danni Deverson, was a delight. It made me feel good about horseracing and I grew attached to

Dutch Art The Thoroughbred

Dutch Art as well, enjoying a vicarious involvement in the season of what Danni called "a dude, just the coolest, most laid-back horse". It may not have been good for the perspective but it was good for the soul. So when Dutch Art *raced in the 2000 Guineas I found surprisingly I was shouting him through the last furlong as loudly as anyone.*

For racehorses the date of 1st January bears more than the normal significance. It is the official birthday for each and every one, the date when they progress from a foal to a yearling, a yearling to a two-year-old, and so on.

For most, their racing career usually takes place when they are still developing physically and against horses within their own age bracket – so the timing of their actual birth is significant. An older horse, even by a few months, has an advantage because they have had more time to mature and grow.

So breeders take care over their mathematics. They know that in the northern hemisphere the thoroughbred breeding season runs from 15th February to 15th July. They know, too, that the gestation period of a pregnant mare is around eleven months. So a simple calculation evidences that the earlier the foal is conceived during the breeding season, the earlier it will be born in the following calendar year. And the earlier the better.

The foal that was to be named *Dutch Art* was born suitably early in 2004 on 18th March at Southborough Manor near Attleborough in Norfolk. He was small (like his father) but a definite looker: an orange-copper chestnut with a splash of white colouring on his forehead and on one of his legs near the hoof.

At the beginning of his life – like all racehorses – he represented a short-term moneymaking business opportunity. That is the nature of thoroughbred breeding. His very existence was sponsored, so to speak, by Cromlech Bloodstock.

They were the company that paid Cheveley Park an amount of £12,000 for one of their resident stallions, *Medicean*, to cover a mare called *Halland Park Lass*, which they owned. They made this investment with the intention of selling for profit once the foal had been born. In fact the foal was sold for 14,500 guineas to the Curragh Bloodstock Agency some eight months after the birth.

Nor did the business transactions end there. The foal was nurtured, developed and then offloaded again – now a year and six months old – for 16,500 guineas at the Doncaster breeze-up sales in September 2005. For the businesses involved in this buy–nurture–sell cycle it was short-term investment to achieve a quick profit.

The purchaser at Doncaster was Tom Goff, working with trainer Peter Chapple-Hyam on behalf of an owner, Matthew Green.

Goff recalls: "*Dutch Art* was by *Medicean*, who we liked. He was a very attractive, nimble sharp-looking yearling and that was specifically the kind of horse we were trying to buy at that sale. Anyway we turned up for the sale and I'm pretty sure that *Dutch Art* was the third horse

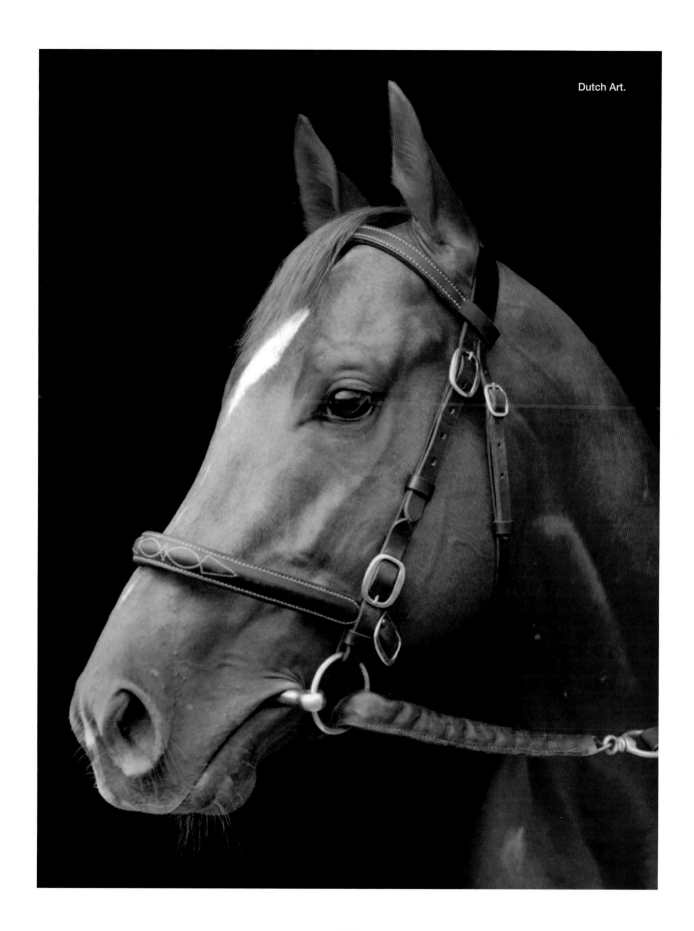

Dutch Art.

out of a long list of horses and we were very lucky to nick him for £16,000. Now I could sit here and spout on about how much we loved him and what geniuses we are – but that would be just bullshit quite frankly. Yes, of course we liked him, otherwise we wouldn't have bid for him. But the reality is that he was a well-bought horse in terms of his price and he's been brilliantly trained. That's the reality of it. We thought it was value and we were happy enough but, no, he was just one of a group of horses that we bought."

Goff's point about being brilliantly trained is well made. Yes, he had unearthed a 24-carat gold bargain – but thereafter it depended on the ability of the trainer to craft and shape raw potential. The young thoroughbred's potential for physical development is exceptional yet it is only with suitable training that it can begin to win prize money.

Dutch Art, then, was fortunate to be placed into the skilled and experienced hands of Peter Chapple-Hyam at St Gatien Stables in Newmarket.

It was there that "little Dutchy" – as he became known – met "little Danni" Deverson, a twenty-five-year-old lightweight stable lass who had worked for Chapple-Hyam for one and a half years, having spent seven years down the road at the stables of William Haggas.

It was Deverson who picked out the newly arrived yearling to tend to on his arrival, because "he was so soft and a sweet horse to look after". She adds, "When I picked 'Dutch' as a baby I just hoped he'd pick up

one or two little races. I fell in love with the character."

In the second year of *Dutch Art*'s life – in addition to being bought and sold on a couple of occasions – he was "broken in". This involved getting used to having a bit in his mouth, used to wearing a saddle and used to walking with long reins. Then he was ridden, progressing through walking, trotting and cantering, up to a gallop.

Throughout his development, Deverson has ridden him out each morning then groomed him later in the day. It is a duty of devotion that has created a deep mutual bond. Her fiancé, Craig Dykes, who also works at the stables, explains: "There's definitely a special connection. He's a lovely horse, a special horse and she keeps him calm. I don't think he would like someone rough or bullying. She's definitely got it sussed."

The fact that *Dutch Art* was "a lovely horse, a special horse" became apparent as he moved from a yearling into a still diminutive two-year-old, being primed to begin his racing career over relatively short distances against horses of the same age. Experts soon began to notice that he had that indefinable something, that X-factor.

Tom Goff takes up the story. "If Peter (Chapple-Hyam) says to me a horse goes well then I know it goes well, because he's a man we know from history that when he makes predictions you need to sit up and listen. Around March time (2006) I went out onto the gallops and Peter said we're just going to give a couple of two-year-olds a spin up here. And this little chestnut went clear of a couple of companions. So indications were good from an early time."

So, by 5th June 2006, the day of *Dutch Art's* first competitive race – a five-furlong sprint at Windsor – astute judges were beginning to pay interest. Goff continues: "I was actually away in the United States when, just after the Derby, he had his first run in a conditions race. I remember Peter saying he would run well but Jeremy Noseda had a nice filly (*Simply Perfect*) in the race. Anyway, our little horse got up and won really well."

Predictably owner Matthew Green was delighted. "He's been showing up nicely at home," he said, "and Peter is an expert at getting a two-year-old ready. We'll be going to the Norfolk Stakes with this fellow, he's got so much speed and he loves fast ground."

However, by the time of the Norfolk Stakes, Green no longer had an official interest in the horse. Paul Roy, another prominent owner, had lost one of his best, *Majors Cast*, to a fatal injury and looked for an immediate replacement. He was one of the experts who had noticed *Dutch Art's* electric turn of foot at Windsor and made Green an offer that he decided not to refuse.

Maybe Green had some second thoughts when the horse won the five-furlong Norfolk Stakes again in fine style at Royal Ascot.

Goff, naturally, was following this progress with interest. "On Norfolk day we were wound up into a bit of a frenzy really and Peter was adamant that the horse would run a huge race – and he did. That was an absolutely fantastic

day at the office." Word is that the trainer was in tears of joy at the end of the race. Anyway, two races, two wins.

Two months later *Dutch Art* was in France contesting the group one, Prix Morny at Deauville. Goff, of course, was also there. "In the Morny," he recalls, "the main issue was the ground. It came up very soft and we were very worried about it. Peter was as sure as you can be that the horse would be able to handle it." And handle it he did, maintaining his unbeaten record, hitting the front with a furlong left and easing to a smooth success. The Morny was a startling victory.

Not only was it over a longer distance – six furlongs – but it was on what racing folk call "bottomless" ground. It suggested that he was not just a fast-track sprinter, that he could cope with longer distances and "give" in the ground. His jockey that day, Christophe Soumillon, said that he thought the horse would be able to "get" a mile the next season (the distance of the 2000 Guineas) and with that *Dutch Art's* credentials for the 2007 running of the race were becoming established. William Hill cut his odds from 25-1 to 20-1 and ante-post punters were beginning to track his progress with interest.

Those odds were cut again after his fourth consecutive victory – and his second group one – a month later. This time it was on the Rowley Mile course at Newmarket in the Shadwell Middle Park Stakes where he began as favourite despite more soft conditions. After

racing just behind the leaders he quickened when asked by jockey Frankie Dettori about two furlongs from home. He held a clear lead with a furlong left, and won by two lengths. Four out of four. Total prize money earned thus far: £278,000.

With a summer of success behind him and cause for optimism in the future, Cheveley Park cut a business deal with the Roys that meant shared ownership and also provided them with stud rights once *Dutch Art* retired.

By the time that he went into winter quarters – having raced flawlessly on four occasions – his odds for the Guineas were down to 9-1, third favourite behind the outstanding Irish pair of *Teofilo* and *Holy Roman Emperor*.

Through that debut season, the post-race quotes of owners, trainer and jockeys usually began by expressing their pleasure with how well he had run. They then followed with an opinion on how effective he would be over a mile compared with shorter distances. There was a question mark here. Of all the variables that affect a horse's ability to run at its best the distance of the race – along with the "going" – is probably the most critical. The difference between a race of five or six furlongs and one of a mile or beyond equates to the difference between an Olympian contesting a 100-metre sprint and a middle-distance event; the needs range from the explosive surge of a Linford Christie to the stamina and last-bend kick of a Sebastian Coe.

Trevor Jones' photograph of
Dutch Art, taken after he had gone to stud.

Dutch Art The Thoroughbred

Certainly for many two-year-old horses even a seven-furlong race is a feat of endurance. They only develop the stamina to cope with longer distances when they grow older and stronger. However, the degree of that capacity varies greatly from horse to horse. For an indication it is always best to analyse the bloodline.

Dutch Art's sire, *Medicean*, won six races in his career including two of group one standard and amassed more than half a million pounds in prize money. Critically two of those wins were over one mile and one mile two furlongs. Since his retirement he has gradually created

a reputation as a stallion and, by 2007, cost a fee of £30,000 to cover a broodmare. The dam, *Halland Park Lass*, ran only twice but was a daughter of an impressive out-and-out sprinter, *Palacegate Episode*, who won eleven races, all over five furlongs. The bloodlines suggested speed more than stamina, but way back through the generations the 1957 Irish Oaks Winner (contested over a longer distance) *Silken Gilder* could be found.

So the genetics were sound but inconclusive in determining whether *Dutch Art* would be able to "get home" at the conclusion of the longest straight and the stiffest mile in racing

---

DUTCH ART'S ANCESTRY

DUTCH ART

Medicean (GB) 1997 SIRE	Machiavellian (USA) 1987)	Mr Prospector (USA) 1970
		Coup de Fole (USA) 1982
	Mystic Goddess (USA) 1990	Storm Bird (Can) 1978
		Rose Goddess (USA) 1979
Halland Park Lass (IRE) 1999 DAM	Spectrum (IRE) 1992	Rainbow Quest (USA) 1981
		River Dancer (USA) 1981
	Palacegate Episode (IRE) 1990	Drumails (IRE) 1980
		Pasadena Lady (IRE) 1983

---

on Guineas day. If he could "get home" there he would "get home" anywhere – but there was an undoubted question mark.

Over the winter he rested, played, grew three inches taller, worked over seven furlongs and a mile in training and by Easter 2007 – as the racing media began to turn their attention away from National Hunt and the Grand National to the springtime flat racing classics – trainer Chapple-Hyam was upbeat about his chances.

"I'm very pleased with *Dutch Art* – I couldn't be happier," he said, "but they're all champions at this time of the year. I have no doubts about the trip, and if he gets it, he wins. He's a natural and I measured him the other day and he is standing nearly sixteen hands now."

For thoroughbreds, the yearling season is one of development, the second is one of progression and the third is time for delivery as it is the only year when they are able to contest the classics. In that respect it is now or never. Dependent on ability and fitness, they may stay in training for ten years. However, the stars commonly retire at three or four so they can maximise their potential at stud. So there was a chance that the 2007 season would be the last for *Dutch Art* even though he would not become a fully developed physical specimen until the age of five. That is just the short and sharp nature of flat racing.

During January, February and the early part of March, the bookmakers' ante-post odds on the 2000 Guineas were pretty much frozen. *Teofilo* and *Holy Roman Emperor*, who had contested the

Dewhurst Stakes in such thrilling fashion on Champions' Day the previous October, were identified as the most likely winners, with *Dutch Art* deemed the next most likely.

Then as racing shed its winter coat the kaleidoscope was constantly shaken and the odds changed, often quite dramatically. The whole serendipity of the sport was illustrated in the contrasting fortunes of the three ante-post favourites.

Firstly, the Irish global breeding operation, Coolmore, issued a statement. "In the very early stages of *George Washington*'s stud career his fertility has been questioned ... He has been suspended from covering and *Holy Roman Emperor* has been retired to take his place."

George Washington had won the previous year's 2000 Guineas and had been the three-year-old star of 2006. His inability to "cover" was a blow for Coolmore and the decision to retire *Holy Roman Emperor*, their leading classic contender for 2007, said much about their priorities. The message was loud and clear: the strength of their breeding operation and portfolio of available stallions was paramount.

Holy Roman Emperor's exit from the race merely reinforced the feeling that *Teofilo* would dominate – and this domination was expected to spread wider than just the Guineas. Many – including his trainer, Jim Bolger – felt that he had the potential to become the first to win the colts' Triple Crown (the 2000 Guineas, the Derby and the St Leger) for thirty-seven years. Only fifteen horses have ever managed this: the first in 1853; the most recent, *Nijinsky*, in 1970.

Only remarkable equine all-rounders are capable of winning classics over a mile (1000 Guineas), a mile and four furlongs (The Derby) and the mile and six and a half furlongs of the St Leger. and many felt *Teofilo* fitted the bill. Some described him as a "monster", some as a wonder horse. Certainly, for the three-year-old class of 2007, *Teofilo* looked to have it all at his feet. Then, quite suddenly, he did not. On 17th April after he had been trotting he showed some discomfort in his left fetlock.

Teofilo's injury emphasised the fact that thoroughbreds are both muscularly powerful and delicate creatures, in the same way Olympic 100-metre sprinters can run like the wind yet are always predisposed to injury. And if there is going to be an injury the load-bearing legs are an obvious pressure point. The great cable of the main tendon, the one that runs through the back of the forelegs, is where the weight and power is absorbed at impact.

It is also where the spring is generated for the next stride. Tendons need to be as strong, straight and flexible as a guitar string to support them as they hurtle along at speeds approaching forty miles per hour, covering twenty-eight feet in a single stride. It is a repetitive and instinctive biomechanical movement but with almost every landing there is a danger of damage to joints, ligaments, tendons or, worst of all, some form of fracture.

After a spell of recuperation and a few days of optimism after *Teofilo* returned to full training, the injury flared up again and he had to be withdrawn from the race (and indeed the Epsom Derby).

So, no triple crown for *Teofilo*. Indeed, no *Holy Roman Emperor* or *Teofilo* for the Guineas. The two horses deemed "most likely" would not even make it into the starting stalls.

In view of this *Dutch Art* seemed well positioned to start as favourite – but, despite these notable absentees, by the eve of the race he was out of fashion, judged only half as likely to win as he had been two weeks earlier. Not one tipster in the national press was even recommending an each-way bet. *Adagio, US Ranger, Major Cadeaux, Diamond Tycoon, Haatef* and *Strategic Prince*: all leapfrogged him in the betting.

This sudden fall from favour was entirely due to an unsatisfactory preparation race in the Greenham Stakes on 21st April at Newbury. There had been considerable debate between owners and trainer over whether to run him. Chapple-Hyam's instincts were to just give him a non-competitive racecourse gallop but others were keener on a more formal run-out at Newbury – and they had the final say.

Yet the horse was far from his peak. Chapple-Hyam told the media he was not yet race-fit, that his tailored preparation for the Guineas was incomplete and that it should be viewed as nothing more than a warm-up race. In addition Deverson recalled that on the day the colt was distracted. "He'd had a long time at home since his last run," she said. "At Newbury he didn't have his mind on the job. He was unsettled. All the fillies were around him and he was more interested in them and getting upset."

Dutch Art, with Frankie Dettori on board, wins the Shadwell Middle Park Stakes at Newmarket in September 2006.

As a result, Newbury did not see the all-conquering *Dutch Art* of the previous season. It was a race of two halves: the first at snail's pace, the second a headlong dash for the line. *Dutch Art* never threatened and finished a comfortable second behind *Major Cadeaux*, one of the horses more favoured in the betting for the Guineas.

"It wasn't run to suit him. I wasn't disappointed with him at all," Deverson said. "It was such a small field that there was nothing to make the pace. They went no gallop early on and then it turned into a three-furlong sprint. He didn't blow hard after the race."

Despite Deverson's protestations and visual evidence that *Dutch Art* had grown three inches in size and filled out, potential punters now had another question to consider: had he regressed since last season? That would not be unusual; many outstanding two-year-olds stagnate and

93

are overtaken in their development. As some stand still, others take several leaps forward. Certainly the media and gamblers lost interest in *Dutch Art*'s chances.

Chapple-Hyam was less concerned. The race had not gone well but with two weeks of preparation ahead he said that "he'll be a different horse for the Guineas". The trainer had history on his side to support this confidence. In 1992 one of his horses, *Rodrigo De Triano*, fared equally badly in the Greenham Stakes but went on to win the 2000 Guineas.

It was Lester Piggott's last classic victory, Chapple-Hyam's first. Despite runners through the 1990s he had been unable to repeat that Guineas success and since returning to England at the end of 2003 – having spent four years in Hong Kong – to train in Newmarket for the first time, his motivation was all the stronger.

Whilst 2004 and 2005 provided group victories, 2006 was the year that he came back to the fore, largely through a vintage crop of two-year-olds of which *Dutch Art* and *Authorized* were arguably the pick. "I want a classic this year," he said, "and to stand in that winners' enclosure again. What would that mean to me? Everything really. I've dreamed about doing it again for so long."

As the Greenham disappointment began to fade in the mind there were more positive signs from *Dutch Art*'s preparation. Deverson explained: "Newbury put his mind straight as to what he was supposed to be doing at the racetrack." Between the Greenham and the Guineas he began to take a real hold on the gallops and display a turn of foot that was so impressive that Chapple-Hyam became concerned. How could a horse displaying such speed also be gifted the necessary stamina for the Rowley Mile?

If that was a headache for the trainer, then he was not alone. The week before the Guineas was a week for headaches. Clerk of the course, Michael Prosser, for instance, had cause to reach for the aspirins.

The problem was the positioning of the starting stalls. When it became clear that there would be a large field he decided to continue with the policy of the previous two years and place the stalls in the centre of the course, even though it was likely that the field would then split into two groups.

If this seems a minor point, then think again. Through no fault of Prosser the splitting of the field was to become a critical factor in the running and eventual outcome of the race.

"With a bigger than usual field in prospect on Saturday, we did consider positioning the stalls on the stands side rail," he told the media. "However, it has worked so well for the last three years that we see no reason to change it. Of course there is the possibility of the field splitting, but realistically that might well have happened even if we had positioned them on the stands rail. Our aim is to try to ensure that the best horse wins the race and by positioning the stalls in the centre of the track, the potential for scrimmaging is minimised."

Unfortunately splitting the field becomes all but inevitable with a large entry, the Roman straightness of the Rowley Mile and centrally positioned stalls – and when it does the horses end up hugging the nearest running rail. Those who end up in the larger group get the unfair benefit of a more competitive race and the spectacle is diminished because the viewing angle makes it difficult for spectators, both at the racetrack and watching on television, to tell who is leading. And for the horses there are two races within one. They compete against the horses in their group with little or no awareness of the other "race" taking place across the track.

So, even though the consistency of the Rowley Mile's surface means that there is no bias in the going from one side to another, the luck of the draw assumes more significance than is ideal. It is unfortunate and unavoidable. The only viable alternatives are to funnel the rails so that the horses converge in the last few furlongs or reduce the size of the field. Six of the horses in the 2000 Guineas were priced at 100-1 or longer, so it could be argued that their chances of winning were minimal – but Prosser gave no credence to either idea.

Danni Deverson also had a headache. One that she had suffered from all week. Despite early nights and painkillers it had shown no signs of relenting. Fortunately the exertions of decorating her house helped her to sleep well on the eve of the Guineas – but next morning she was still awake, mind racing, before the alarm…

Race day: Stan James 2000 Guineas. Saturday 5th May 2007.

The day of the Guineas dawns dry with heavy cloud cover. Deverson is awake, still accompanied by that unwelcome thump-thump above the eyes, and arrives at the stables at 7.15am to ride out her other two horses – *Sophie's Girl* and *Bay of Light*.

By the time she returns after second lot, the inescapable fact that this is not a normal Saturday is evident as she spots Chapple-Hyam being interviewed by Channel Four presenter Derek Thompson next to *Dutch Art*'s stable. The interview will be televised later in the afternoon, minutes before the start of the race. Viewers will be able to watch the horse playfully nibble the interviewer's buttons on his coat.

After "lots", Deverson walks *Dutch Art* in gentle exercise for a while before going home. On the way she stops at a petrol station and bumps into Tom Goff. Optimistically, they agree their chance meeting must be "a good omen".

At home, she showers, gets ready for race day and travels to the racecourse to meet friends and family before returning to the stables at 1.30pm, now dressed in a grey pinstripe suit and mauve shirt that will match the silks worn by *Dutch Art*'s jockey. When she reaches the horse's stable she laughs. He is fast asleep on his bed, conserving his energy. This is so typical of "Dutchy", she thinks, and captures the image on her mobile phone. He always likes to sleep. It is one of his characteristics. Just as he likes to roll over in the stable first thing after exercise and then poke his head out

"Little Danni"
with "Little Dutchy".

of his stable door in the hope of being fussed over by passers-by.

Deverson grooms him, applies baby oil to his face and puts on the racing bridle. Some highly strung horses, somehow sensing that this is a race day, get excitable. *Dutch Art*, though, remains unconcerned. Deverson loads him into the horsebox and makes the short journey from the stables to the racecourse. By now most racegoers are at the course so traffic is light. If there had been an accident or other congestion they had other routes in mind, so there was no danger of the truly nightmare scenario of the big race starting with the horse stranded en route somewhere along the Bury Road.

They arrive at the racecourse at 2.20, an hour or so before the Guineas. Perfect timing. Arrive too early and the horse could get tetchy, burning energy that could be better utilised during the race. *Dutch Art*'s calmness continues as Deverson walks him round the pre-parade ring.

With the start of the race now just twenty-five minutes away, *Dutch Art* is saddled up by Chapple-Hyam. The sun breaks through the persistent cloud cover and Chapple-Hyam and Deverson agree that the horse looks like a million dollars; ears pricked, with that coppery, orange-tinted sheen to his coat and so cucumber-calm that you half-expect him to be wearing sunglasses. He is undeniably a handsome colt and Deverson says he knows it. "He's a poser," she says. "When he sees a camera he looks straight at it and seems to smile."

Deverson has numerous pictures of him (stable lads and lasses are sent photos of their horses by photographers after a race so that they have the opportunity to make a purchase) but horseracing superstition dictates that none of them can be displayed until his racing career is over.

By three o'clock the horses are entering Newmarket's main parade ring. Crowds of watchers are ten deep. Deverson leads *Dutch Art* round and is in his ear, whispering: "Good boy. Good boy, Dutchy. Walk steady. C'mon Dutchy. Stay calm. Good boy." Normally she does not like crowds but gains comfort from talking to her horse. She is not aware of being on show; she knows all eyes are on the thoroughbreds.

On Channel Four's television coverage, the focus is now firmly on the build-up to the big race and the cameras are trained on the weighing room. Lynchpin, Alastair Down, says: "There's a bit of an edge in the jockeys' room. It's the first major prize of the season awaiting resolution. Plenty of nerves, although they're all seasoned professionals. Careers, incomes, reputations: all on the line. The jockeys: entering the paddock for the Stan James 2000 Guineas."

Trainer, owners and jockey meet in the centre of the Parade Ring. They exchange small talk but little in the way of tactics. That was finalised a while ago. *Dutch Art* will be "held back" in the pack, then released to use his speed in the last few furlongs. They anticipate that there will be no repeat of the Greenham where the early pace was so pedestrian. In the Guineas the pace is always flat out.

By now the Nat West Rowley Mile is packed

with eighteen thousand spectators, the biggest crowd since the Millennium Grandstand was opened in 2000. Epsom's Derby Day has a bigger attendance; Ascot has an even newer grandstand; Goodwood has picture-postcard views across the Sussex Downs and York can boast great viewing – but on days like this racing's headquarters has a feel all of its own.

Indeed Her Majesty the Queen, abroad at the Kentucky Derby in the United States of America, has ensured that she has a live feed of the action. Just at this moment she will be viewing images of twenty-four of the most stunning-looking thoroughbreds walking athletically around the parade ring.

Because the other twenty-three are of a similar ilk it might be possible to overlook the fact that *Dutch Art*'s maturing conformation is a mixture of power and grace, strength and beauty, stamina and speed. He is as far removed from the pet horses found in paddocks around the country as a Ferrari from the family runaround. It is there in the look. A primary aim of thoroughbred breeding has been to decrease bone mass and increase muscle mass because a horse carrying a light skeleton using abnormally strong muscles will inevitably travel more quickly. And as jockey Jimmy Fortune mounts *Dutch Art* this is most obvious in his long pencil-thin legs, gluteal muscles and elongated tendons.

Experts might also notice the slight differences in *Dutch Art*'s conformation compared to most of the other horses. He has the look of a sprinter, with a shorter neck and legs; and a big backside and shoulders. He is compact, a powerhouse.

Sometimes jockeys ask the stable lad or lass (who they appreciate will know the horse better than anyone) "How is he feeling? Is he well? How does he prefer to run?" It can help to define race tactics – but there is none of that on a Guineas day. The trainer's instructions are treated as gospel. Television coverage moves through the field with a quick overview of each one:

"*Dutch Art* – a powerful colt, was a brilliant two-year-old, unbeaten in four races, including two group ones, but he was soundly beaten over seven furlongs in his reappearance and even if fitter has a lot more to do today."

Eventually, in alphabetical sequence, they move out of the parade ring onto the racetrack.

"Months and months of planning and thoughts and arguing the toss about which is the best colt and which is the improver and have they wintered well. Well, it all gets sorted out in the next few minutes. Loads of arguments to be resolved."

Chapple-Hyam and Deverson accompany jockey and horse to the racetrack; and then Fortune and *Dutch Art* are released and gone, sauntering away past the grandstand to the starting stalls; the horse still relaxed, calm and switched off. The same cannot be said for the connections who watch their progress.

Deverson's pulse-rate is sky-high. "It's the worst feeling," she says. "Nothing you can do except watch and wait." She briefly observes the horse's movement then, satisfied, walks briskly to the Minstrel Bar in the Millennium Grandstand where she meets her fiancé, mum, dad and brother to watch the race, mainly on the numerous television screens. Her brother is at the bar purchasing her a double vodka and coke.

This is the nearest Deverson gets to a superstition. She always downs the drink in one large gulp during the race.

Chapple-Hyam wants to be alone. He moves away from the grandstand, across the racetrack, close to the photographers and the finishing post. From there he can view the big screen and watch the race unfold alone with his thoughts. He smokes a cigarette at speed and looks as nervous as an expectant father.

> "They're loading up for the 2000 Guineas and the Rowley Mile is absolutely packed as indeed it should be. For many people this is the purist's mile clash of the year... All that winter of wrangling and thinking and rumours is to come to a complete and utter resolution on this course where they've run it for nearly two hundred years."

This is Jimmy Fortune's sixth ride in the race, though he has never had a sniff of victory. As they circle, preparing to go into the stalls, *Dutch Art* remains relaxed and comfortable under him and he has time to look around and focus on the opposition.

He notes *US Ranger*. Fancied to do well (5-1 second favourite in the betting) and drawn just two stalls away from *Dutch Art*. He is trained in France and is unbeaten there but largely unknown in this country. He, too, will be held up in the race, so not necessarily a good one to track. Nevertheless worthy of noting the colours: royal blue with an orange disc.

Fortune also spots an outsider who will not win the race but might set a decent pace: *Danum Dancer* in the orange and dark green check is drawn next to *Dutch Art*. As is *Haatef*, another fancied to do well. Indeed, if the betting odds are to be respected, then he has better prospects than *Dutch Art*. One to look out for. Royal blue with white epaulettes.

Then, on the other side of the draw, there is the favourite, Sir Michael Stoute's *Adagio*. Stoute, with five previous winners, is the most successful current trainer with a horse in the race and many fancy *Adagio* to become his sixth. Kerrin McEvoy on board. Drawn three. Purple with white seams.

And there is the chestnut *Major Cadeaux*, who beat *Dutch Art* so convincingly in the Greenham. He spread a plate in the morning and his participation was in doubt. Drawn seven. Purple and yellow stars.

It is 3.29pm. All the runners are in the stalls. The race is about to begin.

Channel Four's Jim McGrath begins his commentary:

"They're just about set for the Stan James 2000 Guineas – and away they go. *Diamond Tycoon* away pretty well towards stand-side. Showing speed in the early stages is *Vital Equine*..."

The first furlong of the race sees manoeuvring for position, which is scarcely noticeable to the viewer but will be significant in the long run, particularly as the field splits into two groups as expected.

For instance, *Cockney Rebel*, drawn three stalls down from *Dutch Art*, is boldly switched from the far side to the group on the stands side. Christophe Lemaire, the jockey of *US Ranger*, two stalls up, tries the same manoeuvre but is blocked by another horse and abandons the idea. *Dutch Art* would lose too much ground if he tried to make the journey from one side of the track to the other. So the 2000 Guineas has become a race of two unequal halves. On the stand-side there is a group of fifteen, on the far side a group of nine which contains *Dutch Art*. His mauve colours can be seen at the rear of the field, with the towering *US Ranger* close by; *Cockney Rebel* is at the back of the other group.

One concern has been alleviated. The pace is hot; they are going, as Craig Dykes neatly observes, "like stink; like shit off a shovel". No repeat of the pedestrian pace of the Greenham. This is a mile long out-and-out sprint.

"They run down towards the halfway stage now and *Drayton* has taken over on the far side from *Danum Dancer*. Those two disputing it over there. *Vital Equine* has shot clear on the stands side. Can he possibly keep it up? He's gone four lengths clear on the stands side as they race down inside the final three furlongs. *Dutch Art* is out the back at the moment..."

Deverson's heart sinks. *Vital Equine* is dominating the stand-side race and establishing a significant lead. "Dutchy" has a lot to do to get in contention. As the camera pans away from the far side group she momentarily fears the worst. But it is at that moment that Jimmy Fortune releases his mount and *Dutch Art* begins to make his move. He is not alone. At one and the same time his running mate, *US Ranger*, and, on the stands side, *Cockney Rebel* also accelerate. And as they ease stealthily forward, others hit the wall.

"*US Ranger* making ground on the far side but *Vital Equine* is clear in the Guineas as they run down in the final quarter mile."

About three furlongs from the finishing post the Rowley Mile dips downhill before it gently rises up to the line. Often horses never make it out of that dip. Those that "don't get home" lose momentum and never recover. It is the acid test of a horse's ability to "get the trip" – and, given the speculation and pedigree, the doubts over *Dutch Art* are bigger than most.

But *Dutch Art* does not die in the dip. He does not start to go backwards. Quite the reverse. He is accelerating and slaloming through the field. In his group of nine the mauve colours can be spied moving from eighth to seventh. Sixth becomes fourth. He looks strong and he is becoming a threat.

As the camera pans back, Deverson can now see that her horse is in with a chance. And she is beginning to shout. "C'mon Dutchy! C'mon!" Momentarily she feels a tinge of English embarrassment as others in the Minstrel Bar look towards her. Then she thinks, "This is my horse and I'll scream if I want to."

And Chapple-Hyam, from his position near the photographers, is also taking a close interest. No shouting but an uplifting of spirits and a sense of expectation. Dutchy is in with a chance.

However, it is only a chance because his acceleration is matched by *US Ranger* and *Cockney Rebel*. These three have gone from back to front in the course of a furlong, providing a genuine challenge to the long-time pacesetter *Vital Equine*.

"*Vital Equine* on the stands side, chased down by *Sonny Red. Duke of Marmalade* and *Diamond Tycoon*. Also coming through is *Cockney Rebel* on the stands side. Over on the far side the French raider, *US Ranger,* comes through to lead there from *Strategic Prince, Haatef...* and *Dutch Art* is running on well..."

Dutch Art is not just running on well. With one furlong to go he takes a fractional lead. *US Ranger* is unable to quicken and his challenge is at an end. He is not going to win the race – but *Dutch Art* could; he is not only "winning" the far side "race" but he has created clear daylight between him and the following group.

Who said he would not make the distance? Who said he was just a sprinter? Who said he had regressed in the winter? Who doubted Peter Chapple-Hyam's optimism? As others burn out through lack of stamina or class, *Dutch Art* is in contention.

But now the main problem is that daylight. *Dutch Art* is unaware of the stand-side group and has nothing to race against. He is winning "his" race – and despite the increasingly urgent encouragement of Jimmy Fortune all his instincts and training tell him that all he needs to do is keep ahead of the rest of "his" pack and he will win.

He loses some of his momentum. Meanwhile, stand-side, *Cockney Rebel* has had the benefit of *Vital Equine* to chase down. His turn of foot is massively impressive, coming from last to first in fine style and he "takes it up" decisively inside the final furlong.

"Stands side *Cockney Rebel* gets past *Vital Equine*... As they race up to the line *Dutch Art*, far side, *US Ranger. Cockney Rebel* in front, *Dutch Art* far side.
"*Cockney Rebel* wins The Guineas, *Vital Equine* second, *Dutch Art* on the far side, *Duke of Marmalade* behind those..."

THE 2000 GUINEAS RESULT					
Pos.	Horse	Draw	Trainer	Jockey	Betting
1	Cockney Rebel	15	G A Huffer	O Peslier	25-1
2	Vital Equine	6	E J O'Neill	C Catlin	33-1
3	Dutch Art	18	P W Chapple-Hyam	J Fortune	14-1
4	Duke of Marmalade	11	A P O'Brien	M J Kinane	14-1
5	Eagle Mountain	13	A P O'Brien	C Soumillon	14-1
6	Major Cadeaux	7	R Hannon	R Hughes	10-1
7	US Ranger	16	J-C Rouget	C-P Lemaire	5-1
8	Strategic Prince	14	P F I Cole	E Ahern	8-1
9	Diamond Tycoon	2	B J Meehan	J Spencer	15-2
10	Haatef	17	K Prendergast	D P McDonogh	7-1

So close and yet so far. *Cockney Rebel* has won in a time of one minute and thirty-five seconds, the third-fastest recorded 2000 Guineas victory in one hundred and ninety-nine runnings. *Dutch Art* has finished third.

Deverson's initial reaction is of joy and elation. She knows that her horse has run a "blinding race". She also knows she still has work to do and does not want to become overwhelmed by emotion. So she avoids eye contact with her family and pushes her way out of the Minstrel Bar back to the racetrack to greet horse and jockey and lead them back into the parade ring.

She tells the horse: "I love you Dutchy, very proud of you mate." Fortune asks where they finished. He thinks it was second but has struggled to see across the track in a tight finish. Deverson tells him it was third. Fortune is certain that had they been stand-side, racing directly against *Cockney Rebel*, they would have won.

This bittersweet mood is also prevalent in the parade ring as *Dutch Art* takes his place in the third-place area. Along with the pride there is frustration that, given the rub of the green and a "fairer" race he might just have won. Chapple-Hyam, surrounded by press, makes the point: "Jimmy Fortune said he would have won if he was drawn on the stands side. He got there and then he had nothing to race with. Halfway through the race, Jimmy looked across and he saw they were just so far clear. He's a very, very good horse and I'm sure we'll meet some of them again in either the St James's Palace Stakes or the Irish Guineas, where there won't be a draw advantage.

"There is no doubt that he stays, and Jimmy said he'd get a mile and a quarter by the end of the year. It was an outstanding performance, but take nothing away from the first and the second – they've beaten us on the day."

Chapple-Hyam's words – looking ahead to the next race before the horse has even left the winners' enclosure – highlight the essential nature of racing. Largely to satisfy the needs of punters the speculation over the big races begins months in advance and multiplies up to the moment the stalls open. A flat race takes somewhere between one and three minutes to contest. Then, no sooner are the horses unbridled, than the speculation begins again, assessing the impact of the race on future targets. The sport spends a lot of time looking back to try and predict the future. Only for a few glorious minutes does it allow itself to enjoy the present.

Deverson goes about her business with *Dutch Art*, who, she observes "looks pleased with himself". She washes him down after the jockey has unsaddled him, "takes a turn" and provides water. For a few precious moments – as the cameras and plaudits are directed at the winner – it is just "little Danni" with "little Dutchy". And it is then that she wells up. "We just had a little one-to-one in the

Cockney Rebel (3) wins the 2000 Guineas but Dutch Art (8) wins "his" race on the other side of the track.

winner's enclosure," she confides later. "I just told him how proud I was. It's a real privilege to have something to do with him. It's a once in a lifetime thing."

Deverson gets a kiss from Chapple-Hyam and then leads *Dutch Art* around for thirty minutes until he stops blowing. Then it is back to the yard where evening stables are taking place. Chapple-Hyam invites all the stable lads and lasses into the tack room for some champagne. Moments like this are not to be forgotten. The feeling is one of pride and pleasure with the performance, tinged with "if onlys".

Deverson reflects: "Because he's so laid back he's got two or three lengths ahead and thought 'right they're not catching me' and that was that. He's thinking 'I'll just stay in front'. He thought he'd done enough. He still thinks he won! I was pleased because he thinks he's won his race and to me it's more important that he thinks he's won. Mentally it's very good for a horse to think they've won because if a horse gets beat it knocks its confidence a bit. He didn't have a clue there was another race going on the other side of the track."

Danni says goodbye to Dutchy at 4.30pm and celebrates in the evening by partying with her brother and fiancé in Newmarket town centre until 3am. In this small and close-knit community Deverson knows most people and the revelling is punctuated by congratulatory texts and phone calls. One thing is missing:

about an hour into the evening festivities she realises that the week-long headache has dispersed along with many of the question marks that had existed over her horse.

From a financial perspective *Dutch Art*'s ability to contest a world-class race over a mile as demanding as the Rowley Mile, allied to his proven speed over shorter surfaces, establishes him as a horse likely to win prize money during the remainder of the 2007 season and possibly beyond.

And when he eventually goes to stud with Cheveley Park he will inevitably be in great demand – and at a significant cost – as a stallion that provides future generations of thoroughbreds. From a punter's perspective he will be carrying a lot of their money in some group one races.

And from Danni Deverson's perspective? Well, in truth, it has not made a lot of difference to her. She will receive a percentage of the prize money from *Dutch Art*'s third place. Yet, a week on she had not even calculated how much that will be. For her it is irrelevant. Her number one priority was always that he came back safe and sound from his exertions and, barring a bit of stiffness and tiredness that will drain away over the following couple of days, *Dutch Art* took the race in his impressive stride.

The relationship between Danni and Dutchy is based upon something much stronger and deeper than winning, glory and prize money. Victory or defeat will never affect the bond between these two.

EIGHT

GUINEAS DRAMA

"I WOULD MUCH PREFER TO HAVE BEEN IN GOOD NICK AND RUN
AND BEEN BEATEN FAIR AND SQUARE THAN NOT BEEN THERE
AT ALL. THAT'S THE DISAPPOINTING THING; TO HAVE BEEN
ROBBED OF THE OPPORTUNITY TO HAVE A GO."

Race day: 1000 Guineas. 8.30am. Shalfleet Stables, Bury Road, Newmarket. Throughout the winter even a trainer as seasoned and proven as Jeremy Noseda has relished the prospect of this day. It seemed likely to provide him with a realistic possibility of following up his first classic (*Sixties Icon* in the St Leger in September 2006) with a second in Newmarket's 1000 Guineas.

Moreover, this time he would be there to enjoy the moment in person. For *Sixties Icon's* victory he had been away on business at the Keeneland Sales and had watched it alone on television.

So much optimism, so much to look forward to – and yet now that the day has arrived, suitably under a leaden blanket of grey cloud, the acrid smell of anticlimax is in the air and there is not a hint of spring in the Noseda stride.

It is at 8.30am that the examination of *Sander Camillo* is completed. In conjunction with owner Sir Robert Ogden the agonising decision is made: she must be withdrawn from the 1000 Guineas. The formal calls are made. Within minutes the news appears on the wires of the Press Association and the ripples from this heavy-hearted conclusion begin to spread throughout the racing community.

For the two men who make the final decision, owner and trainer, it is a crushing blow. In the winter Noseda had envisaged having three strong entrants in the race. *Rahiyah*, though, has now been entered for the French Guineas, one week later, and *Sander Camillo's* absence means that all hopes now rest upon the grey, *Simply Perfect*. She is an outstanding filly and there is reason for hope that she will run a strong race. However, now is there just hope, whereas before there had been positive optimism.

"It's been a very tough week," he reflects. "One of the toughest weeks I've had in racing. It's extremely disappointing for it to go this way. It makes you think, could I have changed things and done things differently? I know I couldn't but it is very disappointing for everyone here – for my wife and me. When this has been your ambition for a long while and you do not even have a go at it then it is a disappointing day.

"By Friday I had it sorted in my mind that it was going to be bloody disappointing but if it didn't happen, it didn't happen and you just have to accept those things and move on. However, I would have much preferred to have been in good nick and run and been beaten fair and square than not been there at all. That's the disappointing thing, to have been robbed of the opportunity to have a go."

If anything, his wife, Sally, feels the pain and frustration even more keenly. She has ridden the horse out over the last two seasons and grown emotionally attached. Sally knows just how good she is.

There are also implications outside of *Sander*'s "connections". Ante-post punters will lose their money. In total £3 million worth of bets have been wasted with the withdrawal of *Teofilo* and *Holy Roman Emperor* from the 2000 Guineas and, now, *Sander Camillo* from the fillies equivalent.

Of course, losing three thoroughbreds of this standing affects the whole spectacle and quality of the racing. The Rowley Mile has always been, and should always be, the stage where the crème-de-la-crème contest the first classics of the season and write their names large in the legends.

So how did it happen? How did the optimism of early spring turn so sour? In fact, it happened quickly, within seventeen rollercoaster and highly stressful days, beginning with the Nell Gwyn Stakes during Newmarket's Craven Meeting.

This was *Sander Camillo*'s warm-up race. The day before Noseda had described it as "a horrid race". To win was expected. It would merely confirm her sparkling form on the gallops. Yet an unexpected defeat could be damaging. Little to gain – other than the run out – and plenty to lose.

Superstitiously he wore the same tie that he had worn for *Sander Camillo*'s victories in the Cherry Hinton on the July Course and at Royal Ascot. However, the tie lost its powers that day and despite being ridden with increasing alarm and urgency by Frankie Dettori the filly never threatened to get past *Scarlet Runner* (trained by Noseda's ex-mentor, John Dunlop) once the winner surged for home two furlongs out.

In the post-race interviews Dettori told the press "two out I thought we had everything in trouble. But she was rusty and got beaten by a fitter horse on the day. It's good that we ran here". Noseda, uncomfortably surrounded by media in the parade ring, added: "I'm not going to pretend it's ideal. I was expecting more, but we'll not panic. It was only a prep, and I believe there is improvement to come."

The racing press were more damning. They saw it as more than just rustiness. One journalist wrote that she had run "like an old man with his legs tied together". "Limp", "awkward" and "lacking in the previous swagger" were other descriptions. Some of this was unkind but there was no doubt that for a talented and classy filly to run so poorly was cause for genuine concern. As a result there was a revision of the 1000 Guineas betting market and she lost her place as favourite to Jim Bolger's *Finsceal Beo*.

Noseda had seventeen days to solve the riddle of what went wrong and put it right. What complicated matters was that Sander was found to have "tied up" during the race, which means that she suffered some form of cramp and seized up. This condition can be attributable to several things and is usually caused by a build-up of lactic acid in the muscle tissues.

Indeterminate tests were undertaken, her subsequent work was impressive and cramp-free and one week before the Guineas she was outstanding during a workout at the Rowley Mile. However, more tests were required after she seemed "very flat" after her final piece of "work" three days later with Dettori on board. She had not tied up but demonstrated none of

Sander Camillo (centre: pink hat) in her warm-up for the 1000 Guineas – the Nell Gwyn Stakes at the Craven meeting.

the flair of a classic contender, let alone a long-time favourite. Noseda reported his concerns to the owner and, by now, he had diagnosed that the peaks and troughs in performance were related to hormonal problems caused by her menstrual cycle.

A filly may be in season for between four and ten days and the cycle may be as little as three weeks. Whilst some run just as well in season, others are badly affected. *Sander Camillo* had not suffered as a two-year-old but as a three-year-old her first cycle was intense and, alas, she suffered more than most. She was declared for the Guineas at Friday's

107

forty-eight-hour stage as tests were awaited. The hope was that she would emerge through the cycle by race day and perk up. Alas, it proved to be forlorn and there was only one realistic decision to make.

Later, when the dust had settled, Noseda provided some background to the bare facts: "She was in season three days before the Craven meeting," he said. "She ran in the Nell Gywn and got tied up. At the time we felt it was unrelated. I think afterwards it clearly was related but with her just starting cycling properly we didn't know for sure. We've had no issues with tying up since and I'm sure the problems were related to a first season and her not feeling comfortable.

"We'd already discussed prior to the Nell Gwyn that there was a chance that she'd be in season in the lead-up to the Guineas. We were discussing whether to try to change her cycle, but with what happened in the Nell Gwyn it seemed pretty tough to do in a two-week space. We decided to go with nature but sadly she is one of those fillies who are affected extremely badly by her season.

"She worked spectacularly between the two races. Then, sadly, when she came back into season, the season was very tough on her and she lost her sparkle in the week leading up to the race. Although she was coming out of season she wasn't back to her best so we decided that it was unlikely that she was going to be able to run her very best race and had no option but to miss the race. And we had to make a call this morning when she wasn't in tip-top form."

Though he would not be so arrogant as to predict it, you sensed that Noseda's gut feel, at least until that ill-fated warm-up race, was that *Sander Camillo* was going to win the Guineas. To not have even had the chance to contest it represented one of the bigger blows of his professional life.

The challenge, now, in the wake of that 8.30am withdrawal, is to continue to be businesslike and upbeat through the remainder of the day.

Noseda begins by making a call to Frankie Dettori who was due to ride *Sander Camillo*. The jockey is deeply disappointed, of course, but the conversation soon turns to *Sixties Icon*, who Dettori is riding for Noseda in a significant group two listed race, the main support for the 1000 Guineas.

Sixties Icon will always hold a special place in Noseda's heart because he provided his first classic victory. This will be the horse's first run since that day and his first of the 2007 campaign. Trainer and jockey talk tactics and Noseda later explains: "Frankie and I decided it was simple. We knew what we were going to do. I didn't want the horse to make the running and I just wanted him to get the horse relaxed wherever it was, to ride his race from there."

All of this is dependent on the condition of the racecourse. *Sixties Icon* likes a bit of give in the ground. So Noseda drives to the Rowley Mile to check that the "going" is suitable. Michael Prosser did not water the course after the 2000 Guineas, perhaps in the expectation that there might be some late morning drizzle.

He stated confidently in the press: "It's dried out overnight, there is a great covering of grass and it's still a lovely racing surface. There ought to be no excuses for any horses. Those who like fast ground will revel on it, but the soft ground performers will not be inconvenienced either as there is no jar whatsoever."

When Noseda reviews the surface – poking and jabbing into the surface with boot and stick – he concurs: it is safe. It may not suit *Sixties Icon* and Noseda remains concerned about the impact of the ground on his chances of success – but it is safe to run.

With that he returns to Shalfleet for rest, lunch and preparation for the afternoon ahead. He is back at the racecourse at 1.20pm, now dressed immaculately in dark blue suit, powder blue shirt and a pink tie – most certainly not the "lucky" tie he wore for *Sander Camillo*'s successes last season. You suspect that has been binned. He meets a couple of owners and then at 2pm it is time for business in the pre-parade ring where *Sixties Icon* is being led around in preparation for the 2.30 race.

As the horse is saddled, Noseda enters the stable to oversee putting on the tack. He chews gum and remains stern-faced. The next scribe who describes Newmarket trainers as aloof and arrogant will not be the first or the last. However, Noseda's icy distance is not attributable to this, it is just an indication that he is focused on the job in hand. Even though there are eighteen thousand racegoers packing out the racecourse and worldwide media coverage, you sense that Noseda is barely aware of them and is certainly not here to "savour the atmosphere" or "enjoy the sense of occasion".

To him this is business, and his whole attention is trained on the preparation of his horses and working with their jockeys, so they have the best chance of success. He shares pleasantries with the owners and stable lads but you sense that the rest of the throng are just blurred images in the periphery of his vision. In fact, if the crowd, the cameras and the officials slipped away and left the racetrack you would not stake your mortgage that he would notice.

"It's a day of work," he confirms. "What goes on outside is of no interest to me and no consequence. I don't have an interest in what's going on, or an interest in races not involving my horses. We're there for only one thing and that's to run in those races. The occasion is only worth enjoying if you're going to go and compete at the right level. What point is the atmosphere unless you get the job done?"

The chances of *Sixties Icon* getting the job done do not look promising. The "going" is not to his taste, he is not yet at peak fitness, he carries a group one penalty, and has drifted in the betting. Indeed, to add to that, on Channel Four's television coverage they state that Noseda's stable is "not yet in tip-top form. Just two winners out of twenty-five since mid-February".

Noseda speaks to owners Paul and Susan Roy (also the owners of *Dutch Art* who had run so splendidly the day before in the 2000 Guineas) and then briefly exchanges a few words with Frankie Dettori, now wearing those distinctive all-mauve colours. The tactics have already been decided in the early morning phone call and when Frankie gets onboard – given a leg up, as is tradition, by his trainer – he says, "C'mon let's go, I'll just amble my way down in my own time." So Dettori and *Sixties Icon* leave the parade ring early and ease to the start at their leisure.

Owners, trainer and his wife split up to watch the race unfold from different vantage points around the Millennium Grandstand. They see a sedate pace in the early stages with none of the five runners keen to go on. *Sixties Icon* settles in third. Dettori moves him into second shortly after halfway, content to track the leader – and he shifts easily through the gears when Dettori lets him loose at the two-furlong pole. From then on the result is never in doubt as he quickens and leaves a classy field in his wake with a minimum of fuss, securing £40,000 in prize money. In the process he also makes an eloquent case for consideration in the season's top races, starting with the Coronation Cup at Epsom. It is a sight for the sorest of eyes.

Television pictures zoom in on Dettori's joy as he passes the finishing post, his face illuminated by the widest of smiles. Channel Four's Derek Thompson interviews him as he makes his way from the course to the winner's enclosure. They discuss the quality of *Sixties Icon*'s performance and then the impact of *Sander Camillo*'s withdrawal.

"I must say that Jeremy and Sally are devastated – but we're looking forward to seeing her back," Dettori informs viewers. By the time Thompson finishes the interview *Sixties Icon* is entering the parade ring and is reacquainted with his trainer who escorts him to the winners' enclosure. Noseda pats the horse then touches hands with Dettori. Seconds later the jockey performs his trademark celebratory starfish leaping dismount for the cameras, a trick he saves for high-profile winners.

"Devastated" he may still be but *Sixties Icon*'s victory immediately restores that photogenic smile to Noseda's face and you can sense the stress of the previous two weeks begin to drain from his body. The last few minutes have been therapeutic. Later he confirms: "It cheers you up; this was the kind of result I needed after what had gone on." On cue, a weak sun peeps through the cloud cover for the first time.

Noseda fulfils his media obligations with an interview with Alastair Down and before the award of the trophy, he slips away to oversee preparation for *Simply Perfect*'s challenge in the 1000 Guineas.

Noseda came second in this race in 1999 with the unfancied *Wannabe Grand* who failed by a whisker to overhaul Henry Cecil's *Wince*. Legend has it that when someone congratulated him for such a heroic attempt he snapped angrily and pointed out that, in fact, he had been beaten. "I want to win and finishing second is not enough."

He has had only one runner since and even without *Sander Camillo*, *Simply Perfect* – now bubbling around 10-1 in the betting – appears to provide him with the best chance of success in his racing career so far. Again he

Finsceal Beo wins the 1000 Guineas from *Arch Swing* with *Simply Perfect* in third.

helps saddle up the horse and then issues last-minute instructions to jockey Johnny Murtagh. Their discussion appears calm and relaxed, but *Simply Perfect*, as is her wont, is sweating and on her toes in the parade ring. She is led around by two handlers and is not helped by a delay in getting on the racecourse caused by one of the sponsor's signs blowing over in the 25mph winds. When *Simply Perfect* eventually makes it onto the course Noseda makes sure that she is last to go down and that Murtagh keeps her nice and slow on a tight rein.

Once *Simply Perfect* has left his charge Noseda prefers to find some solitude to view the race – just as Peter Chapple-Hyam did the previous day with *Dutch Art*. He does not want to be around people where his reaction to victory or defeat will be witnessed and captured. He just wants to be alone with his thoughts. "I prefer to be just watching it and not be having to talk to people about it when it's going on," he explains. "I can just concentrate on it myself." So, as many of the Newmarket crowd move from around the parade ring into their preferred vantage point to watch the race unfold, Noseda walks against the tide and returns to the parade ring, at the back of the Millennium Grandstand.

At the entrance to the parade ring he spots Dettori, ten yards away, now in jacket as well as his racing silks and black boots, signing autographs for two small boys. He calls out and the two chat. There is a noticeable warmth between the pair and Noseda is clearly a fan. "I've known him for a very long time and I love him riding horses for me. I get on well with him. I think he's a fabulous jockey, the most naturally talented jockey out riding. A gentleman and a fabulous guy as well."

Their chance meeting has some poignancy. If sport was just, Dettori would now be cantering down to the starting stalls on the star of Noseda's stable and would have had every chance of returning a few minutes later riding the winner of the 1000 Guineas. Yet sport, and particularly horseracing, can frustrate just as easily as it can delight – so here he is, all dressed up with nowhere to go. They spend little time discussing their absent friend. Instead they talk about the performance of *Sixties Icon*. "Thanks, Frankie," says Noseda as they part – and then he stands, impassive and solitary, in the parade ring to watch the action unfold on the big screen.

What does he see?

Significantly he spots that the twenty-one runners do not split up into two groups when they are released from the stalls. Within the first furlong all have moved towards the stand-side rail. The purple and white colours of *Simply Perfect* are tucked in within a large group, just behind *Finsceal Beo* who, in turn is tracking the pacesetting *Scarlet Runner.*

Noseda admires *Simply Perfect* as a "tough and competitive" filly and she needs to be as she suffers some bumping and interference during the mid part of the race. Two furlongs out the strong favourite, *Finsceal Beo*, eases past *Scarlet Runner* and takes the lead. Her jockey's racing silks of dark blue and emerald green hoops can be easily identified as a gap develops between them and the rest of the field. As the race intensifies and the punters shout home their favourites, *Simply Perfect* keeps going admirably and moves into third place. Alas, she never threatens to make up the necessary ground.

This is to be *Finsceal Beo*'s day. From two furlongs out the result is not in doubt, her domination just as apparent as that of *Sixties Icon* some thirty minutes earlier. She eases away from a strong field in the last furlong and jockey, Kevin Manning, is able to coast to a comfortable victory through the last seventy-five yards.

Simply Perfect finishes third, a strong and creditable performance and all that Noseda could have expected. He accepts she has been beaten fair and square. "On the day she wasn't good enough," he admits. "She ran her race and that wasn't quite good enough on the day."

Certainly it would have taken some filly to have upstaged *Finsceal Beo*. The winning time is one minute, 34 seconds; 0.14 seconds quicker than the fastest ever 2000 Guineas, the fastest recorded time for any Newmarket classic and only 0.4 seconds outside a course record. Awe of these statistics should be tempered by the fact that a 25mph wind was behind the field on ground that had dried out from the day before. Nevertheless it has been a magnificent performance by the victor. In the winners' enclosure owner Michael Ryan leads a one hundred and fifty-strong travelling posse from Ireland in a loud and enthusiastic rendition of "Dungarvan – my home town".

But the words that might resonate most loudly with Jeremy Noseda are those of *Finsceal Beo*'s successful trainer, Jim Bolger. "I've always said that the 1000 Guineas is the most difficult to win. So much depends on things out of your own hands. You're coming out of winter and very much dependent on the weather in the spring time. Fillies don't always peak for you."

"Things out of your own hands" – what pertinent words.

The most diligent and brilliant trainer – and one pressman described Noseda as a "genius" in the week preceding the Guineas – can only do so much. Even if the preparation is spot on, the racehorse is a deceivingly frail animal and sporting performance can be subject to the whims of fate. That is part of horseracing's charm and also one of the reasons why it can frustrate and disappoint. There is only one winner in a race – so losing is always more likely than winning – and when your horse does not even get the chance to compete it hurts.

As the Irish singing continues from the winners' enclosure Jeremy and Sally Noseda slip away into the crowd; pleased with the performances of *Sixties Icon* and *Simply Perfect* but accompanied, no doubt, by thoughts of what might have been.

Later Noseda put the day to bed: "*Sixties Icon* cheered me up. I still can't say that I enjoyed it. A bittersweet day but more a disappointing day. We never got the filly there and we wanted to compete so it was a let-down. It wasn't the day we hoped and expected it to be. So it was disappointing with a nice result to put a better light on things."

THE 1000 GUINEAS RESULT

Pos.	Horse	Draw	Trainer	Jockey	Betting
1	Finsceal Beo	8	J S Bolger	K J Manning	5-4f
2	Arch Swing	19	J Oxx	M J Kinane	10-1
3	Simply Perfect	10	J Noseda	J Murtagh	9-1
4	Treat	14	M R Channon	J Spencer	14-1
5	Indian Ink	13	R Hannon	R Hughes	17-2
6	Yaqeen	3	M A Jarvis	R Hills	12-1
7	Scarlet Runner	9	J L Dunlop	K McEvoy	14-1
8	Puggy	5	R A Kvisla	S Pasquier	150-1
9	Satulagi	1	J S Moore	S Donohoe	200-1
10	Theann	12	A P O'Brien	C Soumillon	20-1

The Nat West
Rowley Mile.

NINE

GREAT EXPECTATIONS

"I'M VERY BAD UNTIL ABOUT THE DAY BEFORE, THEN I'M FINE.
ON THE NIGHT BEFORE THE BIG DAY I'M FABULOUS. I'M
BRAND NEW. AS HAPPY AS LARRY. THE WAITING IS
OVER AND I'VE DONE MY THINKING AND NOW I JUST
CAN'T WAIT TO GET ON STAGE AND PERFORM."

THE DAY AFTER THE 1000 GUINEAS the mini-six-week drought ended and the remainder of May was showery. Then, as if by royal decree, hot, dry weather returned for the meeting at Epsom Downs in early June when the third and fourth classics of the season were contested.

Epsom made an immediate impression. It had character, as, of course, it should have, having hosted race meetings for four centuries. This is particularly true of the racetrack. On Friday, before the Oaks, I walked the course, primarily to try and understand the big deal about the famous Tattenham Corner. Sure enough, from the five-furlong pole the ground drops steeply downhill before taking a sharp left-hand turn into the finishing straight. I negotiated it without difficulty, hugging the near rail in creditable fashion, but this was an on-foot meander at significantly less speed than a young and inexperienced pack of racehorses. For them negotiating that turn is a test of nerve, skill and balance. Then, once into the straight, the camber draws them to the inside rail. Gradients, camber, twists and turns: full of character, quirky and interesting.

"Interesting" was also a decent description of the two main characters I was at Epsom to follow. Both had a testing childhood. Both left the country of their birth to pursue a career in racing in Newmarket. Both have a fascinating life story, as full of vicissitudes as Epsom's racetrack itself. And both ended up in the White Lion pub in their adopted hometown on Derby Day evening in an inebriated state.

One is a rich and famous celebrity, known across the world. The most recognisable face in horseracing. An honorary Member of the British Empire. A millionaire. The other is a less heralded stable lad. However, their fortunes on Derby Day offered equal fascination.

The idea for the theme of this particular chapter had emerged on the morning of the 2000 Guineas when walking the Rowley Mile course. A diminutive man was testing the going by prodding his heel into the top surface with concern on his face. Upon enquiry he said: "I'm the jockey, Eddie Ahern. I'm riding Strategic Prince *in the Guineas."*

We got talking. "Are you nervous?"

Frankie Dettori The Jockey

"A bit," he replied. "In classics I've always ridden 100-1 shots before, and then you can just enjoy it. But today there's a lot more pressure."

Incidentally, he also said he was more hungry than nervous – but his initial comment gave cause for reflection on the stress jockeys face on Classic race days. They have their careers and reputations to consider and the greater the expectation, the greater the demand to deliver.

So in this chapter I have tried to get into the psyche, inside the head if you like, of a professional sportsman placed under the pressure of a big occasion. And for one jockey this was serious stress. Willie Carson said on BBC's television coverage that no jockey had ever been under more pressure than Frankie Dettori in the weeks before the 2007 Vodafone Derby Stakes. And it was Frankie I was following.

His personal insight into the build-up to the Derby and the race itself was fascinating. What became clear is that the public persona of Frankie as a camera-loving celebrity is somewhat misleading. No doubt he is comfortable with the limelight. However, he is primarily a clear-thinking, strong-minded and dedicated athlete. Indeed, how could he have been at the top of the profession for so long if he was not?

I suspect that my abiding memory of the summer will be standing near the finishing post on Derby Day as the Newmarket-based jockey rode the Newmarket-based horse for the Newmarket-based trainer and tried to make his one remaining sporting dream come true.

Earlier generations of the Dettori family came from modest stock. Frankie's grandfather, Mario, was a mineworker in Sardinia and his son, Gianfranco moved to Rome where he started by working as a dishwasher. Nevertheless, through hard work and talent, he became a multiple champion jockey in Italy and a winner of the English 2000 Guineas in 1975 and 1976. He never won the Derby though, leaving Epsom in tears in 1976 when he rode the favourite, *Wollow*, into fifth place.

Gianfranco married Maria, a circus trapeze artist, and they produced Lanfranco, born in Milan in 1970, though they later divorced when the boy was six years old. The three-year-old Lanfranco wanted to be a petrol pump attendant. However, he also inherited his father's feel for horses and his mother's sense of balance and putting on a show – and like many Italians he wore his heart on his sleeve, brimming over with emotion and animation.

He was bought a palomino pony when he was eight and by thirteen he had left school to become a groom and apprentice jockey. It became his childhood dream to win the King George VI and Queen Elizabeth Stakes, the Prix de l'Arc de Triomphe and the Derby Stakes. He recalls, "When I was fourteen my father said 'You have got the talent and I can give you the chance to go and ride in England and in France to see how you like it'."

He arrived in Newmarket, armed with an unsteady grasp of the English language, a bicycle and a starter fund of £366 in his back pocket, to work as an apprentice (and then a stable jockey) with trainer and fellow-Italian Luca Cumani.

Frankie Dettori's trademark dismount.

His first win came at the age of sixteen in Turin in 1986, his first in Britain the following June. Two years later he was champion apprentice with seventy-five winners and the following year, at the age of nineteen Lanfranco (or Frankie as he was nicknamed in Britain) became the first teenager since Lester Piggott to ride one hundred winners in one season. That was just the start.

He won his first classic (the Oaks on *Balanchine*) and became champion jockey in 1994 (with a massive two hundred and thirty-three winners) and 1995. Nowadays Dettori is Godolphin's stable jockey and does not chase the jockeys' title, focusing on quality rather than quantity.

So it is easy to forget the hard yards he put in to establish his reputation. No one becomes champion jockey without a whole season of tenacity, perseverance and sheer, bloody-minded desire. And Dettori had these qualities in spades. He was not just talented; he wanted it badly and was prepared to make the necessary sacrifices.

The inspiration and genius followed the next season. Most athletes have experienced a day, a time, when mind and body work in spontaneous coordination and they can do no wrong. Their mind is clear and alert and their body, in turn, performs any feat, no matter how testing, with such ease that they wonder what they ever found so difficult. On 28th September 1996, Dettori was "in the zone". He won all seven races on a single day at Ascot, a 25,095-1 accumulator that put many bookmakers out of business. "Horses have the ability to catch your mood," he says, "and the horses caught my mood that day. I wasn't even on the ground – I was flying and they were just running that little bit faster."

The remarkable feat acted as the final confirmation to doubters that Dettori represented a prodigious natural talent. To those in the know it had long been evident in his balance and the perfectly poised position of his body. And the fact that he kept winning. Race after race after race.

The racing CV developed with classic and group one victories all over the globe – but it was not just high achievement that elevated him. Down the years jockeys had typically been deadpan figures, visibly deferential towards owners and trainers. Dettori was different. He neither knew nor cared about class or status. His joy and zest for the job oozed out of every pore and his natural charisma and exuberance made him known outside the close-knit racing community.

He became the face and the voice of racing as his popularity snowballed. Walk down any British high street and chances are that young and old would recognise the face of Frankie, with his wide, ever-present smile. His accent – a unique Anglo-Cockney-Italian linguistic cocktail – was also unmistakeable. He was not just a jockey or even a sportsman any more. He was a celebrity, appearing on BBC's television programme, *A Question of Sport* as a team captain amongst other commercial ventures.

However, the high-flyer came back down to earth with considerably more than a bump when, on 1st June 2000, Dettori and his fellow jockey, Ray Cochrane were aboard a Piper Seneca plane which crashed on take-off at Newmarket on its way to Goodwood. The pilot, Patrick Mackey, was killed but the jockeys survived miraculously. Dettori was pulled from the wreckage by Cochrane and escaped with a fractured right ankle and an injured thumb.

He recovered physically but, of course, he was deeply affected by the tragedy. His focus turned towards his loved ones (in 1997 he had married Catherine Allen and they were to have five children: Leo, Ella, Mia, Tallulah and Rocco) and, for a while, he appeared to lose his passion for horseracing.

"My wife, Catherine, knew the spark was still there," he explains, "but she had to give me a kick up the backside and that gave the freedom and energy to really go for it seven days a week. I was trying to be half-family man, half-jockey and as a result I wasn't fulfilling my potential."

Catherine did the trick. In 2004 Dettori became champion jockey for a third time and at the end of the 2006 season, when he rode Jeremy Noseda's *Sixties Icon* to St Leger success, he could boast eleven English classics to his name. They included four St Legers, three Oaks and two wins in both the 1000 and 2000 Guineas. And he also fulfilled two of his three childhood ambitions by winning both the King George VI and Queen Elizabeth Stakes and Prix de l'Arc de Triomphe on *Lammtarra* in 1995. His CV now stretched to several pages as well as thirty personal scrapbooks. An amazing record, with one glaring omission. He had never won the biggest race of all.

Dettori's fortunate break came in May 2007 after the Dante Derby Trial when he rode the Peter Chapple-Hyam trained *Authorized* to an imperious victory. As the stable jockey

for Godolphin, Dettori would normally have ridden the best of their entrants in the big race. However, 2007 was a fallow year for Godolphin. They had just one runner, *Eastern Anthem*, which was judged a long-shot (and ultimately was withdrawn from the race). So, after the Dante, Sheikh Mohammed rang Dettori and told him that he had decided not to enforce his contractual right. Magnanimously he gave Dettori permission to ride *Authorized* in the Derby.

Few phone calls could have made the Dettori pulse rate rise so quickly. This was the dream opportunity for which he had been yearning. Yet with opportunity came high expectation, the like of which he had never known before and surely will never have to endure again. Between Sheikh Mohammed's phone call and 4.21pm on Derby Day, when the starting stalls clanked open to begin the big race, the media spotlight intensified, day by day, hour by hour. In their eyes it was a one-horse, one-jockey and one-result story: "Dettori's Derby". The rest of the combatants were merely a supporting cast and were paid scant attention.

But, of course, sport does not work like that – and a unique accumulation of circumstances created a psychological examination of Dettori's mental strength and resilience, spunk and bottle, well beyond the sporting norm.

The first reason for the pressure was the very stature of the race. The Derby is easily

Frankie Dettori and his
father, Gianfranco.

the most famous and prestigious of the classics. It is part of the nation's heritage, contested two hundred and twenty-seven times since 1780 and the number one flat race in the world. One hundred thousand flock to the Downs each year and three million in the United Kingdom watch it live on television. Little wonder that it was one of the three races that Dettori dreamed of winning as a teenager.

And yet he had never achieved it. Indeed scarcely had a sniff. Fourteen times Dettori had travelled to Epsom on Derby Day, usually more in hope than expectation. Fourteen times he had left disappointed. Two favourites; one second place and three thirds. No wins.

"I haven't had too many decent chances in the Derby," he said. "Normally mine is the horse dropping away exhausted with five furlongs left to run. Each year I turn up thinking it will be my turn."

This year, though, the famous jockey was paired with the best horse, an outstanding three-year-old bay colt. Trainer Peter Chapple-Hyam had no doubts: "I've always said *Authorized* could be the best I've trained. He just has so much class and anything he does he does so easily. He's improved too from the Dante to Epsom; there are no worries about that. The opposition are good solid horses but I just think this horse has a bit of class."

Certainly the colt appeared to fit the identikit of the sort who could handle Epsom. For two hundred years the requirement has not altered:

Speed – to take up a good position in the hectic early stages, and, later, kick for the line.

Agility and balance – to handle the slopes, Tattenham Corner and the camber on the home straight.

Stamina, fortitude and persistence – to continue with the lung-bursting effort through the final furlongs and the tunnel of noise.

The bookmakers agreed, making *Authorized* favourite. Even with the most inexperienced jockey onboard the odds would have been short but the "Frankie-factor" reduced them to around even money.

However, the excellence of *Authorized* added to Dettori's burden. As Eddie Ahern explained there is a big psychological difference between riding an outsider and a fancied runner in the race. And there is another quantum leap between riding a fancied runner and the strong favourite, with the expectation and hopes of the "connections" and punters (around £50 million is gambled on the Derby) resting squarely on the jockey's shoulders. Moreover in the previous forty-one runnings the race had been won by the first or second favourite twenty-seven times.

Dettori was acutely aware that he would never have a better companion to help break his Derby hoodoo – but Epsom is such a quirky racetrack that much can go wrong. It poses unusual challenges that test the experience and tactical nous of a jockey.

Dettori said: "I remember explaining the

course to Japanese ace, Yutaka Take, who was shocked when he rode there for the first time. I told him it was like climbing up Mount Fuji. First you sprint up a steep slope. Then you sprint down the other side. Nor in the straight are you ever running on a level surface. From twenty runners, eighteen will have a problem, unable to handle the twists and gradients, but the first two finishers tend to be ones that cope. They are the best."

Even *Authorized* would need his jockey to manoeuvre him into the best position. Dettori could not win the race alone but he could hinder his mount's chances by poor decision-making. And one of the downsides of a long career is that even the most successful sportsman inevitably carries some psychological scars from the past. Of course there have been times in the past when Dettori made mistakes. Such as when, on *Swain*, after over-using the whip, the horse came off a true line in the 1998 Breeder Cup Classic and lost a race he should have won.

Dettori rationalised the possibility of pilot error maturely and said: "I've lost a lot of races that I should have won, but I've also won plenty. And a few bad days at the races doesn't compare to the really bad things that happen in the world."

But those psychological scars could be unhelpful on Derby Day, because then he would not be able to count on favours from some of his colleagues. There is a remarkable camaraderie between race-riders and in addition to looking after themselves they will also respect and watch out for colleagues. However, the Irish trainer Aidan O'Brien had entered an unprecedented eight runners, all competitive, from his Ballydoyle stable.

Quite aside from their individual threat it also opened up the possibility of team tactics to block *Authorized* and Dettori. The Ballydoyle bunch – ridden by Irish-based jockeys with little kinship with Dettori – would see no romance in a "Frankie wins at last" storyline. The senior stewards spoke to them about the rules over interference but some felt they might enjoy pooping on his party.

So, accumulate the circumstances. Start with the sheer stature of the race, Dettori's fourteen previous failures and his all-consuming desire to win. Multiply that by the quirkiness of the track, placing unusual demands on horse and jockey. And do not forget that psychological baggage and the possibility of a tactical roadblock. In all, ample reason why Dettori would carry extra weight when he rode *Authorized* on Derby Day; the weight of history, the weight of expectation and the weight of circumstance.

Of course, it would all have been less of a big deal had he been an unknown, but Dettori cannot fly under the media radar. So his quest to win the Derby not only made headlines on the sports pages, it was also front-page news. He felt the eyes of the world upon him. Analysing. Expecting. Watching.

Authorized's win in the Dante and the quality of his work back in Newmarket underlined that he was at the top of his form in the build-up to the big day. But the same could not be said of his jockey. Dettori fell at Goodwood nine days before the race, pulled a lateral ligament in his knee and received intensive ultrasound, ice-treatment and acupuncture. There were doubts over whether he would be able to ride and he missed several days' racing.

In addition, by Derby Day he had gone two weeks and thirteen rides without a winner. For a jockey with Dettori's glittering record this should have been no more than an irritation – but, more than most, the graph of his success during each season moves in peaks and troughs in synch with his confidence and mindset. He draws faith from success, and when he is on form, in "the zone" as he was at Ascot on the famous, "magnificent seven" day, he moves to another level. However, leading up to Derby Day, he was in a trough.

Little wonder then, that Dettori later agreed that in the week leading to the big race he had never been as nervous. "My family and friends knew to stay out of my way", he recalled. "The last ten days were a nightmare. It was mad leading up to the race. Absolutely mad. It was plain obvious to the world that I had the best horse in the race. I just had to point and pull the trigger. But the Derby always carries a bit of the unpredictable, and so many things went wrong in the run-up. I had never known such a media spotlight on me – and I had never

been more nervous. Four or five days before I was the most nervous."

Inevitably he mused ahead, picturing the race in his mind. Often this can be helpful. Visualisation techniques are often employed in sport. The athlete imagines success in his mind to make it more likely to happen for real.

Dettori explains: "Every time I put my head down I was riding round Tattenham Corner. I must have ridden that race a million times. You just want everything to be right; from the horse getting to the races in one piece, the race to run well and to ride the race well. I had the best horse so you try to think of every situation so you are prepared mentally for anything that the race throws at you. It never comes out the way you thought, but you always think of the worst scenarios so you are mentally prepared to find another way. I would say every sportsman would think like that."

But it can work the other way too. Along with the excitement and anticipation an inner voice, absent in more relaxed times, can arrive to plant mischievous thoughts and ideas into the mind, prompting with unwanted questions: wouldn't it be terrible if?

For instance the jockey who worries about getting boxed in coming round Tattenham Corner unconsciously gravitates towards it and is more likely to become faced with their concerns in reality.

Dettori says that he managed to avoid these kind of demons and his experience reassured him that any nerves would probably dissolve

On the way to the start of the 2007 Derby. You can see the tension on the faces.

on race day. However, it is little wonder that he lost sleep. Even though he could fall back on the comfort of thousands of winners, eleven classics and a reputation as one of the best jockeys in the world, human nature means that only the most laid-back character could be immune to a tightening knot of angst in these circumstances. And Dettori has never

been laid-back. He is a bottle of champagne, normally fizzy, only occasionally flat.

Of course, his colleagues in the jockeys' weighing room did not miss the opportunity to wind him up. Late one evening, with his brain still in overdrive as he tried to relax into sleep, fellow jockey Martin Dwyer sent a brief text. It simply stated "tick tock, tick tock".

That is why the contest for the 2007 Derby took place not just on the green turf of Epsom but also in the grey matter between Frankie Dettori's ears.

Days before the race, Peter Chapple-Hyam said: "The horse is fine, and I'll be okay, but Frankie's like a two-year-old. He's that wound up, he keeps ringing every minute. Keeping Frankie calm will be the problem. But on the day, I'll tell him 'You're the best jockey in the world, go out and ride like the best jockey in the world.' He'll be fine."

And by the time he woke on Saturday 2nd June Dettori was indeed at ease. "I'm very bad until about the day before, then I'm fine," he says. "On the night before the big day I'm fabulous. I'm brand new. As happy as Larry. The waiting is over and I've done my thinking and now I just can't wait to get on stage and perform."

He felt "on another planet" with excitement, "buzzing" and could not wait to get to Epsom. He flew there by helicopter with his mum and dad (who were over from Italy) and was at the racetrack by 11am, immaculate in grey pinstripe suit and pink shirt and tie, laden down with gifts, good luck wishes and superstitions. The lucky omens included as ever a small coin bearing a St Christopher attached to his skullcap. It was around then that a bet of half a million pounds was placed on the nose of *Authorized*. The pair's popularity with punters was not dwindling.

By midday Epsom was a colourful and noisy jumble of humanity, relaxing under strong sunshine.

In the Queen's Stand there were the rich, the famous and the aristocrats dressed in their fine dresses, top hats and morning suits. On the inside of the racetrack – on "the Hill" as it is known – entrance is free and families enjoyed picnics in T-shirts and shorts. Here there were the sights of the funfair, the smell of hot dogs and popcorn and the noise of a rock concert.

Perhaps liquid consumption during the meeting illustrates the differing ends of the social order in attendance: fifteen thousand bottles of champagne, three thousand bottles of Pimm's, served with five tonnes of ice, and forty-four thousand pints of beer. However, the two have always coexisted harmoniously, enjoying the racing and sense of occasion in their own ways.

Dettori had four rides on the Epsom card before the Derby and his barren, winless run continued. He was thinking, "Don't fall off, don't get hurt, and don't do anything stupid". The five-furlong sprint was a particular concern. Some of the jockeys were "kids" and, before the start, Dettori told them – somewhat paradoxically – "If you kill me, I swear to God I'm going to strangle you."

At least he survived without injury and by 3.30pm, he knew that only a freak mishap could prevent his opportunity of a lifetime. The path was clear. He could now focus all his energies on trying to win that elusive Derby.

3.58pm – Parade Ring, Epsom Downs. The jockeys leave the weighing room and enter the harsh summer sunlight of the parade ring. Wearing the olive green silks of *Authorized*'s owners Saleh al Homaizi and Imad al Sagar, Dettori talks to the connections, who look nervous and pale. They say little. Trainer Chapple-Hyam tells Dettori to keep the horse relaxed, regardless of what position he is in, and to ride him as if he owns him – a phrase the Italian will remember.

4.00pm – Dettori mounts *Authorized* and his demeanour reflects his focus. His mouth is dry and he feels divorced from proceedings, in another world. Members of the crowd circling the parade ring shout "C'mon Frankie" and other wishes of goodwill. However, he is concerned that the noise will spook *Authorized*, who dances on the spot and flicks his white splashed forehead around in annoyance. So Dettori raises a finger to his lips to quieten the well-meaning supporters.

4.03pm – Now in alphabetical order, the colts leave the parade ring and follow the curve that takes them out onto the track, in front of the Grandstand. *Acapulco, Admiralofthefleet, Anton Chekhov, Aqaleem, Archipenko* and then *Authorized*.

As the lead horse sets foot on the racetrack the trumpeters herald their arrival with a fanfare. They parade slowly in front of the Queen's Stand.

4.07pm – The horses are released from the pageantry of the build-up and begin their U-shaped long canter around the course past the stands, round Tattenham Corner, up the hill and then down to the starting stalls. Dettori purposely keeps *Authorized* down the centre of the track, as far away from the

noise as possible. It is all down to Dettori and the horse now. The waiting is over. No turning back.

On BBC television, the camera focuses on *Authorized* and their articulate anchor, Clare Balding says: "This is going to be such a fascinating tactical race, with these eight jockeys riding for Aidan O'Brien. So many who have not ridden in the Derby before. Will Frankie Dettori get the gaps when he needs them? We are going to find out very, very soon because the trainers have done everything, the stable lads have let the horses go. It's all down to the jockeys now and it's in the hands whether they experience glory or defeat today... *Authorized* making his way down to the start and he (Frankie) looks like he's got him perfectly under control."

At the start it is eerily quiet and remarkably still. *Authorized* is led around by stable lad, Mark O'Reilly. Dettori takes his feet out of the stirrups to ease the weight on the colt's back. He tries to make use of this sanctuary to draw breath and compose himself. "This is it", he thinks, "don't balls it up."

At 4.18pm the seventeen-horse field begins to load up. *Authorized* is third last into the stalls, entering as a 5-4 favourite. A micro-camera inside the stalls focuses on Dettori, deadpan behind his goggles.

Clare Balding gives the last pre-race word to co-commentator Willie Carson and asks him, "What do you think is going to happen?"

"If everything goes one hundred per cent

for him, he's going to win," he replies. "But of course everything has to go for him and that's why Dettori has been given the ride on this horse. Because you always try to put the best jockeys on the best horses."

4.20pm – All the horses are loaded. There follows a momentary pause, as one hundred thousand people at the racecourse – not to mention millions of television viewers – hold their breath and wait for the stalls to clank open.

4.21pm – And then, quite suddenly, the two hundred and twenty-eighth running of the Derby is not just a delicious prospect, it is actually in progress. Here and now. Two and a half minutes to make and break reputations. Certainly two and a half minutes that will help to define Dettori's career.

The BBC's Jim McGrath starts his commentary: "That's it, they're racing..."

The crowd roars in the way that greets kick-off on cup final day. There is a frisson of excitement. *Authorized* inches out of the stalls and makes a sluggish start.

"It's a furious pace early on..."

Dettori expected the swift, early tempo and finds it reassuring. Walter Swinburn, who won the Derby on *Shergar*, *Shahrastani* and *Lammtarra*, once said: "The Derby is won and lost on the climb up the hill during the first half-mile. If you go up the hill using petrol to get a position you will be in trouble."

With a strong pace over the first few furlongs the rise of the ground will drain "petrol" from *Authorized*'s rivals and help to sort the wheat from the chaff. It will also spread the field and reduce the chances of getting boxed in.

Authorized finds his stride and settles into a rhythm, nice and relaxed, easing uphill into a gradual right bend and then moving to the other rail towards the top of Tattenham Hill.

Dettori decides to pick a horse to follow. He sees some of the Ballydoyle quintet towards the front, then spots Eddie Ahern's *Strategic Prince* and decides "He's a good miler, he'll take me to the straight." So he slots into his slipstream. It is astute and mature thinking. A good choice and a good sign.

Over the last thirty years riding a thoroughbred has become as unconscious to Dettori as driving came to his Formula One hero, the late Ayrton Senna. It is what he does. As soon as he gets "into" a race, his brain spends little time on the act of riding. Instead it computes at split-second speed the mass of incoming data, received through his senses, to help him make and execute the correct judgements.

Again it is not a conscious act. It just happens. The danger was that today's pressure would paralyse and inhibit the process – but even in this defining race of his life it would appear that Dettori's onboard "computer" is functioning correctly.

There are only six horses behind *Authorized* as he climbs the hill through the first quarter of the race but he is well out of harm's way on the outside of the rail and in cruise control, conserving energy.

Frankie Dettori The Jockey

"They're climbing towards the highest part of the course. And Frankie Dettori, right in the middle of the pack in about seventh position. *Kid Mambo* the leader from *Anton Chekhov* and *Lucarno* and then *Acapulco*. *Aqaleem* is on the outside, followed by *Soldier of Fortune*. Then *Strategic Prince* on the outside there."

After four uphill furlongs the field breast the top of the hill, five hundred and two feet above sea level, before the turf levels out, they pass the mid-point of the race and begin the left-handed, downhill descent towards Tattenham Corner.

For nearly seven furlongs Dettori's tactics have been safe and steady; he has stayed off the rails without covering excessive extra ground, whilst keeping towards the rear of the field. As the field begin the descent he counts the horses in front of him: two, four, six, eight, ten. Down near the finishing post, trainer Chapple-Hyam thinks this is further back than ideal. But Dettori decides that as long as the group ahead keeps up this gallop there will not be a problem. They must surely tire and he will benefit from their exertions.

"As they charge downhill to Tattenham Corner and *Authorized* in about eighth position. It's *Kid Mambo* out in front here from *Anton Chekhov*, flat to the boards..."

Tattenham Corner and Frankie (green with beige stars on sleeves) and *Authorized* are poised to strike.

Frankie Dettori The Jockey

Dettori recalls later: "Five furlongs out, just entering Tattenham Corner, it runs downhill and I looked at the horses in front. And as I looked at them I could see the jockey's body language and I knew that I had them all covered. And then I had a quiet, cheeky look about the four and a half to see the other nine, what they were doing, and I could see a bit of a gap, and I was able to freewheel round Tattenham Corner..."

It is about now that Dettori feels the first surges of anticipation, because it is about now that he can confidently predict the future. He has seen that there is nothing ahead to worry about and nothing behind and feels, in racing parlance, that there is "a lot of horse" under him with petrol in the tank. In short, he knows that, barring accidents, he is going to win.

As the colourful carousel of vivid racing silks rounds the corner to come within full sight of the grandstands, Dettori's green colours can be spotted, still towards the back but beginning to take closer order.

> "*Authorized* comes round Tattenham Corner in about eighth or ninth place and plenty of room on the outside. As they straighten up for home now and it's *Kid Mambo* who kicks away by four lengths..."

Once into the straight, the field continues downhill until the ground levels out. However, Epsom has one final test up its sleeve: in the straight the course slopes down from the stands side, causing tired horses to hang to the left.

The temptation is for Dettori to make his challenge here and now. However, he adheres to the words of Martin Dwyer, who won in 2006 on *Sir Percy*. He advised, "In the straight so many jockeys want to push on but it's deceptively long and it pays to bide your time. It's important not to kick too soon. People said you couldn't come from as far back as I did on *Sir Percy* but I'd watched some old videos and seen it done. It's a long way up the straight."

The unanswered question is whether the horse will have the expected va-va-voom when Dettori does press the accelerator. The answer is emphatic. He gives him "a couple of flicks" and gets the response of his dreams.

The decisive burst down the centre of the track, over a furlong and a few giant strides, settles the contest. Tongue rolling out of his mouth; in less than a quarter of a mile *Authorized* sweeps past eight of the finest thoroughbreds on the planet and takes the lead.

> "*Authorized* on the outside, in the clear... He's cruising up to them, the favourite, as they race up with a furlong and a half to go now. *Authorized*. Frankie says go and he races into the lead and careers away..."

Now Dettori just needs to keep a lid on his adrenalin.

"I remembered the words that Michael Hills had said to me," he says later. "He won the Derby on *Shaamit* in 1996, and Lester Piggott had given him this advice: 'Ride the horse; don't ride the race.' So that's what I was thinking on the straight. Just be patient, don't do anything stupid, be professional. I got him balanced going to the two-furlong marker and he stretched away.

"Then I was just thinking: just think, keep it simple, don't let the race get to you, push him out to the line because a hundred thousand people are throwing hats and everything and I don't want to spook the horse and him do anything stupid. Just get him from A to B as smooth as you can."

All Dettori can see is a huge sea of people right and left and a strip of green leading to the finishing post. The deafening noise from the crowd would not be out of place at the newly opened Wembley Stadium. By now his blood is pumping with pure adrenalin and he is so excited he can hardly breathe. "When I got past the furlong marker the world stopped, my heart stopped, I knew this was going to be my moment," he reflected later. "Everything went so smoothly. I expected a dogfight but it was like an oil painting, beautiful and smooth."

As the red circle of the finishing post becomes closer, Dettori screams with eyes wide open. But there is no celebratory arm in the air. He does not want to attempt anything flash; he just wants to get to the line in one piece.

"It's all *Authorized*. Frankie Dettori, at the fifteenth attempt, lays to rest his Derby ghost. Up to the line, and *Authorized* wins at a canter by five or six lengths!"

As he passes the post, Dettori feels as though he is in a dream. Everything stops for a few seconds. He can hear the other jockeys trying to say "well done" but they seem so far away. He is overwhelmed with joy and relief.

Peter Chapple-Hyam fires an imaginary six-shooter after peering above the top hats to enjoy the finish and then dissolves in tears of joy. The winning time is two minutes, thirty-four seconds and the prize worth £700,000.

"You have to give it to horse and rider. Both of them rose to the occasion and Frankie Dettori came there, cruising on the outside. Racing has the story it desperately wanted and this run has got the prize. What a fantastic performance by *Authorized*."

Dettori has done it! He has won the Derby!

Images of the aftermath and celebration that followed will remain easily in the mind of those who either were at the racecourse or watched on television:

Dettori, breaking with protocol to take *Authorized* back in front of the main stands, so the fans can share the celebrations.

Dettori, entering the winners' enclosure, and leaping off the horse – bad knee and all – with the cameras clicking and whirring all around him.

In a dream; Franie Dettori wins the Derby.

Dettori, embracing his father who so wanted to win the Derby thirty-one years ago but never quite made it and left in tears.

Dettori, kneeling in front of the clerk of the scales as if he were at an altar and telling him "I've won the f'ing Derby, sir."

Dettori entering the jockeys' weighing room and shouting "Get the f'ing bubby open!"

Dettori, on the winners' rostrum, with the other connections, being interviewed and receiving his medal.

Above all, Dettori enjoying the intoxicating relief and joy of successfully fighting the demons of high expectation to secure the biggest prize of his career.

This is why all the travelling and being away from the family, the wasting and the threat of injury is worth it; for priceless moments such as these. The limping and somewhat exhausted little figure left Epsom carrying a glass of champagne in one hand and a trophy bag in the other. By then his mobile phone contained eighty-six unread messages.

And of course, once the cameras had stopped whirring and the crowds began their long journey home the celebrations continued, away from the limelight at last.

"When I got back home on Saturday night I knocked on the door of all my neighbours and invited them in the house," Dettori recalled later. "I stayed there, drank everything I had in the house and then went down to the White Lion in Newmarket, staggered down to the yard to see 'Chapple' and my wife put me in a taxi at 1.30am and sent me home."

The morning after the night before brought the expected extensive coverage in the sports sections and front-page headlines on the Sunday broadsheets. "Dettori has his day of days," said the *Independent*; "Dettori lives out a dream," said the *Mail*; "Frankie's first," said the *Observer*.

Despite the remnants of a heavyweight hangover, Dettori travelled to Longchamp the next day to win the French Derby on *Lawman*; the perfect end to a perfect weekend. And on the Monday he went to see the horse that made it all possible. Dettori kissed *Authorized*, who promptly bit him. No matter, he was able to consider the magnitude of the achievement at his leisure.

And, in spite of a hangover, the French Derby follows the next day and Frankie Dettori says thank you to *Lawman*.

"I feel really drained," he said. "But this is the most satisfying moment of my career. When my five children grow up I want to be able to tell them that I won the big honours in sport."

Once the dust had settled he considered how it compared with the "magnificent seven" at Ascot? Was it the pinnacle of his career?

"Well, the Derby was just one race; Ascot was seven in one day. Of course the Derby is close and it was a huge notch on my CV. That was the only one I was missing. But in three hundred years of horseracing I'm the first one to have ever done it (all seven winners in a day) and I'm probably the first living person to have a statue (Dettori's statue, commemorating the achievement, stands at Ascot). Normally you only have a statue when you're dead!

"I was just thinking this morning, I've won every classic twice or more, bar the Derby, and I was thinking four King Georges, four Gold Cups, four QEIIs, six Breeders' Cups, three Japan Cups, three World Cups – it's not a bad record."

What would be his abiding memory of Derby day in, say, thirty years' time?

"Having my dad there, my mum and dad there for me, was *really* special. My dad tried in 1976, he had an odds-on shot, same as me, on *Wollow* and he failed. So it was great to put the record straight, great to have him there."

And did the Derby win change the way he thought about race-riding?

"Not really. I still enjoy it. I love it. I still get nervous before big races and I guess I won't be riding any more if I ever lose those nerves."

TEN

LIKELY LAD

"FRANKIE WAS KISSING ME AND TELLING ME HOW SORRY HE WAS
FOR BEING AN ARSEHOLE THERE, DOWN AT THE START. AND I SAID
'DON'T WORRY ABOUT IT, LITTLE MAN. LOOK, AS LONG AS YOU GOT
PAST THE LINE FIRST I DON'T CARE WHAT YOU SAID TO ME.'"

THE FIRST TIME I MET Mark O'Reilly was in the depths of winter, on a wet evening. That day he had got up in the dark, and, following his second shift at the stables, arrived home in the dark. At that stage the heat, sunshine and big race days of summer seemed distant and each new morning was not met with undiluted exuberance.

The second main discussion was four days after the 2007 Epsom Derby and even a seen-it-all, done-it-all, got-the-T-shirt racing veteran like O'Reilly was still positively buzzing with schoolboy enthusiasm.

Well, that's racing for you. When it's good, it's great; but there are times – normally during the winter – when people wonder why they don't find something else to do for a living.

Regardless of the circumstances, Mark was always good to interview. People react differently to this process. Some clam up and give little away. Others, like Mark, are keener to unburden. In addition to his personal perspective on Derby Day, he revealed that he suffered a harsh and unhappy childhood, that he learned to ride on the bare backs of travellers' horses and that he left the country of his birth to create a new life for himself in Newmarket.

In the eighteen years since he has worked (as a "rich man's slave" as he puts it) for a range of trainers, most notably Henry Cecil. He's now a "mucker-outer" with Peter Chapple-Hyam, looking after three horses: a pair of two-year-olds, Tame that Tiger *and* Declaration of War *and a three-year-old sprinter with serious attitude,* Hamoody. *"He'd have you at the drop of a hat," O'Reilly explains.*

Apart from horseracing, his passions are his family and a blossoming role as a boxing coach. As a result our discussions were often interrupted by boxing-related phone calls – once, impressively, by a young fighter called Rocky!

In short, O'Reilly has a story that deserves an airing and one that he needed no second invitation to share. Like many Irishmen, he can spin a yarn. "I like to talk," he says – and talk he did; at speed, at length, in lucid tones and with little need of prompting.

Mark O'Reilly The Stable Lad

Wednesday 7th June, Astley Club, Fred Archer Way, Newmarket. Mark O'Reilly's Derby Day began at St Gatien Stables at 4am and finished, in a drunken haze some twenty-one and a half hours later, at 1.30am the following morning. In between *Declaration of War* won the listed Woodcote Stakes on the Epsom undercard. In addition, he was involved with *Authorized*, who, of course, carried Frankie Dettori to that long-awaited first Derby victory. If you look at pictures of the successful connections of *Authorized* on the winners' podium you can see O'Reilly amongst the top hats and tails and the euphoric faces.

"In racing for every high there's twenty lows, but that's one of the best days' racing I've had for many, many years. It helped me rekindle feelings of why I came into racing," he says, sitting in a quiet room in the Astley Club on Fred Archer Way in Newmarket. Below him is the gym where he now spends so much of his time coaching young boxers.

Even within the one, opening sentence there were clues that begin to provide some context and background to the O'Reilly story. "Many, many years," he says – confirming that he has been around the racing block a few times. And when he talks of "rekindling" there is an implied suggestion that there have been times when his flame of enthusiasm for the sport had dimmed, if not been entirely extinguished.

And so to explain just how much 2nd June 2007 meant to him and why he rewound back to his beginnings: 8th March 1964, more than forty-three years ago, when he was born in Dublin.

He was brought up in a small flat in Dún Laoghaire, with his father, who worked for an electric company, his housewife mother, three brothers and a sister. This was the 1960s/early 1970s and in the less prosperous areas of southern Ireland many families were on the breadline. Money was as scarce as laughter and O'Reilly admits that the emotional scars remain with him to this day.

"I had a shit upbringing," he recalls, with Irish eyes that are most definitely not smiling. "I was never a child. I wasn't allowed to be a little boy. I was an adult when I was born and working at nine because there was no money. My father used to beat us up. It's still very hard and I still get very depressed about it."

There was also danger outside of the family flat with an undercurrent of violence, crime, drugs and political unrest in the community. O'Reilly says, "I had to be clever, streetwise. I stayed out of trouble. There's a lot of people that I went to school with who are either dead or inside. I was on the fringe of all that. With the troubles in Ireland and coming from the area that I came from it was always around, in certain ways. You could be involved to a certain extent but any further and you'd be putting yourself in danger. It was just common sense; knowing where your boundaries were without upsetting anyone. I've never been in trouble enough where I'd need to be worried about it. I knew a lot of people who were involved,

Mark O'Reilly, stable lad and boxing coach.

but I was clever enough to just keep on the edge of it."

His haven was sport: football, golf and particularly running. He ran hundreds of miles, perhaps symbolically expressing a desire to get away. He also took a shine to horses. "On a Saturday morning," he says, "when the milk wagon used to come round, it was pulled by a horse and I used to be mesmerised by them. I thought they were fantastic and just loved to be around them." By the age of nine he could ride. Of course, there were no plush riding schools for the young O'Reilly. Even had they existed there would have been no money to fund his attendance. No, for him and his friends the craic was to seize impromptu opportunities to ride pretty much any horseflesh that came into sight in the open fields of the Irish countryside. "There were lots of travellers where I lived and I just used to jump on the horses' backs and away I went," he says. "Young kids don't have fear and we didn't. If you saw a horse in a field we just put a rope on its neck and got on it. Simple as that. I just loved the feel of it."

Unconsciously he was developing an understanding and empathy with horses that have held him in good stead through his working life. Having left school at fourteen, he began by riding out in various stables, pocketing back of the hand cash and experience. There was also the fresh air and exercise to be enjoyed and the inspirational victory of *Desert Orchid* in the Gold Cup made up his mind that whatever he did, it needed to involve horses. Certainly a four-year spell working shifts in a factory confirmed that the alternative was not to be countenanced. He loathed factory life.

As a result he moved to the British mainland at the age of twenty-five and the obvious choice of destination was the home of the horse, Newmarket. O'Reilly began his formal, bona fide career in racing by riding out for trainer Dr Jon Scargill. His resolve was tested on only the second day when a loose horse was hit and killed instantaneously by a car right in front of him. He rang his mother in tears and said he was coming home. Fortunately he was persuaded to stay and began to feel comfortable in his new surroundings.

Within six months Kerry – then his partner, now his wife of fifteen years – joined him and they have remained in the town ever since, bringing up their two daughters, eight-year-old Aisling and five-year-old Kiera.

In addition to Scargill, O'Reilly worked for Michael Bell (as second head lad) and then Mick Ryan before spending fourteen years in the opulent stables of racing legend, Henry Cecil.

Little wonder, then, that Cecil's success in the Oaks (the day before) was a topic of conversation as O'Reilly began 2007 Derby Day in a horsebox travelling to Epsom Downs. In the back were two horses, *Authorized* and *Declaration of War*. In the front were O'Reilly, Noel O'Connor, stable lad to the Derby favourite, and the travelling head lad, Ronan Meehan, who also spent a year with Cecil.

They left the stables at 5am, early enough

to beat the traffic jams that blight the M25 and the little lanes around Epsom before and after such a big event. More than one hundred thousand were expected to attend and it was critical that they dodged the traffic. After a problem-free run they arrived at Epsom at 7.30am. A relatively quick journey but still more than enough time to reflect on Henry Cecil's headline-making win with the filly, *Light Shift*.

During his pomp Cecil had been leading trainer on ten occasions between 1976 and 1993. He could boast twenty-three victories in the English classics, including four Derbys and seven victories in the Oaks, the last with *Love Divine* in 2000 – and after each one the family standard (depicting the Horn of Leys, an heirloom given to one of Cecil's ancestors by Robert the Bruce in 1323) was raised outside Warren Place. It became a familiar sight.

But famine had followed feast with a depressing, seven-year, public decline. He became yesterday's man. No flying of the standard, fewer owners, fewer horses. In addition he suffered with stomach cancer and was still recovering from the effects of chemotherapy. So only the coldest heart could have viewed his return to a classic winning enclosure with apathy.

"The man could train horses," says O'Reilly. "I must admit when he came into the winner's enclosure, near to tears, I felt a little lump myself, because I know what it meant to the man. Hats off to him. Everybody had him retired, pipe and slippers, years ago and he's proved them all wrong. I've got the greatest respect for him as a trainer."

O'Reilly's fourteen years on the payroll coincided with Cecil's halcyon days and it was "a huge eye-opener to work with some of the best horses there's ever been". These included Derby winners *Commander in Chief* (1993) and *Oath* (1999). He also rubbed shoulders with the rich and famous. Jockeys like Kieren Fallon (who remains a good friend), Steve Cauthen and Lester Piggott and owners such as Sir Alex Ferguson and Kevin Keegan. There were also royal visitors to the yard: Her Majesty the Queen and princes from Dubai.

Many of the stable lads and lasses in the yard were veterans who had been in the game for thirty or forty years; genuine characters who had seen it all and were happy to tell the story. O'Reilly reminisces, "Racing people can be very witty. There are some characters that will have you in stitches. It's our sense of humour; we're all on the same wavelength and you can have a bit of fun. You get all sorts of stable lads and lasses; there's banter and fun as well as some bitchiness and jealousy."

However, towards the end of his time at Warren Place, progressively, day by day, O'Reilly grew stale and disenchanted. What had been a labour of love became just a way of paying the mortgage. He does not know quite why this happened but his dissatisfaction – and you sense a bristling against authority that he traces back to his father's influence – led to conflict with his 'Guvnor'.

He recalls: "I had to call Henry Cecil 'Guvnor' for fourteen years and 'Sir' if an owner was there. Why? What's the difference? He just has the name of a man who's trained a lot of winners. He's just a human being like the rest of us. We had our differences. I don't take crap off anyone."

So the parting was less than amicable but that was several years ago and, on his way to Epsom, O'Reilly could take some pleasure in his former employer's rejuvenation.

By 7.30am, having arrived at Epsom, the horses were unloaded and settled at the stables, suitably guarded by security. O'Reilly's main concern was his own charge, *Declaration of War*. He says, "He's so straightforward and laid back it's unbelievable. An absolute gentleman." He also likes the fact that he is a fighter, a trait close to O'Reilly's heart. *Tame that Tiger* is "a backward two-year-old who won't run until later in the season" – but it is *Hamoody* which presents the biggest challenge of his three charges. He is a highly-strung and – to someone with less experience – a highly dangerous thoroughbred.

"*Hamoody* came from the breeze-ups last year," explains O'Reilly, "and he's a very dodgy character. When he first came I and another fellah had to do him because he'd have you if you did him on your own. Now he knows the rules he's a bit better. But you have to be careful; there's some days when you can't touch his head and days when you can't touch that side of him or that side of him. It's just him. He's a horse of habit. If you change something that you did yesterday he doesn't like it. For someone else it might be off-putting, but to me it's second nature.

"On race days *Hamoody* gets so tense in the parade ring that he puffs himself up to three times his normal size and sweats freely. It's very off-putting because people think he's boiling over. But that's just him. Riders like Frankie Dettori have quiet hands and just let him go and once he's on the move down to the start he's fine. He's a coil that just wants to release itself."

Hamoody's volatile nature at least provides a challenge for experienced horsemen like his work rider, the chirpy scouser, Johnny Lowe. Lowe is an ex-professional jockey, now fifty years old, who still rides out three times a day. He has horse sense, an ability to interpret a horse's psychological make-up and handle them accordingly.

O'Reilly is the same and that is how he adds value in his own job. He enjoys the challenge of fathoming them out. "I get on well with horses, particularly dodgy ones," he says. "Someone who's experienced can walk into a box and know if a horse is ill just by looking at them. You just know. Any horse. It's about spotting things. Hearing a horse cough. It's programmed into you. It's just experience and little things like making sure under their girth is clear of any sand, because it's tender there and they'll get sore. You also make sure their ears are sponged out because they get sore there too."

In his time with Henry Cecil, O'Reilly

Mark O'Reilly with *Declaration of War*.

was an exercise rider like Lowe, riding three lots each morning, and this is also the role of most of the Chapple-Hyam crew. They are known as the "rider-outers" and earn ten to fifteen pounds more than the "mucker-outers", which can now boast O'Reilly in their midst. Certainly his experience comes cheap. "Mucker-outers" in Newmarket – regardless of whether they are a seventeen-year-old wet-behind-the-ears rookie or an O'Reilly with a lifetime with horses on his CV – are not paid well. And he gets one day off every fortnight.

He says: "I don't ride out any more since I put on a few pounds. So I get in at about twenty past seven and muck eight horses out. I give their boxes a clean out and give them fresh water and hay. I make sure they're neat and tidy and sweep the yard up."

By 10.30 he has finished the morning shift. "It's not that it's hard graft and it's not danger-ous because we're used to it," he says. "But the job does grind you down because you're there all the time. It's constant. Horses, horses, horses. Nothing different." Just occasionally he travels as a stable lad on race days, which provides a welcome variation to the normal routine. He adds with a resigned smile, "Es-sentially we're all in the same boat – underpaid and overworked. We're all looked at as rich man's slaves. At least that's what I call us."

He returns to the stables for another shift at 4pm – this time for just an hour – to look after his three horses. "I tie them up, make sure their beds and mangers are clean," he explains, "then dress them up. I brush them, making sure there's no sweat marks on them,

shine them up, put the rugs back on them and leave them alone.

"My own way of doing things is to leave them alone as much as I can. Some shine them up like a new pin but horses don't want to be stuck there for forty-five minutes being brushed. They get agitated, particularly the fillies. When a horse is well it looks well, it's not achieved by what humans do to it. It's like looking at an athlete who's one hundred per cent fit. They might be tired but their eyes will be shiny and gleaming and their skin will be clear. I can tell by looking in a boxer's eye how fit he is. It's the same with horses; that's how they are in the wild."

Hence, at Epsom, O'Reilly was happy to leave *Declaration of War* to settle himself in the stables and then meet his travelling companions for breakfast. Straight after they walk, under warm, early morning sunshine (the preface to one of the hottest afternoons of the summer) the one and a half miles of the Derby course from the starting stalls to the finishing post.

What does he think of Epsom? "It's a horrible place to run horses," he says, "but at the end of the day, one, you've got to stay a mile and half and, two, you've got to handle the contours. It's like a bad rollercoaster and when you're going at speed on four legs it's not the easiest thing in the world to negotiate. You need a horse that's extremely well balanced, if not you can forget it. And it has ruined many a horse because they've never got over it."

Added to that, of course, they have to

cope with the size and noise of crowds that can spook a two-year-old. Epsom can be both education and ordeal. So when, after a long morning and early afternoon of anticipation and waiting around, the race card eventually reached 2.30pm and the two hundredth running of the Vodafone Woodcote Stakes, how did *Declaration of War* cope?

"He played up a little," says O'Reilly. "With a big crowd there he reared up and pulled away from me once or twice. He was just well in himself. He's only a two-year-old, it's only the second time he's ever ran in his life – and he's got this massive crowd looking at him. He was really showing off: 'Look at me, pay me attention.' They're little boys."

And did he expect him to run well?

"Not really. We were drawn really badly. At eleven. Rule of thumb round Epsom is that if you're drawn wide on the six-furlong course forget it. You can't win from there. You've got to come too far round. You're going straight down the hill, going flat out and then you've got to come round the bend – and then the camber of the track is the wrong way."

During the race one of his rivals, *Baytown Blaze*, hung to the right so severely that he struggled to make the turn around Tattenham Corner at all and, at one stage, seemed to be heading to Epsom Station before he eventually straightened up on the stand-side rails.

Declaration of War also toiled to make the turn. He ran wide and veered off into the centre of the track, losing ground as a result, before he finally straightened, regained balance and surged through the final stages to claim the £17,000 prize, one length ahead of the Dettori-ridden *Bespoke Boy*.

The crowds were so large and voluble that O'Reilly, down by the winning post, neither got to watch the race nor hear it on the tannoy commentary. But he saw the racing silks of his jockey, Robert Halvin (red with black and yellow stripes on the arms) flash over the line ahead of the chasing pack. Of the many images that O'Reilly will store from the day, he thinks that is the one that will be retained the longest. It meant a lot. In fact he punched one fist into his hand so hard that he wondered briefly if he had broken it.

Why so happy?

"I was pleased for the owner (Mickey Mercer) and pleased for the boss (Peter Chapple-Hyam). It was a great start to the day. The owner and his mates are really, really nice men. All young West London people. The owner comes to the yard quite regularly, goes to the Baker's Oven in town, buys three bags full of sausage rolls and pies, and brings them to the yard for all the lads. Little touches like that go such a long way. Really, really nice fella. You'd wish him all the luck in the world, y'know."

O'Reilly's joy as he collected his medal was evident and he kissed it as he left the rostrum. "When you get to Derby Day and you've got the favourite and you've just won a two-year-old race it gives you a buzz," he adds. "You'd have to be very cold not to get excited. For me that was fantastic. That's what racing is all about. You've got your highs and lows. In the winter, it might be pissing down with rain – not a nice time – and you think 'I've had enough of this'. And then this comes along and gives you such a boost.

"It's like when *Dutch Art* ran well in the Guineas and *Authorized* won the Dante. Our yard started laughing and joking again. It gives you that spark. That's what you need sometimes.

"It's also great to be involved with nice horses – and, at the end of the day, when you have nice horses you earn money (stable lads receive a proportion of prize money). I'm not greedy but I'm interested in looking after my wife and family."

However elated he was, O'Reilly kept some emotions in check, aware that this was the precursor to the Derby, which was now just ninety minutes distant. Although his main work was finished, he was given responsibility for walking *Authorized* around at the starting stalls (special permission needs to be provided from the stewards to allow this). So once he had offered his good luck to Noel O'Connor, he walked across the Downs and through the crowds to the start and sweated under an unrelenting sun for the completion of the pre-race parade, and for jockey and horse to arrive.

When they did, what state were they in?

"*Authorized* was very warm but he wasn't boiling over. *Montjeu*, the breed, can boil over but he took it all very well. But it was a ridiculously scorching hot day. I put a lead rein on him. Frankie was telling me what to do,

making sure he didn't stand on his plates. To be honest, he was being a bit of a pain in the arse but he was nervous, so you put up with it. I'm a very experienced lad; I don't need to be told how to lead a horse round. But he was nervous. I don't mind that. He was only being careful.

"I wiped *Authorized's* neck down and I took the neck strap off him. I was just going to wipe his reins, but Frankie told me his reins were fine – and, all I said to him, which I also say to all my fighters, was 'Believe in yourself'. That's all I said to him. I said nothing about the horse. And he said 'Thank you'.

"He was concentrating. It was quiet down there. You could hear a pin drop. And they started loading up as quickly as possible. The stalls handler came and took him off me. And then the rest is history. The stalls released and off they went over the hill."

So how did O'Reilly watch the race? Truth is, for the second time that day, he didn't – at least not until later when he glimpsed the video replays on the big screens. It was only when he was back home on the Sunday that he sat in front of the video and absorbed it all at leisure.

He had planned to watch on a portable television set next to the start, but felt the urge to get back to the winning post so managed to persuade the starter to give him a lift in his jeep that follows, albeit from long distance, the race down the track. O'Reilly was not alone. There were three stable lads, including one from Marcus Tregoning's yard, sitting in the back listening to commentary

on the jeep's radio. Of course O'Reilly's loyalties were obvious: "I was screaming out of the back of the van 'Go on Frankie, go on Frankie'. I was screaming my head off as he passed the line."

The main reason that O'Reilly wanted to get back to the finishing post was to take *Authorized* from O'Connor, in case he needed to go and pick up a prize. Once Dettori and *Authorized* had stormed to victory, finished their unscripted bow in front of the main stand and entered the winners' enclosure O'Reilly was on hand to offer to take the horse away and allow O'Connor to enjoy the moment.

But that was not the way it panned out. "Noel said, 'I can't be doing with this, you stay here' and so he took the horse away and I got announced on TV as the stable lad and collected the medal."

How did he feel?

"Elated. That's the tenth classic winner that I've been involved with – but only the second time I've been there and seen it all unfold. And the first time at the Derby. With these (the Chapple-Hyam connections) it was fan–tastic. We were all hugging each other. It

147

was absolutely fantastic, just an honour to be there."

How far back does O'Reilly have to go to find a better racing day?

"I remember a great day in 1994 on Churchill Downs when Dettori won the Breeders' Cup on *Barathea* and the noise was deafening. And winning the Sussex Stakes with *Distant View* was special. But, barring my children being born, standing in the winning enclosure is something I'll never forget."

And had Frankie relaxed a bit by then?

"Oh yes. He was one hundred per cent relaxed by then! We were all under a lot of pressure, and Frankie in particular. If he had lost people would have questioned his bottle. The horse was that good that I could have ridden round and won on it. He's so far in front of those other horses. We knew it, but though you see it you're frightened to say it. He's got so much natural ability. He's always had it. He's not even the finished article. Give him another three or four months on his back and you'll see a better horse."

After a glass or two of champagne, the stable lads whisked *Authorized* and *Declaration of War* out of Epsom, the horse box arriving back at the yard at 7.30pm, welcomed by many stable staff who turned up to witness their arrival.

Once the horses were settled back into their stables, the festivities began in earnest, with drinks at the yard being followed by a heavy social night in Newmarket, predominantly at a favoured watering hole, the White Lion, with Chapple-Hyam and Dettori involved in the merriment.

As might be expected details are somewhat sketchy, but O'Reilly recalls, "Frankie was kissing me and telling how sorry he was for being an arsehole there, down at the start. And I said, 'Don't worry about it, little man. Look, as long as you got past the line first I don't care what you said to me.' I eventually got home at 1.30am, er, shall we say, in a little bit worse state than when I left."

You sense that although the celebrations were clearly exuberant O'Reilly actually relished the build-up to the race as much as the carousing that followed. "It is relaxed in this yard," he says. "It makes such a difference. You feel part of a team and you're allowed to enjoy it."

Certainly O'Reilly looks back at his move from Henry Cecil to Peter Chapple-Hyam with relief and he speaks highly of the trainer's man-management style. "Peter is the total opposite of anyone I've ever worked for," he says. "He's just a normal, everyday, run of the mill bloke. He leaves you alone and gives you no trouble, no hassle. I probably speak to him once a week. Peter's very relaxed and I much prefer it."

He also speaks highly of his ability as a trainer. He says, "He's very, very talented. He knows how to handle good horses, and he knows how to handle bad horses. And that's where he's clever, in knowing how to get the best out of bad horses and winning a race for the owner. He's excellent at finding races for people who can't afford the elite horses."

Probably up to £150 a week more is available down the road at Godolphin but O'Reilly wouldn't countenance such a move. He says that "At Godolphin you're just a number whereas Peter treats you like a human being."

This kind of respect and appreciation clearly means a lot to him and days like the Derby victory remind O'Reilly why he is in the job. Whether it elevates horseracing up his list of priorities is another matter.

Family O'Reilly clearly comes first. He loves his wife and adores his two daughters. He says, "I hope and think I'm a good dad. I've seen the other side of it. I'm not afraid to tell my children I love them; not afraid to hug and kiss them, although I never had any of that. I'm not frightened to show my feelings; I'd give them everything I've got."

And if the wife and girls come first then over the past few years, boxing has become a clear second. His voice crackles with enthusiasm as he describes how he has become an ABA coach and aspires to become an England coach. The first spark of interest in the sport was more than thirty years ago when he woke at 3am to watch the Muhammad Ali v George Foreman "Rumble in the Jungle" with his father on their grainy black and white television. "Probably the only good times with my dad," he ruminates.

The spark ignited when he became involved with boxing in Newmarket at the Astley Club. By then O'Reilly was carrying various battle scars that are all but inevitable after a life of dealing with horses. "I've got crushed in the stalls," he says, "done all my ribs, had a horse rear on top of me. I've been kicked in the thigh twice and stood on hundred of times. There's nothing worse! Oh the pain of it! That's why I wear steel toecaps. They're extremely strong animals. I've also been bitten."

So maybe it was some relief that he was spared from further punishment because he was too old to box competitively. Instead he sparred to keep fit before coming a coach. He is taking a senior coach's course in 2008 and it is clear that the sport usurped much of the affection he used to have for horseracing. He now runs a jam-packed gym and "dabbles" in the professional game. "Boxing never stops," he explains, but the rewards of developing young talent justify the effort. He says, "Boxing is good and bad. It's a fantastic discipline – and I'm a firm disciplinarian with them – but it's also a hurt game."

Certainly O'Reilly's efforts offer some antidote to the social challenges in Newmarket. He lives happily on the outskirts of town and enjoys the history and open spaces of the heathland but says, "It's not the town I came to. It's completely different. There's drugs in the town, a lot of trouble. It's very concerning for a father with young children. There's people fighting at the weekends. Of course you get that everywhere, but it's worse here at the moment."

Of course, Newmarket has been home to various degrees of rowdy behaviour since the time of Charles II, four centuries ago, so little changes. Nevertheless any activity that encourages youth off the streets and instils personal discipline and maturity is to be commended.

Maybe O'Reilly sees some of the protégés in his gym in the same way as some of the juvenile thoroughbreds that he looks after; young, strong-willed, rebellious and craving support, guidance and direction. And maybe when he looks at them he occasionally gets flashbacks to the young Mark O'Reilly of the early 1970s in those dark days in Ireland. You sense that whilst he is living in the present he is also purging the past and helping others to enjoy a better upbringing than he endured.

So if anyone deserved a day in the sun it was Mark O'Reilly. The names of Dettori and Cecil will be writ large in the legend of Epsom 2007 – but there were a host of backstage players who all played a part in this remarkable sporting theatre. O'Reilly was one of them and worthy of his fifteen minutes of fame.

ELEVEN

HOBBY HORSE

"I'VE NOT A CLUE HOW MUCH WE'VE SPENT ON HORSES BECAUSE
COLIN IS MY 'RACING MANAGER' AND LOOKS AFTER THE
FINANCES. I'D GUESS AROUND HALF A MILLION POUNDS. I
DON'T ALWAYS THINK ABOUT COSTS. IT'S ABOUT FUN AND, AT
TIMES, A LITTLE PROFIT. THIS IS PRIMARILY OUR HOBBY BUT
IF WE CAN COVER A FEW COSTS THEN THAT'S GOOD."

*ONE OF THE BENEFITS of following the people in this book was getting uncommonly close to some
great sporting theatre.*

I was next to the Derby winning post when Frankie Dettori and Authorized *breezed past – one screaming with joy, the other with a big tongue lolling out of his mouth (you can work out which was which). I was
there on the rails as* Dutch Art *spurted for home in the 2000 Guineas. And when Jan Harris (with her
family) went to Royal Ascot for the first time as an owner I was there too; enjoying the ambience, pageantry
and glamour and tucking into rather too many chicken legs during their car park picnic. I was also with
them in the parade ring, listening in as trainer provided jockey with last-minute, pre-race orders.*

*It should be stated, in my defence, that I did drive them back from Ascot – so I was not a complete free-
loader and it was certainly educational to be there.*

*Of course their main objective was to enjoy the day. For me it was to get an insight into why people want
to own horses. I think we were both successful and in the unlikely event that I ever win the lottery, purchase
a racehorse and make it to Royal Ascot "for real" then the Harrises have provided a useful blueprint of
how to get the most from the day:*

1. *Travel in hope more than expectation. To have a runner – let alone a winner – at Royal Ascot is a
   privilege few ever get a chance to enjoy.*
2. *Relish everything about the day. Soak it all up.*
3. *Dress up to the nines, enter into the spirit of the social occasion, and enjoy the sense of being part of
   Britain's heritage – but don't take it too seriously. Recognise it for what it is.*
4. *Take the family.*
5. *Enjoy the racing – that's always the number one priority – but also eat, drink and be merry.*

Jan Harris The Owner

Some fifty thousand people own all or part of the fourteen thousand racehorses currently in training in Great Britain. Most have dipped their toes into the deep waters of equine investment by co-owning in a partnership or syndicate, which is an increasingly popular option. Members are rewarded for a comparatively modest outlay with a personal stake in a horse's career. Bills and earnings are shared amongst the syndicate along with some input into decisions about trainers, jockeys and where and when the horse runs.

At the other end of the spectrum are the multi-millionaires who build up strings of superbly bred horses through their own breeding operations and invest heavily at bloodstock auctions. As a result, on the flat at least, elite horses are owned by elite owners and the classics tend to be contested by jockeys sporting the colours of the likes of Godolphin, which operates out of Dubai and Newmarket and was set up by Dubai's ruling family, the Maktoums.

Their success is reflected in the list of champion owners over the past ten years. Godolphin has topped the list five times and the other champions have been Hamdan Al Maktoum (twice) Sheikh Mohammed, HH Aga Khan, and Khalid Abdullah. These foreign interests are the Roman Abramoviches of the racing world, using wealth and status to powerful effect.

They are not alone. Monarchs, celebrities, aristocrats and mega-rich businessmen have always been prominent in ownership in Britain and the current list features Her Majesty the Queen, an array of lords, dukes and earls plus famed headline-makers such as Sir Alex Ferguson. Horseracing ownership has always had a whiff of "them and us" about it; of snobbery and privilege, elitism and class – and certainly these people move in exclusive circles. Little wonder it is often known as "the sport of kings".

Someone in the middle of these different ends of the spectrum is forty-six-year-old Jan Harris and her husband of twenty-three years, Colin, who is a highly successful businessman who runs the largest manufacturer of darts in the world. He also owns a property company and Jan is currently coordinating the purchase of a Caribbean holiday resort on his behalf.

They used the resultant financial prosperity to begin their adventure as racehorse owners five years ago when Colin received an invitation from a friend at his golf club to purchase a third share of an unborn foal with an impressive pedigree, coming out of the Irish stallion *Montjeu*. The cost would be £35,000.

Jan had been fascinated by horses since going to riding schools as a child. Colin liked "the odd bet" and his father was a bookmaker. So there was already a family affection for the sport.

As a result they decided to accept the invitation and take the gamble but sell for profit when the foal became a yearling. She was entered into the prestigious Houghton Sale in Newmarket and it was anticipated she might be sold for around £300,000. That was before the foal injured herself in the stable and went lame. She was withdrawn and did not go under the auctioneer's hammer. Tensions within the syndicate resulted in the Harrises ultimately purchasing her outright for £60,000 at auction. They have not entered into co-ownership since then. But, in a sense, the damage was done. They were captivated from the moment that they saw the tiny baby foal that became known as *Ti Adora* and won five races under Jan's ownership.

They were reeled in, hook, line and sinker, after they also enjoyed success with a filly, *Diamond Lodge*, whose purchase they made after two days at the Tattersalls breeze-ups, stopwatch in hand, timing and logging each horse as it went past them. Those statistics were a useful guide and as Jan recalls, "*Diamond Lodge* moved well and she looked good. She stood out for us, being a filly as well, so we got her conformation reviewed by a bloodstock agent. He said 'Yes she's OK', so we bought her. At that time we did not claim to know much about conformation and action and what is needed to make a good racehorse but just went on gut instincts. If we made a mistake we would have nobody to blame but ourselves."

This was their first purchase as sole-owners and she proved to be an inspired choice, winning four of eight races, including victories at Windsor, Sandown, Goodwood and, best of all, the July Course where she won the one-mile Newmarket Trophy at long odds. As a result the 17th July 2004 was a red-letter day, one when it felt special to be an owner.

Jan recalls, "Colin's mum and dad were in their eighties and we brought them down to Newmarket. We sat them in the kitchen to watch the television in our house in the town and we went off to the July Course. An hour later we were back. Colin's dad is an ex-bookmaker who advises against betting. But that day we did have a bet and *Diamond Lodge* won at 14-1. We returned with the trophy and the money and placed it all on the kitchen table in front of them. It had all happened in the hour. We couldn't believe it."

Diamond Lodge went on to amass £43,000 in prize money and then, having suffered an injury, was prepared for sale and bought by John Warren on behalf of the Queen at Tattersalls for use as a broodmare. She now resides in the North Norfolk opulence of Sandringham where, in February 2007, she produced a colt. The Queen does not sell any of her horses and the colt (as yet unnamed) will start training at two years old and will then run in Her Majesty's colours. A real success story, made all the sweeter for Jan and Colin because they made the initial decision to buy her.

Subsequently the Harrises have always bought fillies in the hope they will be successful in races and sold as broodmares to studs so that they can maximise their breeding potential. Horses that have won group or listed races tend to be worth as much at stud as they are on the racecourse and their long-term ambition is "to have a listed or group one filly and breed a good foal".

Because of their growing addiction to

Jan Harris dressed for Royal Ascot.

horseracing they purchased a second home in Newmarket (they also have a house in Nazeing in Essex), perfectly situated on the doorstep of the entrance to the Rowley Mile. The couple visit the house regularly in summer and winter.

Five years on they are now sole-owners of four thoroughbreds and, in total, at the time of writing horses under their ownership have run one hundred and twenty-six times and they have been in the winning enclosure on twenty-six occasions including victories on the big stages at Goodwood, Newmarket and Ascot…

Wednesday 22nd June, Nazeing, Essex.
… however, there is an important difference between Ascot and Royal Ascot. Ascot is an elite racing venue but the Royal Ascot meeting each June is a class apart. It provides a quality of racing that is unmatched anywhere in the world. It does not boast a flagship, headline-making race in the way that Epsom has the Derby and Aintree the Grand National. Nor does it host any of the flat racing classics but the meeting is an annual, five-day Olympics for the top thoroughbreds, with numerous group one races spanning all distances, ages and genders.

It features the St James's Palace Stakes, the Coronation Stakes, the Prince of Wales's Stakes, the Gold Cup and the Queen Anne Stakes – yet to single out one in particular would be spurious; each one is prestigious and exclusively contested by the equine crème-de-la-crème. So for Jan Harris to have a runner here represents the highpoint of her time as an owner so far – though that, of course, would instantly be superseded if she were to enjoy a winner.

Horseracing tradition dictates that sponsors invite the winning connections to view the race again on video while they enjoy celebratory champagne. To taste the bubbly at Royal Ascot would really be something for the scrapbook, and it is the kind of pleasant muse that swims around Jan's brain as she slumbers in bed – having woken at 5am – on the morning of her debut.

Pleasant though it may be Jan generally tries not to get ahead of herself. "I don't ever have any expectations," she says, "I just go and hope it'll be a nice day whatever the outcome. If you expect to win you'll often be disappointed."

Much of the time she visits the likes of Lingfield, Nottingham and Haydock supporting her charges in action. "I go everywhere to watch the horses, come rain or shine," she says. "If it's somewhere like Southwell then I'll dress up smart, just go for the relevant race and come back. I don't stay all day."

There is something gritty and rewarding, pure and focused about attending bread-and-butter venues. There is little distracting pomp and circumstance. It is all about thoroughbreds and the contest – and this suits Jan, who instinctively places the health and fortunes of her horses foremost in her mind. It was her passion for horses which first drew her to racing.

She says, "They're just such beautiful creatures. They're stunning. All the different breeds you get – the shires, the Shetlands, different sizes. They just fascinate me." Whilst she has little interest in gambling or the unrelenting politics of racing, she has become knowledgeable on breeding, training, feeding, riding and conformation.

However, setting aside the earthy delights of the all-weather racing at Southwell on a wet Wednesday in winter, there is also a feel-good factor in having a horse run at one of the top venues. For one it suggests a certain status and standing. The connection between a man's worth and the worth of his horse goes back centuries. In AD 1250, a Knight-Farmer wrote to Emperor Frederick II stating "No animal is more noble than a horse, since it is by horses that Princes, Magnates and Knights are separated from lesser people."

Even though Jan is remarkably self-effacing and ego-free, she was pleased to appear in the racing *Pacemaker* magazine pictured on the same page as Zara Phillips and Sheikh Mohammed. The framed page hangs up in the living room of their Newmarket home. She also confesses to getting an inward kick from the simple fact that punters back her horses. She explains, "On race days after I've seen my horse leave the parade ring and go down to the start I walk through the crowd to view the race. If I go past the bookies I can hear people putting money on my horse and I think it's quite funny."

Jan ponders and decides that, overall, her preference is probably for the elite venues, where she can enjoy both the racing and the socialising. "My favourites are Ascot, Glorious Goodwood and the July Course at Newmarket. For those days I might purchase a new outfit and often meet friends. If it's at Newmarket then they'll come down the night before. We have some great parties and there's more of an atmosphere which I like."

And today, of all days, is about atmosphere, outfits and friends just as much as the sport. The whole immediate family will be travelling to Ascot and there are associated logistics to consider: transport, food, drink and clothing.

By 8am there is purposeful activity in the Harris household and outfits are being taken out of wraps. Each one has been carefully selected to match the occasion and meet the strict dress code at Ascot. The Royal Enclosure, which the Harrises will visit, is notoriously authoritarian on attire but even for general admission women must dress smartly and most wear hats. Men wear a shirt and tie, preferably with a suit or jacket. Sports attire, jeans and shorts are forbidden.

This is symptomatic of the style and flavour of the occasion. Media interest in who is wearing what often exceeds that of the racing. More than three hundred thousand people make the annual visit to Berkshire during the week and some of them do not know a bridle from a saddle. Nor do they care. They are there to socialise and drink large quantities of champagne; to dress in apparel befitting the eighteenth century; to see and be seen.

As such it forms part of the busy and exhausting British social calendar which, according to the peerage guide, Debrett's, also includes Glyndebourne, the Proms, the Royal Academy Summer Exhibition, the Chelsea Flower Show, Glorious Goodwood, Badminton, the Grand National and the Royal Windsor Horse Show, Trooping the Colour, the Garter Service, the Boat Race, Henley Royal Regatta, Wimbledon, Cowes Week and the Lord's Test matches.

9am – In most households the kitchen is where families make early-morning contact. Outside the kitchen window in the Harrises home at Nazeing, a tennis court and indoor swimming pool can be seen adjoining the back garden – but the activity is taking place inside the kitchen this morning. The family bustle and buzz around, briefly visiting the breakfast table to drink coffee or eat toast.

Colin Harris is first to settle, talking optimistically, cheerfully and at speed, as he will do through most of day. He wears a morning suit and a crisp, white shirt, open at the neck. Jan Harris is next down, wearing a light beige dress with light beige and gold jacket. Later, at the racecourse she will add a brown feather hat and accompanying handbag. She looks keyed up and just a little pensive.

Soon they are joined by their two daughters along with their guests for the day. Sarah Harris wears a multicoloured green, purple and pink vintage strapless dress and sister Louise a cream tiered dress, with accessories of a beige and orange hat and matching bag.

They are joined by Louise's friend, the Ladies Champion point-to-point jockey, Clare Hobson, who wears an orange off-the-shoulder dress with black hat and bag, and Damian Ara (Sarah's fiancé) in top hat and tails. They are a photogenic group and within the kitchen, where there is a soft-spoken hum of excitement and anticipation, it both feels and looks like the morning of a wedding.

Breakfast complete, they pack the two silver jeeps that will take them to the racecourse. It is clear that they will not be short of food or accessories for the traditional car park picnic at Ascot, which takes place before, after and often during races. Picnic tables, folding chairs, chicken legs, sausage rolls, a vast array of meat, salad and fish-filled sandwiches, crisps, strawberries, cheesecake, fourteen bottles of champagne and fine wine, numerous bottles of beer. Soft drinks as well. All top of the range food; a feast fit for Ascot. One of the jeeps heaves under the weight of the refreshments; the other contains clothing accessories.

The plan is that Jan and Colin will travel in one jeep with ex-jockey, now trainer, Paul D'Arcy and his wife Sue. Their daughters will follow in the other jeep with friend and fiancé. The planned departure time from Nazeing – suitably early to beat the worst of the traffic – is 9.30am but the D'Arcys call en route from their Newmarket base to explain that a horsebox of trainer Clive Brittain has broken down on the M11. The road has been closed to allow the horse to be manoeuvred from one

The Harris party at Royal Ascot. (left to right): Clare Hobson, Louise Harris, Paul D'Arcy, Jan Harris, Colin Harris, Sue D'Arcy, Damian Ara and Sarah Harris.

box to another. As a result the kitchen clock has ticked round to ten past ten by the time they arrive.

Sue D'Arcy wears a lilac dress with matching jacket and hat and bag; her husband remains in the same work clothes, jeans and T-shirt, he wore at 5am when he oversaw dawn gallops at his Newmarket stable on the Hamilton Road. Swiftly he showers, changes into his morning suit and cuts pink roses from the garden, which he makes into suitable buttonholes for the men.

It soon becomes obvious that the relationship between the D'Arcys and the Harrises is constructed on a foundation of trust and friendship. Its strength can be traced back to *Ti Adora*. Initially the horse was placed with Peter Chapple-Hyam. But with all due respect to the bigger names, the Harrises found that their personal preference was to use D'Arcy, who has just twenty horses in his care.

Jan explains their thinking: "He's a small trainer but we like him because we can talk to him. He knows his horses; he rides them all and he's an expert on the veterinary aspects."

D'Arcy had an immediate challenge when *Ti Adora* – then a two-year-old – was moved into his yard. Until then Jan says that the filly "hadn't been placed in a race and was underperforming. Several people said to us, 'You won't win anything with that, she's a headcase.' But Paul D'Arcy turned her around, calmed her down, brought her on and now she's just a different horse."

The stats support this view and act as confirmation that *Ti Adora*'s impressive pedigree has been fulfilled. So far she has won five times in twenty-two starts, along with four second places and four third places. In total she has brought in £39,240 in prize money.

The turnaround in the horse's fortunes gave Jan and Colin confidence in the trainer. For Jan the key is that the size of the stable encourages flexibility in his training methods. "That's why I like him," she says, "because he looks at a horse and says 'What does that horse need?' Every horse is different. They all have different needs and he treats each one differently. Because he's only got twenty horses he's got time to do that … I feel that with a larger trainer they're relying on their staff too much for feedback on what's going on. But Paul's in there with it. He rides every horse, making sure that everything is OK."

Though it is down to each owner to decide how much to be involved, most like to keep in touch with the trainer regularly by phone or make trips to the yard, as well as seeing the horse run at the racecourse. The Harrises are no different and that is another reason why they think less is more. "With bigger trainers," says Jan, "they'll see you at an arranged time but you can't just call in. It's a more businesslike relationship than a friendship. Paul phones us regularly. We have big discussions about where and when we're going to race, though ultimately we always seem to end up where Paul wants to go as we recognise him as the expert."

D'Arcy also helped Jan to fulfil her ambition of galloping on a thoroughbred. She says: "I hadn't ridden for ten years but they found this big, placid horse and I felt comfortable on it. So we moved from a trot to a gallop. It was fantastic. I galloped on him on four consecutive days."

How did it feel? "They've got tremendous power. You only have a small saddle and you can feel more of their frame. When they go from a standstill to a gallop it's just amazing. And the most amazing bit was still being on it at the end of the gallop. That was a big surprise to me!"

A more traditional perk of ownership is the pleasure of naming the horse. In their early years thoroughbred foals and yearlings are unnamed, referred to by their colour, sex and the name of their sire and dam. However, when registered to race, they have to be named in line with a strict set of rules governed by Weatherbys. The name cannot be longer than eighteen characters, viewed as obscene or insulting, or duplicate existing names on the register or big-race-winners from the past. Names are constructed in all sorts of ways. Some reflect personal associations, the owners' name or nickname, or maybe advertise a company – and the Harrises used another idea when they came up with *Sir Duke* for a three-year-old purchase. Jan explains: "We were at the races and a horse named *Walk like an Egyptian* won a race. Everyone was walking around singing the song – and we thought that's a good way of naming a horse. Colin likes Stevie Wonder, so we looked at a few CDs, found the song 'Sir Duke' and went for that."

However, the most common way is to try and combine elements from the sire and dam. The Harrises have done this with their filly who is running at Royal Ascot this afternoon: *Kylayne*. Her parents were *Kyllachy* and *Penmayne*.

And, as the clock ticks round to 10.45am and the twin silver jeeps leave Nazeing to negotiate the delights of the M25 and the M3 on the fifty-mile journey to Berkshire, *Kylayne* gets plenty of mentions.

She is a "small, sharp sort" who cost a bargain 15,000 guineas in 2006. The price was reduced because an injury to one of her feet put off some potential purchasers. But it was diagnosed by D'Arcy as a short-term problem. So far she has run only once – and the family watched the video of the race after breakfast this morning to reassure themselves what an impressive outing it was. The camera never lies and it showed her storming to a one and a half length victory at Warwick, leading throughout and raising her stock significantly.

D'Arcy reports that her recent work has been good, she is at peak fitness, in good spirits (she demolished two and a half buckets of breakfast this morning) and thinks she has a much more realistic chance this afternoon than the bookmakers' odds of 40-1 suggest.

D'Arcy has taken a horse to Royal Ascot before just because the owner wanted a day out at such a prestigious event. However, having tried it once he will not repeat it again. He hated travelling just to make the numbers up. He needs to be competitive and thinks *Kylayne* can be just that today, even though she will be challenging stronger and bigger horses.

Indeed, when D'Arcy assisted the Harrises in buying the horse he had this specific race in mind. It is the Queen Mary Stakes: a group two sprint over five furlongs and the fixture's most prestigious two-year-old prize for fillies with a total prize fund of £70,000 with £31,000 to the winner.

D'Arcy thinks with good fortune *Kylayne* will be worth around £50,000 to breeders by the end of the season, which will bring in an overall £35,000 profit, paying for his training fees and helping to fund the next purchase. That is D'Arcy's modus operandi. He helps owners to buy, race and then sell for profit, which encourages the cycle to continue. He says it works well most of the time. But beware: Jan Harris is spot on when she describes racehorse ownership as a "hobby with occasional money-making potential", because whilst the potential for return does exist it should never be budgeted for.

Rather like the purchase of lottery tickets, some regard horse ownership as a serious busi-

Colin and Jan Harris

ness investment. Alas, they display a mindset of wilful self-delusion and blind innocence – and their judgement is fundamentally unsound. Common sense and a careful analysis of the laws of probability can only lead to one conclusion: that if ownership is evaluated in terms of cold finance then the odds are heavily against making a profit.

On the debit side there is a long list of costs to be covered, starting with the initial purchase. The average price of racehorses sold at public auctions in Britain is around £20,000, though this varies depending on pedigree, physical make-up and form. Whilst horses with little pedigree have defied the opinion of experts and won some of the world's greatest races, generally buyers get what they pay for. And they have to pay plenty to buy a decent thoroughbred with a decent chance of winning a decent race.

Once the horse is purchased a trainer is required. Jan Harris says the cost of keeping each horse in training each year is around £15,000 regardless of whether using an all-inclusive rate or a base rate with additional items added as and when. Obviously the owner pays for the skill, experience, knowledge and time of the trainer and their staff and the cost of feeding the horses – but that is just the beginning. Budgeting also needs to include:

● Heath Tax – the public gallops at Newmarket are owned by the Jockey Club Estates and owners are charged £95 a month per horse for use.

161

Jan Harris The Owner

- Veterinary Care – routine veterinary care needs to be administered, procedures such as vaccinations, blood sampling and respiratory investigation.
- Horseshoes – shoeing of all four of a horse's hooves provides support and protection to the hoof and leg when the horse is in training and racing. The shoes need to be renewed about every four to six weeks and a new set costs between £40 and £60.
- Transport – there are costs to move the horses to and from the races and to cover staff overtime whilst they are there.
- Race entry fees – these vary from £20 for a lower grade race to thousands for the Derby.
- Jockey Fees – a jockey receives £125 from the owner for riding their horse in a flat race.
- Ownership registration fees – these cover the ownership, colours, racehorse and its name.
- Insurance – this covers death of the horse but tends to come at a heavy premium.

These costs accumulate endlessly and opportunities to recoup them are limited. There is prize money for horses placed in a race but Jan Harris's only gripe with horseracing is that prize money is low and, of course, trainer and jockey take their cut of any winnings.

A realistic owner expects to regain no more than a quarter of their costs so no sane financial adviser would recommend ownership as a reliable and intelligent way of boosting the bank balance.

Jan and Colin Harris are bright sparks.

They know the ups and downs of racing: that only one in ten thoroughbreds actually win a race; that troughs follow peaks and that peaks are few and far between. They know there are shares and ISAs and savings accounts and a hundred sound investment opportunities out there. And that if you are looking for more fun with your investment there are another hundred more viable options before you would buy racehorses. There are boats, wine, cars and holiday property, to name just a few. But they overlook these financial health warnings because they recognise that being at the sharp end of horseracing gives them a buzz that cannot be measured solely by pounds and pence.

"I've not a clue how much we've spent on horses because Colin is my 'racing manager' and looks after the finances," says Jan. "I'd guess around half a million pounds," she adds without batting an eyelid. "I don't always think about costs. It's about fun and, at times, a little profit. This is primarily our hobby but if we can cover a few costs then that's good."

Racing owes a massive debt to people like Jan and Colin. Through their investment they provide racecourses with runners, jockeys with rides, trainers with clients, the media with material to write about and photographers and racegoers with a spectacle to watch. That puts them in the dominant position in racing's food chain. Indeed the whole premise of big-business professional racing is that people are willing to subsidise the sport by splashing their cash in pursuit of their entertainment and pleasure, their kudos and kicks. But no one should be under any illusion, the key word in the paragraph is "subsidise".

11am – Predictably there is congestion on the M25 but a call confirms that *Kylayne* at least has arrived at Ascot from Newmarket. There is a sigh of relief. There are so many obstacles that can block a horse from making it to the starting stalls: traffic, injury and illness to name just a few. The story of *Sander Camillo*, Jeremy Noseda and the 1000 Guineas emphasises that. It has been a nagging concern for Jan Harris that misfortune will scupper her day. Now, though, even the most ardent pessimist would have cause for optimism. She will have a runner at Royal Ascot and *Kylayne* will, as they say in racing parlance, be able to "take her chance".

By 12.45 the jeeps have crawled through the leafy lanes of Berkshire to car park 2 at Ascot, lining up alongside the vast array of Mercedes, Bentleys and Rolls-Royces, often labelled with personalised number plates. Even the car park is top of the range: grassed, spacious and situated under vast, old trees that provide – on days like today – both shade from sun and shelter from showers. Skilled champagne poppers (and there are many of those at Ascot) might just be able to launch a cork from the car park across the road into the grounds of the racecourse. Certainly from the car park it is possible to hear the tannoy system and the roar of the crowd for the finish of races.

The scene here conveys the essence of Royal Ascot. For those who have been coming here for a while you sense one-upmanship at play. The group next to the Harrises, for instance, have their own gazebo, catering staff to prepare the food – including some of the biggest prawns in the free world – and waiters and waitresses to serve their needs. It is, in all but name, a top-quality restaurant situated underneath a tree. Some groups bring candelabra and if anyone has any doubts that a class system still exists in Britain then a day at Royal Ascot should clear up the mystery.

It is the only race meeting which could conceivably continue without the horses or, indeed, the grounds of the racecourse. Just as the band played on as the *Titanic* sank, you fancy that if, one evening at Ascot, word spread that the end of the world was nigh then the men in top hat and tails and their ladies in fashion finery would finish their glass of champers and enjoy one last taste of lobster before heading for cover. There is something timeless, stoical and very English about it all and on such occasions it is difficult to believe the days of the Empire are over.

1pm – The Harrises' family picnic is punctuated frequently by laughter and the sound of popping corks as pink champagne begins to flow and nibbles are nibbled. They are getting into the spirit, though their primary subject of conversation remains *Kylayne* and her chances. Colin Harris reveals some personalised number plates that he has had created, bearing the name "KYLAYNE". They are pinned to the back of the jeeps.

Jan Harris The Owner

At 2pm the sound of the national anthem can be heard in the middle distance as the Queen, Prince Philip and their entourage travel down the racetrack in open landau carriages to kick off this right royal occasion. It has ever been thus. It was Queen Anne who put the Royal in Ascot in 1711 when she took a carriage ride through Ascot Heath in the forest near Windsor Castle, came upon a large clearing and decided that it would be ideal for horseracing. The next time the court was in Windsor, racing at Ascot began with the "Her Majesty's Plate of 100 guineas". The Royal meeting developed through the eighteenth century and in 1825 George IV instituted the tradition of the carriage procession. The current royal family always attends the meeting, arriving each race day since the Second World War in a horse-drawn carriage.

The nearby arrival of the Queen spurs the Harrises into action and after an hour of lunchtime refreshments they collect their various admission badges at the entrance of the racecourse and join the throng of forty thousand spectators enjoying the feel of an Edwardian garden party – though the extensive (and expensive) recent redevelopment has also made the racecourse corporately functional and entirely capable of coping with Premier League-sized crowds.

Elletelle (nearest camera) wins the Queen Mary Stakes at Royal Ascot.

Jan and Colin have paid out to gain access to the Royal Enclosure this afternoon on the basis that this may be a "once-in-a-lifetime" experience and they wish to make the most of it. As they enter, the horses are just returning to the parade ring after the opening race. The enclosure is unashamedly elitist and swanky; an area where it is possible, as Paul D'Arcy will testify, to almost literally bump into the Queen. Morning suits and top hats are de rigueur. Guidance to attendees states:

"Ladies are required to dress in a manner appropriate to a formal occasion. This means that a hat must be worn, strapless dresses are not permitted, midriffs must be covered, and trouser suits must be of full length and of matching colour and material. Gentlemen are required to wear either black or grey morning dress, including a waistcoat, with a top hat which must be worn at all times when you are in the Royal Enclosure other than within your private box or facility. Overseas visitors are welcome to wear the formal national dress of their country or Service dress. Those not complying with the dress code will be asked to leave the Royal Enclosure and will be relieved of their Royal Enclosure badge."

3.40pm – Having watched a couple of races, hob-nobbed with the gentry and absorbed the atmosphere Jan and Colin leave the Royal Enclosure. Jan has enjoyed the experience but reports that "I was a bit disappointed with it as it seemed that anyone could get in. The security was not very good."

They meet up with the rest of their family, leave the racecourse, cross the road and return to their jeeps to tuck into more refreshments. It is easier and cheaper than buying food at the course. Besides, the first hour of lunch barely made a dent in the provisions. The D'Arcys remain at the racetrack, sorting out declarations and generally tending to training business.

4.20pm – Now just thirty-five minutes before *Kylayne*'s race. The Harrises leave the car park and return nervously to the racecourse. Ten minutes later they stand in the centre of the shady Ascot pre-parade ring as *Kylayne* circles, loosening limbs with the rest of the field. And ten minutes after that *Kylayne* and the Harrises enter the parade ring, the bell rings and the jockey Daryll Holland arrives.

Like D'Arcy, Holland is another favoured with the trust of the Harrises. Jan says: "We've used John Egan, Daryll Holland, Frannie Norton, Eddie Ahern and Shane Kelly. For me John and Daryll are top of the list. They listen to Paul D'Arcy and do what he says. They work well with Paul and know how he wants them to ride."

This afternoon there is barely a minute between Holland's arrival and the signal to mount the horse. Trainer speaks to jockey in hushed, businesslike tones; two experienced professionals at work. Jan and Colin lean forward to catch the nuggets of advice like boxing seconds around their man in the corner. They hear that the plan is that *Kylayne* will be "tucked in" and then, hopefully, use her acceleration towards the end of the race.

Holland's silks are in predominantly white colours, registered by the Harrises in keeping with strict rules. In the eighteenth century, when silks were first worn, subtle shades could be used: straw for the Duke of Devonshire, apricot for Lord Howard de Walden and maple leaf green and beaver brown for the Canadian Lady Beaverbrook. Nowadays, though, owners select from eighteen colours: white, grey, pink, red, maroon, green (light, emerald, dark), blue (light, royal, dark), mauve, purple, yellow, orange, beige, brown and black. The design is also standardised and the cap, for instance, can only be plain, hooped, striped, checks, spots, quartered, star(s) or diamond(s).

Ideally the Harrises would like an entirely white jersey and cap but they found that single colour ensembles are much sought after and tend to be purchased by the big players, so they compromised with all white with purple epaulettes.

Instructions complete, the white and purple can be seen as *Kylayne* leaves the parade ring and saunters down to the starting stalls. It is about now that Jan's pulse races, like a parent attending a Christmas play, anxiously hoping that their child does not fluff their lines. Owners can usually watch from their own viewing gallery, but Jan feels "cut off from it" there and prefers to go and watch from the rails. In those final few furlongs she always gives her lungs a workout. She says: "I'm always screaming and shouting. It's very exciting and I always shout them home whether they're winning or not. Many owners have never had a winner, and I count myself very lucky to have had twenty-six of them so far."

At Royal Ascot, the crowds mean that a close-up view from the rails is not possible so once Colin Harris has placed his bet, the family and trainer climb to the elevated viewing area to watch the action unfold. They overlook both the finishing line and a big screen.

In precisely one minute and one second the race has been run. It would be a delight to report that *Kylayne* settled in the pack before making a decisive late burst to secure a famous victory. Alas, that is not how it pans out. A large blanket could have covered more than half the field at the finish, but it would not have covered *Kylayne*. She does not get even a mention on the commentary.

In the pack for the first two furlongs she is one of three fillies who suffer interference in a rough race and, along with *Cristal Clear*, is close to being brought down at the halfway stage. The lead is only held by two horses and *Elletelle* gets up to edge past the front-running *Starlit Sands* close to home. *Kylayne* finishes sixteenth out of twenty-one.

It is a disappointing result. The Harrises have not had a run for their money and they have learnt little about the quality of their horse because it did not get the benefit of a fair run. Not having seen the video they can only speculate on what might have been.

After the race, jockey Daryll Holland returns

to the unsaddling enclosure for the normal post-mortem before weighing in. In victory it is all smiles with no explanations required. Today he talks about the interference and explains that the filly has "speed to burn" but was "a bit green" and may need to drop in class. That said, any meaningful analysis must carry a health warning. In a five-furlong sprint there is no time to recover from the slightest interference. So when the horse is nearly brought down it loses all momentum and with it the opportunity to contest the race.

5.45pm – Back at the picnic area there is a quieter, deflated air for a while, born out of frustration. They talk of what is next for *Kylayne*, and that is the nature of racing: months of build-up, one minute of racing, then the build-up begins again.

It is a warm, sun-blessed evening of soft shadows and a gentle breeze, and even after the racing is over few leave the car parks. Pockets of owners, trainers, jockeys and bloodstock agents all socialise. Aristocrats too. Anyone who is anyone in the racing world is here, enjoying food, drink, laughter, anecdotes, jibes, racing politics and gossip – and, at the same time, business takes place, albeit in a subtle, understated manner. Movers and shakers operate, easing around in their top hats and tails. Owners are wooed, new acquaintances are formed and existing relationships are nurtured.

The charming, veteran trainer, David Elsworth (who had the great *Desert Orchid* in his care), comes over to commiserate with Paul D'Arcy over *Kylayne's* bad luck. D'Arcy and Elsworth are trusted friends and arrange a game of golf.

6.15–8.15pm – The Harris family enjoy two hours of eating, drinking, chat and, just before the jeeps drive off, family charades. The car parks remain over half-full more than two hours after the end of the last race.

Jan Harris dozes some of the way home, exhausted by the preparations, and misses some of a wide-ranging discussion which includes vigorous debate and large dollops of common sense, most notably from Paul D'Arcy. He is happy to share his experience and opinions from a lifetime in the racing industry, both as a trainer and a jockey riding top-class horses for Sir Michael Stoute, Barry Hills and Sir Mark Prescott.

What, they debate, makes a top trainer? Answer: difficult to define. It is all about the owners they serve and the quality of the horses they train. Largely horses that cost more are more likely to perform well in races.

What was it like to ride in the Derby? Answer: the roughest race ever and one that demands both speed and stamina of a horse.

Owner and trainer muse over what they would like from a jockey and who is most likely to provide it? Answer: a winner; someone who is talented, professional and genuinely wants to do as well in each race as the trainer and owner. Ryan Moore is one who all feel fits the bill.

And there is also a light-hearted discussion

167

on the thinly veiled coded messages that jockeys provide to trainers and owners when they return to the parade ring to pass judgement on the run. They agree that "he moved well up on the way to the start" represents a coded message for "but not very well during the race" and that it is rare for a jockey to state "he just got beaten by better horses" or "it was all my fault, I rode him badly".

In some way the pleasure of having such an informal and fascinating insight into the world of racing helps to answer the fundamental question – what is it about horseracing ownership that makes it worth the outlay? Well, this is it. Having access to the inside of the sport. Being right at the core. Talking to the people who really know. Living the dream.

Jan sums up: "It's the whole thing from choosing your two-year-old, finding out what sort of character and temperament it has, watching it being broken in and schooled and eventually being entered into a race. They go from their baby-like frame into a grown-up racehorse and we are lucky enough to watch this happen at a very owner-friendly yard. There is much excitement and anticipation on the day of a race. No matter how well the horse is or how well you think it will do, you just never know what is going to happen in the race and, of course, if you win it's just fantastic. Being patient is also very important.

"I suppose it's about what makes you happy. Above all I get to spend time with my husband and time with the horses. We're pleased we've got into it and it's become a big part of our life. We are not doing this to make money – although if they cover their costs it's a bonus – but to enjoy our good fortune and go to different places and meet people that we would not have had the opportunity to meet."

By 9.30pm the Harrises are back in their Nazeing home, ending the day as they began it: drinking coffee, and watching a video of *Kylayne* in action. The morning re-run featured the promising maiden victory at Warwick. Tonight's watching, though, is a video-nasty of today's action: just a flurry of interference (the horse rather than the television) and an anonymous finish in the chasing pack. Certainly the tape verifies jockey Daryll Holland's evidence.

"It showed us that *Kylayne* did not get a good run at all," Jan confirms later. "Early on in the race she was knocked by a couple of horses and nearly brought down. During the race she also lost a shoe. The jockey knew he had to look after the horse and brought her home safely."

Did it ruin the day? Certainly it left a bittersweet taste. "*Kylayne*'s race was both the highlight and low point," she says. "Racing at Ascot is very different to any other day's racing as the emphasis is on clothes, picnics and people-watching. I found it difficult as an owner to concentrate on the race with so much going on. Although it was a very enjoyable day – one which every owner would love to have his or her horse run at – it was exhausting. It was very disappointing that *Kylayne* was knocked in the race as I now know she would have got a place – but that's racing."

TWELVE

FRONT RUNNER

"IT'S NOT ABOUT PATTING HORSES' HEADS AND SAYING HELLO TO
FRANKIE DETTORI. IT'S ABOUT RUNNING A £12 MILLION POUND
BUSINESS THAT JUST HAPPENS TO HAVE RACING AT ITS CORE."

OUR FIRST DISCUSSION took place in Lisa Hancock's office in Westfield House on the outskirts of Newmarket on 3rd December 2006. With one season just finished, sights were already fixed on the next – and even then there was a particular challenge that stood above all others.

Anyone who observed the endless saga of the construction of Wembley Stadium, every Olympic venue or, indeed, has added an extension to their house knows the likelihood of frustration, delays and spiralling costs.

So, as managing director of Newmarket Racecourses, Hancock was entitled to allow just the faintest trace of anxiety to enter her voice as she considered the £10 million phase one development of the July Course. There were now precisely two hundred days until its anticipated opening.

Certainly the development was much needed. On race days during the 2006 season, Hancock was on tenterhooks anticipating the next problem. She knew circuits might fuse and drains might block. The course needed essential maintenance and a makeover to elevate it to the standards that visitors to racing HQ expect.

"May 24th is D-Day," she explained, "when we get the course back to us from the contractor. And then we have a month to gee it all up and get it set up for the first race day. Amazingly £10 million doesn't go very far – Ascot spent £200 million on their development – but it's a big project because the July Course is loved by everybody. If we get it wrong they will never forgive us. We keep telling the contractors 'Look after this place for us, it's very special'. You don't get any second chances. People are very unforgiving at Newmarket. They have high expectations of us. They expect top, top, top in every area and it's up to us to deliver."

Her words reflected the memories that she carries from Newmarket's last redevelopment. Hancock inherited the newly built Millennium Grandstand – which cost £16 million and overlooked the Rowley Mile – when she took over in 2000. It was imposing but unpopular. Corporate customers enjoyed panoramic views of the racecourse landscape, but little provision had been made for the rank and file members and day race-goers who struggled to find a decent vantage point.

169

Lisa Hancock The Managing Director

As a result Hancock's first year as managing director was soured by constant criticism and she spent a great deal of time dealing with issues not of her own making. Six years on she thought the problems had long since been rectified and felt more well-disposed to the work being undertaken on the July Course.

"I think it's quite a clever project," she said. "It's not one grandstand; it's a lot of landscaping, a lot of small disparate buildings. So what I want when people come on June 22nd next year is for them to think 'What have they done?', barely knowing what we've done to improve it. But suddenly realising that they haven't queued for the loo, they've been able to get a really nice meal for £20 with a cold glass of beer and a cappuccino from a china cup and plate and there's been somewhere to sit down. And they can walk about without bumping into people. I think we'll deliver that."

The words were confident and positive as one would expect of the MD at HQ – but with builders and projects of this magnitude you can never really know for sure. What I didn't know at the time was that wasn't the only major challenge exercising the formidable Hancock brain. But more of that later...

9am, Saturday 23rd June 2007 – July Course, Newmarket.

The race meetings on Newmarket's Rowley Mile are held in the spring and autumn. Summer meetings are held a mile away on the July Course. There are eight double-headers between 22nd June and 24th August, seven of which have an evening meeting on the Friday, featuring a late-night pop concert, and an afternoon meeting the next day. In addition there is the three-day, midweek, July Festival which is the centrepiece of the summer schedule with some particularly high-class racing.

Last night saw the first of the Newmarket nights and the first public use of the redeveloped July Course which had been delivered on time and on budget. After a full race card the Australian pop group, INXS, performed to nine thousand spectators.

Throughout the day Lisa Hancock had been "seriously keyed up". These were first-night nerves on a grand scale. The experience of both Newmarket's Millennium Grandstand and the £200 million vast construction at Ascot (which needed another £10 million to even begin to put right) provided proof that public acclaim cannot be taken for granted. They are tough to please.

And so, on the morning after the first Newmarket night, Hancock is floating on adrenalin and relief as she pays her second visit of the day to the course to survey the aftermath of the race meeting and the concert. She describes it as "like a dream, fantastic" that there were only minor teething problems and positive feedback. She left the course after the INXS concert at around 1am, slept fitfully between 2 and 4am ("wired to the ceiling") and was back on the course by 6am – perhaps to convince herself that it all really happened. Further heartened she went home for breakfast with her husband and two young children and watched Channel Four's *Morning Line*, delivered from Newmarket.

Now, at 9am, she begins to ensure that all is

in place for this afternoon's meeting. Hancock is not one for showy status symbols. She does not drive a high-priced sports car, wear expensive jewellery and, at first glance, she does not cut the stereotypical figure of a high-flying businesswoman. Yet she possesses an air of gravitas and stature and looks in charge as she moves around the empty concourse area behind the stands, where spectators eat, drink and socialise between races.

She begins upstairs in the open air Stravinsky's Cafe where most of the Channel Four team are tucking into breakfast having just finished their live programme. Down below John McCririck walks his dog amidst the on-going clearance and preparation. Vans nose along pathways collecting debris. Engineers crouch over cables. Caterers are setting up for the day ahead, just hours after they have tidied up from last night. One party has not long finished; another one is soon to start.

As she walks around, others confirm that last night went as well as she thought it had. For pretty much all of them the reality exceeded expectation. And her eyes continue to reassure her: somehow the new layout just looks right. Certainly to the untrained eye it is difficult to pinpoint where the join is – even though the landscaping and upgrading has involved one hundred and seventy five kilometres of cabling, two hundred tonnes of steel, two thousand five hundred metres of decking and thirty-one newly planted semi-mature beeches.

The treasured architectural features of the weighing room, the parade rings and saddling boxes have been retained along with the rustic charm and character. However, more space has been created for better crowd circulation together with easier access to new toilets, bars, restaurants, cafes, other food and betting outlets, areas of seating and other facilities.

Twenty minutes later the scene moves from the early-morning July Course to Hancock's office in Westfield House. It is a large room housing, somewhat bizarrely, a sculpted, limited-edition hippopotamus table which belongs to Frankie Dettori; his prize for being top Newmarket jockey in 2006.

For the next hour she thumbs through the *Racing Post* at speed, catches up with emails, makes phone calls (notably to Haydock Park with feedback on INXS – they play there tonight) and chats to key staff such as her personal assistant, the general manager and the finance director.

There is a debrief on the previous night and a review of the all-important numbers, of which the most important is the attendance. It was around budget even with the counter-attraction of Royal Ascot, which led to the absence of many Newmarket members. The police, however, reported a strong American presence following INXS.

However, these are not formal, minuted meetings and the overriding feel this morning is of colleagues wanting to enjoy the after-glow of an encouraging first night in relaxed reflection. Besides they have stories to tell.

There is the one about the lads from

Lisa Hancock was a
very competitive
point to point rider.

Bedfordshire who dressed as pirates, got nicely juiced up, fell out with each other (as pirates often do), had a punch-up on the late-night bus and were turfed off.

And Hancock tells the tale of her visit to the Ocean Swell bar. She fell momentarily when some other well-oiled but friendly lads inadvertently tripped her. They were most apologetic and when they recognised that this was "the boss" they gave her a fireman's lift and swung her around the bar.

The conversation between Hancock and her inner circle is warm and friendly. They share a genuine desire for Newmarket to prosper. Trust and respect has grown over the years so that she can treat them as equals and not need to crack the whip – but few would doubt that she would do so if required. For when it turns to business, particularly outside the inner circle, her words are focused and precise. You sense that each one has been filtered, at high speed, through that sharp brain of hers for ambiguities. She does not ramble, waffle or indulge in prolonged small talk. She says what she means – no more, no less. This is not symptomatic of any iciness, simply a businesswoman who has demands on her time and much that she wants to achieve. Certainly her employees all speak highly of her. They know that she would "go the extra mile" for them.

This morning Hancock is guardedly euphoric, trying not to get too ahead of herself. She worries that the first night at the July Course was "a bit too good to be true" and thinks "it's gone too well". She fears that today there may "be a backlash" and they will be "bitten on the bum".

However, leaving natural caution aside, this is looking like a day to enjoy for the thirty-six-year-old farmer's daughter from a small village in Cambridgeshire whose role in the redevelopment of the July Course acts as more evidence that she is executing the top job at horseracing HQ with distinction.

It must be all the sweeter because this is the job, above all others, which she wanted even when she was in her teens. Her ascent was notable for her willingness, like many high achievers, to back up lofty ambition with action and application. In this respect she bears a similar psychological fingerprint to the trainer, Jeremy Noseda.

Most high achievers – from an early age – consciously or subconsciously set challenges and then pursue them with a single-minded self-belief. They do not just go through the motions. They are desperate to be successful and the pursuit of excellence drives them forward in a way that more laid-back individuals can't even begin to imagine.

Hancock's ambition was defined with remarkable clarity and maturity during her teens as a farming girl in Clavering, near Saffron Walden. By then she was showing an interest in riding, just like her father, the late Hunter Rowe, the embodiment of point-to-point racing in East Anglia, who won a hundred races. His daughter was also outstandingly competitive, winning sixty-five races. However, in her mind, it never provided a potential outlet for a long-term career.

She recalls: "I set my heart on being a racecourse manager from the age of fifteen. I wanted to be involved in racing, didn't want to be a trainer – that never appealed – knew I didn't want to be a jockey. It's incredibly hard for female jockeys to make a really strong career in it and I wasn't that good. I knew that. And so this was the next best thing. At the time it didn't seem unusual, but looking back it is. I have a lot of work experiences with me now and they haven't really got a clue about their future. That clarity enabled me to really use my summer holidays during school and college to best effect. Time that is often wasted I was working at racecourses, getting to know other people and getting my face recognised."

Thereafter the period between the ages of fifteen and twenty-eight acted as a structured grounding for the job she now holds. She says, "Summer holidays were spent here in Westfield House, shadowing my predecessor, Nick Lees, who was fantastic to me and gave me huge opportunities to see what was entailed in running a racecourse and running Newmarket."

At university she took a Bachelor of Science degree in chartered surveying, which was a useful general degree featuring tax, management and law. Her dissertation was on maximising racecourses so she managed to fit in lots of racing work in her three years. The university's location in Cirencester also allowed her to ride out at the stables of David

Nicholson. Best of all she managed to work at three consecutive Cheltenham Festivals, and at the Grand National meetings at Aintree.

She then moved on to Warwick, where, at the age of twenty-two, the driven young woman in an undeniably masculine world became general manager. She stayed for five years, getting a "fantastic grounding" and being responsible for "pretty much everything", from creating the brochures to locking up on race days. She also gained her clerk of the course licence.

She continued her education for another two years, this time in the north-west, undertaking a Herculean workload which included clerk of the course duties at Haydock (where she was also commercial manager) and Chester and acting as assistant clerk of the course at Aintree. At that time she was single and worked from dawn to dusk without a second thought.

Then came the big opportunity. Nick Lees vacated the managing director's position at Newmarket and the job was advertised. At first Hancock was reticent to apply, thinking that her dream job had become vacant too early in her development. After all, when Lees had first taken over as MD Hancock was just two years old.

She recalls: "I missed the deadline date for the Newmarket job. I thought I'm young, I'm female, and they'll never employ me. And then someone gave me a kick up the backside and said 'What are you doing, you've got to put your hat in the ring at the very least.' So

I came down here and I knew the interview went well because I'm passionate about the place and the board recognised that and were prepared to take a gamble with me."

That first summer was difficult. Because the Millennium Grandstand had opened to a chorus of raspberries rather than the anticipated fanfares, Hancock spent much of her induction defending a construction she had no involvement in creating. Then the foot and mouth epidemic hit. But gradually she grew into the role, demonstrating her capabilities to all, not least through that tireless work ethic.

Sacrifices had to be made: she jettisoned her point-to-point riding and much else besides because the role of MD at HQ is not a job to be undertaken at a trot or a canter. It's a full-out gallop each day. Hancock confirms: "I used to burn the midnight oil too much, but you do that when you start a new job. I was desperately keen to make headway and it was all new. Now I'm better at delegating to my team. Yes, I'm on the computer most evenings which I'm not proud of. During the season there's a lot of Saturdays and a lot of evenings and it's a demanding job."

What is it that makes her put in all those extra hours?

"God! Good question! I guess it's because there's nothing worse for me than coming in the morning and feeling that I'm on the back foot. I like to be prepared, in advance of meetings. For my own sanity I like to have got through things. I don't like having twenty emails unread. I'm a hands-on person,

probably too much. But better than I was. I set myself high standards, which sometimes make it pretty onerous for me. But I think that's what makes me good at my job in Newmarket. Because Newmarket is all about high achievers."

Certainly she seems to deal with emails and phone calls day and night. She says that one Tuesday she went to Royal Ascot on a rare social day out, still spent a lot of time on her Blackberry and felt at a loose end when the battery went flat on the journey home. "What shall I do?" she asked her husband, Charlie. "Relax," came the reply – which is easier said than done when the only gear you possess is fifth.

Now this all-out commitment is well and good if you are doing the job you love and able to give it your full attention. But what happens when the job becomes at odds with family life? For Hancock it was the birth and development of her children Sally, now three, and one-year-old Tom, that began to create a conflict that other mothers in high-powered jobs may recognise.

How to reconcile the twin demands? Is it best to be great at the job or a great parent? Is it possible to be both? Imagine the traffic in her mind. On one hand the status, the buzz and the challenge of the role she wanted since her teens. On the other the maternal instinct to nurture her offspring and watch them grow and flourish.

For a while she managed to keep both

Show time. Lisa Hancock on duty on a big race day.

plates spinning and, no doubt, she could have muddled through by delegating tasks – either in the home or at the office – to trusted friends and colleagues. But, remember, this is a high-achiever who is programmed to pursue excellence. So being merely OK at both roles and muddling through just was not an option.

She made the first concession in the autumn of 2006 when the Newmarket board agreed that she could work a four-day week during the off-season. It was not enough and in early 2007 she took what she described as the hardest decision of her life and decided to resign at the end of the 2007 season.

"It's not really been achievable," she says. "Newmarket is a big ship, a £12 million business where something is always happening, and I set exacting standards for myself and the team. I've given one hundred per cent commitment and loved every minute of the job, but I have got a young family and I'm missing out on bringing them up. I made up my mind in February but twice chickened out of telling my chairman. At the third attempt, and after massive soul-searching, I just got out what I wanted to say to him before I burst into tears."

She also shed tears when she told her management team and "was on an emotional rollercoaster for a while". But the decision and the news release are a few months behind her now and, currently, it is business as usual for this most professional of women. There is no sign of her shifting down the gears and her reaction to the success of the July Course redevelopment says much about her mindset. Perhaps she is in a kind of denial. Certainly she is still getting the feeling that used to accompany point-to-point riding.

"I'm a very competitive person and racing is all about competing and winning and priming yourself up for that big event," she explained later. "So it's that huge sense of anticipation for the big race meeting and the big races that really gives me a buzz and turns me on."

Maybe the reality of her departure will begin to hit home this grey Saturday morning because, after she has addressed the one hundred-strong green-jacketed stewards on the day ahead (and thanked them for last night's efforts), she has the first formal meeting with Richard Hambro, the chairman of Newmarket Racecourses, to discuss what is required of her successor. As she does so – with symbolic timing – the heavens open with an hour-long biblical downpour that soaks the racetrack and changes the going from "good" to "good to soft".

Hancock's shoes will be tough to fill. She smiles. "It's certainly not about patting horses' heads and saying hello to Frankie Dettori. It's about running a £12 million pound business that just happens to have racing at its core."

The job has a variety of demands, which involve:

● Hands-on contact with major sponsors
● Managing the senior management team
● Project management of activities such as the redevelopment of the July Course
● Public relations, focusing on the marketing and positioning of Newmarket Racecourses
● Overseeing the financial prosperity of the Racecourses, documented within monthly reports
● Human resource issues for the staff who report to her
● Strategic planning

She sums up: "I'm the figurehead of the racecourse. I don't do all the work but I'm the face of it – so whether it's the press, the trainers or the owners I need to be the key point of contact so that I hear what the issues are and then cascade them out to the team. We respond to them as a team and that's how any good team works."

Of course these responsibilities need a wide range of skills. "I've got a team of sixty people here," she says, "and also on a race day you're hosting this enormous party and there are a number of different customer groups, many of whom have different desires, expectations and wants. And somehow you have to manage all that so that they have an enjoyable and good experience; and that takes some doing. You're on show from the moment you walk onto the course until the end of the day and longer because you don't turn your mobile off in case something happens. You're putting on a good, positive face throughout that whole period and you've got to pitch it right for each group.

"Race days are the most important because its show time – and then behind the scenes it's probably still about man management. It's giving my senior management team enough direction, encouragement, also flexibility, and rope to go and do their own things and have an overview of it.

"I believe knowledge and a passion for horseracing is hugely important here. Probably more than anywhere else in racing because we have so many people who are passionate and extremely knowledgeable and if you are walking around the racecourse or the supermarket or the bank and if you don't know what's happening in the racing world you are extremely vulnerable and can be made to look very silly. So you've got to have a business brain but also an empathy with and a sound knowledge of racing so that you talk the talk. And it wouldn't do to have a shallow, scant knowledge. That would be exposed very early on."

Having completed their 11am meeting, managing director and chairman lunch with sponsors and television executives in the constant quest of nurturing relationships and gathering revenue. Investment in facilities and prize money needs to be funded by income and sponsorship. Champions' Day each October, for instance, boasts more than £1 million in prize money – and that has to be generated from somewhere.

"We are struggling to make enough money to invest in the racecourse facilities and prize money at the level that we would like to," she explains. "It's a hugely expensive operation.

I always liken it to an ocean liner. You pile in the coal, stoke up the furnace and it takes ages to get going and when at last the old ship gets going it's pretty powerful and it takes some stopping. But God, it's hungry. It's really hungry.

"We've spent £10 million on the July Course and that's only phase one of that development and in three or four years another tranche of money will need to be spent to get to the standards that are needed. In the meantime we've got to keep investing in the prize money because racing is now an international sport and if we're not careful the top horses won't run at Newmarket, they'll run in Hong Kong and Japan and America. That would be disastrous and so we're really fighting hard to make it a profitable business so that we can keep our position right at the very top."

These Newmarket night meetings, when the likes of INXS perform to packed audiences after the evening racing, are real money-spinners. Some aficionados treat them with disdain but they deliver a much-needed injection of funds into the Newmarket coffers. The bottom line is critical.

By the time that the working lunch is complete the afternoon racing at Newmarket has begun and the first race is weighed in. Not that it really affects Hancock. Like a dutiful host at a party she spends no time relaxing and enjoying the spectacle. She is always on the move. She catches only glimpses of the eight races on the card and the roar of the crowd as each one reaches its conclusion is generally in the middle distance.

Instead she undertakes "management by walkabout" for four hours, touring the grounds, dodging the showers and speaking to a list as long as the Rowley Mile of key customers and service providers: police, security, owners and trainers, maintenance, ticket sales, bookmakers, the tote, press, bars, fast food outlets, restaurants, car parking, toilets, member areas, sponsor areas and the racecourse office.

If it is management by walkabout it is also management by questioning: "How's it going?" or "Everything OK?" Impressively, she knows the first name of practically every one of the fifty people to whom she talks. She carries a walkie-talkie, a Blackberry, a blue pen and one sheet of white paper upon which all the matters arising are noted. These will be formalised and help to drive the agenda when her team get together in three days' time for an extensive review.

She is often interrupted by phone calls, emails, and impromptu chats. Many spectators also recognise the diminutive figure dressed smartly in black jacket and blouse and a polka dot skirt. Happily for her they are full of compliments on the renovation. Halfway through the afternoon she spots two people who had been fierce critics of the building of the Millennium Grandstand. "What do you think of the changes?" she asks them. Inwardly she braces herself. These two like a moan. She need not have worried. This time they are positively beaming: "It's good; in fact, it's better than good."

Hancock thanks them and moves away with her expression in neutral. But inwardly she gives a little whoop. This is probably the definitive moment that she knows that the day will not "bite her on the bum".

Certainly there are remarkably few issues to resolve. It is not always so. At every meeting there is the possibility of a cold-sweat crisis bubbling up that will have to be addressed at speed, with astute judgement and sound leadership under pressure. In 2006, for instance, 2000 Guineas day was soured by a major brawl involving twenty youths on the second-floor balcony of the Millenium Grandstand.

Today there are a few problems with the cashpoint machines and the disabled lift breaks down briefly. Equally the dodgems in the family enclosure are not stopping – as per the contract – when the horses go to post or during the race.

Someone reports that the beech trees on the far side of the course need some branches trimmed so spectators can enjoy an uninterrupted view and Hancock can sympathise with a member of staff trying to coordinate a Japanese film crew – when they do not speak Japanese and the film crew do not speak English.

But this is run of the mill fare, considering it is only the second day of active use since the racecourse was upgraded. In fact, the only moment approaching controversy is when two jockeys get banned for a fierce on-the-line battle at the conclusion of the 3.50 that ends with one striking the other with his whip.

Crowd movement is free from bottlenecks and the new twenty-first-century facilities are well received. Security, for instance, like the new CCTV. Hancock has just one regret: the Mozart's Bistro, which provides a full sit-down meal, is packed and Hancock reflects that it might have been made more spacious.

Often she gravitates to her inner circle. This includes heads of operations, catering, finance, the director of racing (Michael Prosser) and the head of public relations (who is actually at Ascot today and so keeps in regular contact on the phone). They tend to congregate in the winners' enclosure.

Talk is often of "the numbers"; of attendance and budgets. For each race day there is a budget that is calculated using a three-year average "and then some". The budget involves attendance income, both members and pay-on-the-door visitors, and profits from other sources such as sponsorship and catering.

The team are surprised and pleased by today's attendance. It looks to be around six thousand, slightly above budget, despite a pessimistic weather forecast and that lunchtime downpour which must have persuaded some that an afternoon in front of the TV was a better option.

By 3.20 Hancock admits that she feels "a little footsore and tired". A quiet confidence and satisfaction is beginning to replace the adrenalin high. She makes for the pressroom, gets a drink and a snack and sits for ten minutes watching the TV screen, catching up with the big race at Royal Ascot.

With few pressing, operational issues Hancock is able to look ahead and much of her afternoon is focused on planning for the future.

For instance, earlier in the year the Lester Piggott race day had to be postponed because the great man was in intensive care with a heart condition in Switzerland. Now that he has recovered it has been re-arranged for 22nd September but Channel Four – the normal broadcasters – are already committed to other venues. Without television the day is unlikely to get sponsorship and Hancock feels that it deserves to be high-profile. She is thinking BBC. It is the kind of thing they have always done well but doubts that contracts will allow this. She discusses the options with her team. Resolution will be high on the "to do" list on Monday.

Then there are police fees. Newmarket pays for the support they provide. Coming up is a sell-out Newmarket night when the pop group Madness will be performing. They have not appeared at Newmarket before and intelligence on the demographic of their audience is sketchy. However, these nights do attract a different type of racegoer and, with the gig taking place after a full race card, the potential for excessive drinking is obvious.

The challenge: to create an adequate police presence without dampening the

atmosphere of a fun night. Riot gear and batons would be overkill; one bobby and his truncheon would not be enough. It is about balance and Hancock spends thirty minutes in discussions with the police senior officers. This is all pre-positioning before a formal meeting later in the week, and her influencing and negotiation skills are obvious; the conversation is friendly but when she makes a point her position is crystal clear.

These are just some of an ever-moving conveyor belt of issues that a managing director at Newmarket has to address and it would be a surprise if Hancock does not miss the challenge once she leaves her post in November. She says that in 2008 she will not be seen at the racecourses ("just wouldn't be able to do it and, besides, it would be unfair on my successor") but she may be a more frequent visitor to the town itself and, specifically, the morning gallops. "I take friends up to the top of Warren Hill," she says, "because it does me good to have someone going 'Bloody hell. This is unbelievable' – because it is. It's a good reality check to go up there are see three thousand horses in a huge expanse of open land and walking through the town. It *is* unbelievable."

Will she have feelings of unfinished business?

Certainly, given an unlimited budget, she would have liked to have made further changes. There would have been phase two of the July Course to consider and she would then – in a perfect, cash-rich world – have turned her attention to the Rowley Mile, which has three hundred years of history and top-quality racing in its favour but often a breeze that can cut through you like a lance.

She explains, "The problem with the Rowley Mile is that it is so exposed. You feel cold on it even when it's warm – and the atmosphere just disappears and somehow I'd have liked to have contained that atmosphere, which probably would have meant putting something on the other side of the course to create an amphitheatre, bowl effect. We have the best racing on the Rowley Mile but not the best atmosphere."

However, these tasks will be something for her successor to consider. At least they will begin from a position of strength. The first Newmarket night on the redeveloped July Course occurred just four days before Tony Blair finally left the prime minister's office. Talk of legacies was topical. And when Lisa Hancock handed over power she did so with a strong legacy from her seven years in charge; not only in terms of the bricks and mortar of the July Course but in the team that will continue her good work.

THIRTEEN

IMAGE RIGHTS

"HORSES ARE TERRIFICALLY PICTURESQUE, WHETHER ON A
MISTY MORNING ON THE GALLOPS OR RACING HELL FOR
LEATHER UP CHELTENHAM HILL. YOU CAN PHOTOGRAPH
LOW-KEY HORSERACING AND IT STILL LOOKS GOOD."

ONE MINOR INCONVENIENCE encountered when speaking to the characters in this book was the difficulty several had in explaining how they excel at their job. For instance, ask Tom Goff, Jeremy Noseda or Tony Elves how they spot a yearling that has "got it" and they might struggle. To them it is an instinctive, gut feel. In some cases the skills are executed so naturally that they find it a challenge to dissect them into component parts. Sixty-year-old Trevor Jones is a good example of this.

Trevor is a photographer with a strong reputation within the racing and bloodstock industry. However, when I encouraged him to explain this excellence he looked quizzical. It was as though he had been asked why he was so adept at breathing; or quite how he managed, on a consistent basis, to put one step in front of another and walk in a forward direction.

The truth is that, having been in the business for forty years, photography is not merely an activity he undertakes to earn a living. He has "become" a photographer from head to toe, heart and soul. The art of capturing eye-pleasing images comes as naturally to him as breathing or walking. So when Trevor describes the camera as an "extension of my arm" he is spot-on. The man and his machinery are as one.

Nevertheless he tried his best to self-analyse: "It's just something you were born with, either you have it or you don't have it. Others take pictures for me on big days like the Derby and I help them, set them up, don't put too much pressure on them and they do a nice job. But they are always surprised that they don't get the picture they want. Yet I seem to be able, with the same camera, to get the picture. It's just a question of your eye, the fact that it's like an extension of my arm really. I don't suppose that you are born a photographer but there must be something that makes you able to react."

Regardless of exactly how he manages to "get the picture", the images in this book should act as sufficient evidence that Trevor Jones is a top photographer. He is also universally regarded as a top bloke who has endured more than most with serious illness – and, with this in mind, his main aim for the 2007 season was to continue to accumulate sufficient funds to begin to ease into semi-retirement. He is blissfully happy, living in the countryside around Newmarket, with his wife and numerous dogs and macaws – and the plan is to enjoy them to the full in rude health.

Trevor Jones The Photographer

"Hopefully we'll be able to do more local work," he muses. "That's why we're so glad to be out of London. We're keen to reduce the thirty thousand miles per year. We just want to carry on as we are. It's a really nice life. Sometimes the photography is banal, but then the racing gives a buzz."

However, it has not always given a buzz. Jones explains that when he left school in Eastbourne he had no interest in racing. In fact, he says he had no idea what he wanted to do with his life, though by then had bought his first camera and was beginning to enjoy photography. He worked in an opticians and a building site "buggering about", before he took a job in a camera shop.

He then eased into professional photography, working for the *South Coast News* and *Eastbourne Gazette* before uprooting from Sussex and joining the liberated and artistic *Hampstead and Highgate Express*, universally known as the "Ham and High". This was a local newspaper with the style of the *Observer* and for five years at the end of the swinging sixties Jones photographed the rich and famous.

It was, as he recalls, "a really eye-opening time to be in London for a boy from Sussex. I can remember going to photograph Peter Cook of Pete and Dud fame. He'd broken his leg. I was in his house, I was chatting and about to leave, and the doorbell rang. Because he was incapacitated he said 'Oh, can you get that?' It was John Cleese. So all of a sudden I'd gone from photographing the Eastbourne Rotary Club to mixing with people that everyone knew."

He got married, started a family, moved further into London to work on the *Kilburn Times* and it was here that his interest in sport – and specifically football – began to flourish. Jones was assigned to photograph, home and away, the trendy and successful Queens Park Rangers team which was riding high in what was then labelled the First Division. "As a young man I'd played football – not to any great degree – but I knew my way around," he says. "Photographing football wasn't easy, but it was easier because I had an interest, a knowledge."

He enjoyed the adrenalin of the big occasion and the technical challenge of capturing high-speed action – so it was a natural progression to specialise in this area by moving to *Sporting Pictures* where he was sent, very much in his element, to famous sporting stadia around the globe.

However, his burgeoning career was rudely stopped in its tracks in the mid-1970s when he was diagnosed with Hodgkin's Disease. In some ways he was fortunate: only in the previous six or seven years had the cancerous disease become treatable. Nevertheless the medication regime was severe and provided no guarantee of survival. "I don't think I feared the worst, but my parents did," he recalls. "When you're in your twenties you feel a bit bombproof really. You can't imagine dying."

He had his spleen removed and underwent intensive radiotherapy. He lost his hair and his energy and the pounds dropped off him. He gave up work and moved back to his native

Photoholic, Trevor Jones

185

Eastbourne to rest and recuperate. And his marriage broke up. It was the darkest period of his life, yet he recovered.

When the worst of the treatment had been endured and the prognosis became more promising he began to work again for a local paper – and once he had fully regained strength and spark he returned to *Sporting Pictures*. He stayed for five more years before spending another four at *Allsport*.

These were golden years. Jones travelled the world (he says that cameras have been his passport) capturing the elite sporting events. From World Cup football to Wimbledon, Open golf to the Olympic Games. He loved it. Never more so than during a glorious month following the 1982 World Cup in Spain. "I photographed twenty-one matches," he recalls, "and drove more than six thousand miles – but it was tremendous. As a bloke the football was great and as a photographer there was so much to photograph, with fans like the colourful Peruvians and Brazilians."

In amongst the fun, Jones was gaining experience at photographing the various sports, learning to anticipate where and when the key action, human drama and offbeat moments would occur. He found that he needed many of the same attributes as his subjects: skill, timing and execution – and he also found that there was most satisfaction to be gained with horses and horseracing. "Horses are terrifically picturesque," he says, "whether they're being led on a misty morning on the gallops or racing hell for leather up Cheltenham Hill. You can photograph low-key horseracing and it still looks good, whereas low-key football always looks like low-key football."

Consequently he decided to concentrate on this area, becoming a freelance and creating *Thoroughbred Photography Ltd* in 1987. Twenty years on business is brisk and in addition to Jones the company employs his second wife, Gill, and Laura Green.

A host of clients pay a retainer for Jones's services; most notably the horseracing magazine *Pacemaker*, The British Horseracing Authority, and Tattersalls. Other regular clients such as Darley Stud, *Irish Field*, *Blood Horse* and Juddmonte pay for usage.

Over the years Jones has constructed a million-strong image library of horses at auction, exercise, rest and play plus, of course, race day action. There are photos from the gallops at Newmarket and Lambourn, bloodstock sales at Tattersalls in Newmarket, Deauville in France and Goffs in Ireland – and high-class competition from the English classics, major European races, the Breeders' Cup, Royal Ascot, Glorious Goodwood, Cheltenham and the Grand National. Studies of prominent owners, trainers, jockeys and personalities are also featured.

The library is housed in three electronic repositories – the images "live" on a server, are backed up onto digital tape (which Laura takes home each day) and are also archived onto CD/DVD, suitably filed into sequence for each year. The contents represent a monument to twenty years of hard work and skill – but for a photoholic like Jones a million or so is never enough. He may say he is looking to ease into retirement, but as the summer of 2007 progressed it was clear that he was also beginning to ease towards the second million.

It is the morning of Friday 13th July, 2007 at Trevor Jones's home in Worlington. As it's Friday the thirteenth it would be raining. Not heavy rain – but a steady drizzle out of leaden skies (rather typical of an inclement May, June and July) that throws a dank murkiness over this summer morning. When you take photographs for a living the state of the light is critical and it forces Jones to adjust his itinerary.

He had intended to go to the Darley Stud Parade on the outskirts of Newmarket, and take photographs of the stallions stabled there. Some of the images would have been used in specific publications, some as background material for his library. However, stallions only look at their athletic, potent best with sunlight streaming onto their back, so he decides to stick with yesterday's images.

Jones undertakes regular and profitable work at stud farms, usually photography of stallions for the breeder's glossy brochures. Others who work in this area take formal and posed images that can be time-consuming to capture. Jones's technique is more natural and utilises his unique selling point, the instinct to capture athletic movement that he learnt watching the likes of QPR. He shoots the thoroughbred as it grazes and plays, searching for a more spontaneous image that conveys the essence of the animal. He says: "If I have to go back to the stud farm the next day, then I will – but usually the client is very happy with the images."

Today, though, Jones will give the stud farm a miss. Instead he sips coffee in the office, a converted room in his house in Worlington, nine miles to the north-east of Newmarket. As he does so he wears a pink, tailored shirt and black trousers. He wears glasses, perhaps the result of days in darkrooms squinting at negatives, but his face is lightly tanned which also reflects many hours out in the fresh, open air at racecourses.

Outside the window, in addition to the soothing sound of light drizzle, are familiar barks and squawks from the family dogs and macaws. The Jones's like their pets.

Inside the office what first catches the eye is an action picture, taken by Jones, of Ed Moses, the legendary 400 metres hurdler in Zurich. It made the front cover of *Sports Illustrated* magazine, which, for sports photographers, is the Holy Grail. The framed cover celebrates the fact and hangs on the wall above three, hi-tech computers. Jones sits at one, his flame-haired wife Gill sits at another and Laura Green can be found at the third. They all tap away, dealing with emails, searching for photos, sometimes "topping and tailing them"; making and taking phone calls.

Their roles at *Thoroughbred Photography* dovetail. Trevor's is to focus on what he's best at: taking photos. His skill and reputation is the core of the business, the product. Indeed, without it there could be no business. Gill and Laura devote their energies and knowledge into marketing, communication, travel arrangements, invoicing, and associated administration and logistics.

This morning the three do not say much but there is a relaxed sense of industrious harmony. Jones describes himself as affable, which displays self-awareness because that is the perfect word for him. Whilst he is the key element of a dynamic business he is also generally regarded with warmth and affection within the industry and, as a result, has many friends – including several of Newmarket's headline-makers.

Think of professional photographers and thoughts come to mind of intrusive paparazzi snapping, literally, at the heels of the famous. They seem hard and heartless – but Jones is not cut from that cloth, which, of course, accounts for some of his business success. He gets on with people – and he also works hard to meet and exceed customer expectations. Some would say too hard.

Certainly this quiet, chilled Friday morning is welcomed by Gill, who thinks there are not enough of them. She wants her husband to take his foot off the gas. The calendar on the wall details that since the beginning of May he has attended race meetings (between one and five days in duration) at Newmarket, Chester, Lingfield, Longchamp, York, Newbury, the Curragh, Epsom, Chantilly, Ascot, the Curragh again, Sandown and now back to Newmarket. Between those meetings he has worked on private jobs for studs and other clients and has shown no signs of slowing down.

Gill, with just a hint of resigned exasperation in her voice, says, "He can't say no. He still operates at the terms of the clients, whereas nowadays he should be able to operate on his own terms." Perhaps her unease is driven by the fact that Jones's successful battle with Hodgkin's Disease has not been his only encounter with debilitating illness.

Trevor takes up the story: "I had a stroke three years ago at Ascot. It was the day *Persian Punch* died. The race was happening and *Persian Punch* was clearly in difficulties. After the race I picked up the phone, called Gill, and said 'You won't have seen it on television but they've put screens around *Persian Punch* and it doesn't look good.' She said, 'I can't understand a word you're saying.' I thought it was a problem with the reception on my mobile so I crossed the course and tried again. But she still couldn't understand and said 'I'm really worried, you must find a doctor.'"

The doctor shared Gill's concerns. Jones spent a week in hospital, unable to read or write and having great difficulty in speaking. For the second time he had to recover and continue his job. Fortunately his photography is unaffected, though he tires more quickly and a careful analysis of his speech patterns suggest a hesitancy that did not exist before. He explains, "Sometimes in your brain you have to wait till the correct word comes round. It's like a carousel, waiting for your luggage at an airport."

Maybe this explains partly the noticeable and endearing compassion shown to Jones, not just by his wife but by Laura too. The two

Sakhee's Secret wins the July Cup and Trevor Jones gets the shot.

women joke that they cannot travel together for fear of an accident that would leave him without his "guardians". It is just a joke because he is entirely able and independent, but it betrays how they feel towards him.

As this damp, drizzly morning ticks around into a lighter, brighter afternoon, Jones moves around the office and house finishing his preparation for his visit to the final day of the July Festival. It features the Darley July Cup, the top sprint in Europe and one of the highlights of the whole flat racing season at racing HQ.

By 12.30 he is ready for action, or at least to capture it. Bags and two laptops are packed and loaded into his car. For the record it should be stated that the family of cameras includes:

- Two Canon EOS-1, D Mark III
- Three Canon EOS-1, D Mark II
- Two Canon EOS-20 D
- One Canon EOS-1Ds Mark II

These are supplemented by three Canon EF zoom lenses; a 16–35mm (wide angle), a 24–70mm (mid range) and a 70–200 mm (telephoto). He also has a Canon 300mm F2.8 lens and a Canon 600mm F4 lens – the latter three feet in length and £6,000 in value. In total his equipment is insured for £30,000.

Of less technological merit is the tin ladder that joins the cameras in the boot. However, Jones is uncommonly pleased with it. For a start he bought it for a bargain basement £40 – it should have been £90 – and fits perfectly its purpose, with five steps and a length that just allows it to squeeze into his car. Most importantly it allows him to get above the action and improve the quality of his photos.

Even though he leaves at race day rush hour, the journey to Newmarket from home in Worlington is brief; partly because he has got to know an intricate back route that avoids hold-ups, and partly because it's now on his doorstep.

It was the regularity of visits to Newmarket and the advances in modern technology that encouraged Jones to move out of London. "One September and October I made sixteen visits to Newmarket from London, and said to Gill, 'This is crazy, we should live in Newmarket and go to London as and when we need to.' Previously I had to be within the 01 (STD code) part of London because someone needed to send a bike to pick up the pictures. In those days there were still dispatch riders. However the technology had got to the point where you send pictures to people online through a modem. They were still photographs, not digital, but you digitalized them yourself."

It is a move he has never regretted. Quite the reverse. "If you can be bothered to get up and get out of bed then Newmarket in the early morning with the horses on the gallops is terrific. Warren Hill is the focal point, and the Limekilns where they test the big horses for particular races. Moving was the best thing we ever did. We live in a nice environment, we've got a lot of friends – mostly within racing – and this has been a really good period for us. We've become recognised more and I realize now that being a bit older, people take you much more seriously. When I was in my thirties in the racing game I was a bit of a boy."

Certainly Jones is treated with friendly respect by the other photographers as he unpacks, fifteen minutes before the first race, next to white rails near the finishing post in the advantageous vantage point that is the main benefit of his racecourse accreditation. Of course, being in the right place is one of the critical elements to taking good photographs.

For horseracing on the flat, in contrast to many other sports, the location of the key action is predictable. So Jones knows the critical moments will probably take place on the run-in to the finishing post. As a result he generally positions himself in the fifty yards leading to the line. From there, today, he can look down the July Course to the far-distant starting stalls. The crisply cut turf undulates gently, with emerald inclines that test a horse's stamina. Above them, he is thankful that the morning rain has dispersed. Indeed the clouds have turned pale and begun to part, throwing the odd gleam of sunlight onto the racecourse. It is a warm, humid afternoon.

There are around twenty other photographers there and it is clear from the cheerful banter that Jones knows most of them. Like many of the groups in Newmarket (the jockeys, the stable lads) their behaviour and dialogue marks them out as more of a team than in opposition.

For the first race, a small handicap, Jones just takes photographs to build up the library. He is more interested in determining which side of the racetrack the jockeys will opt for. This is important because it affects where he will take his pictures for the more prestigious races later in the card. Ideally he wants to be on the rail away from where the bulk of the field will pass. The nightmare is when the field splits across two rails – though this is not likely today as the racetrack is narrow and the field can move to the better ground in unison.

The second race is a group two race for two-year-olds. Jones's pictures will feature in the *Irish Field*, a weekly paper, published on a Saturday with a 6pm Friday deadline. So, as a form of insurance, he captures most horses as they go down to post in addition to the frenzied dash to the finishing line that follows. The Darley-bred *Hatta Fort* wins, just ahead of Peter Chapple-Hyam's *Declaration of War*.

Darley are one of the companies who invariably pay Jones for images of their horses winning. They will publish them on their own website and use them to advertise. So straight after the race Jones downloads the images onto his laptop, chooses which frame is most pertinent, crops and enhances the image, sends it to his website and alerts regular clients such as Darley who have the necessary password and can visit the site to retrieve and collect. Nearly all the photographers are at a similar task, stooped over laptops, often with coats over their heads so that they can get a darkroom view of the images and send them off.

Although they have access to more comfortable facilities in the pressroom, most of them can undertake this transfer only yards away from where they actually take the photos. That is the wonder of modern-day technology. It is instantaneous because Newmarket is equipped for wireless internet connection – and there is no doubt that such technological advances have revolutionised professional photography. That said, Jones points out that it is still about taking the right photo. "It was always the images that I liked," he says. "The cameras and technology in the forty years between then and now have changed, but it's still about the image isn't it?"

The third race is the Bunbury Cup, run over the Bunbury Mile and a cornerstone of the July Festival for many years. With this in mind Jones goes on the far side of the track, up his ladder, under the beech trees, so he can capture a finishing shot which includes the spectators, the end of the race and the packed stands of the July Course behind. Location is important, partly because it determines the background. Choosing an atmospheric, or at worst neutral, background to the shot is key and often overlooked by amateurs. Most have taken pictures where the main image in the foreground is fine but the background (perhaps a rogue telegraph pole or a fire exit sign) ruins the shot.

On this occasion Jones is trying to capture the ambience and olde worlde tradition of both race and racecourse. In many ways he succeeds. The foreground is fine, the background is fine. Yet he is no more than reasonably satisfied when he looks at the image. Yes, structurally it is perfect: the silhouetted crowd, backs to the camera, in the foreground as they watch the colourful silks of the jockeys, whips in the air, as they drive their mounts through a tight finish; and the packed grandstand in the background. The *Irish Field* may well use it. However, during the race there were clouds overhead and the image lacks the sparkle that a glint of sunlight would have given it. Illumination and shadow benefits professional photographers every bit as much as the amateur snapper.

The fourth race is the July Cup and whatever happens in the next few minutes will make headlines in the racing newspapers tomorrow. Of course there are more-heralded occasions in the racing calendar – and the July Cup certainly does not match the classics, and particularly the Derby, for applying pressure on a photographer. The Derby is a day that Jones ends with a tension headache. There is a long build-up, camped in position, and just a split second when you really, really need the technology to work and your instincts to help capture "the shot". This year Jones captured his friend, Frankie Dettori screaming in jubilation as he passed the winning post on *Authorized*.

As an aside, that photograph gave Jones considerable satisfaction because the emotional reaction to winning or losing is often a more powerful and significant image than horse and rider passing the winning post. The same is true in football, golf, tennis and the rest. The human response, whether it be tears, elation, frustration or anger, to the ups and downs of sport is compelling because the viewers can relate to the feeling. It is also more of a test of a photographer's ability because these opportunities are often unpredictable. Jones's early development following Queens Park Rangers and then sporting action across the globe has given him experience and instincts that help him get "the shot".

Anyway, the July Cup is the feature race of the whole festival, let alone today's race card, featuring eighteen of the world's outstanding thoroughbred sprinters – and Jones captures each one as they canter to post from the parade ring, past his vantage point near the winning post, down to the starting stalls.

First to post is the handsome copper-orange colt, *Dutch Art*, who was third in the 2000 Guineas. Soon after there is the white-nosed face of Jeremy Noseda's *Sander Camillo*, so unlucky when missing the 1000 Guineas. And, seconds later, all eyes follow the chestnut *Sakhee's Secret*, favourite for the race.

Jones's concentration has moved up a notch now. He is still relaxed but his mind is alert and focused. As the stalls burst open and the five-furlong charge begins, Jones is already up his ladder on the far side of the racetrack. And as the roars of the crowd intensify when the field comes vividly into sight, the Jones camera collects the images that will appear on websites and publications. It sees *Sakhee's Secret* clear of the chasing pack, pursued by a fast-finishing *Dutch Art*. *Sander Camillo*'s miserable season, alas, continues as she trails in last.

Sakhee's Secret is a product of Shadwell Stud and they will certainly want to visit Jones's website to collect the image for advertising. Tonight's *Irish Field* and *Pacemaker* are others who will use the best image. By the time the field has eased to a halt and turned back towards the parade ring Jones has descended his ladder, crossed the racetrack and passed his flash card to his assistant, Laura, to begin to decide which image to use. He then jogs to the winners' enclosure to join the arc of photographers who receive the returning *Sakhee's Secret* and jockey Steve Drowne with a volley of clicks and whirrs.

Back at the finishing line Laura has decided on "the shot". Later Jones will agree. Of course modern technology makes finding this easier than it used to be. "The cameras that I've got now shoot at eight frames a second," Jones explains. "It means that when I come to edit, because there are more frames from a one-second bite I'm able to isolate the better and more fluid stride. What I'm looking for is that elegant stride, rather than when all four legs are pointing back and the horse looks like it's going to trip over."

Later, at home and at leisure, he will download all the flash cards onto the server then review, prune, edit, process, reference and add them to the portfolio. But, now, time is of the essence and within minutes *Sakhee's Secret*'s victory has been released into cyberspace to his various customers. Job done – and Jones's concentration and intensity can drop down a notch.

He stays for the fifth race, then packs up, says his goodbyes to his colleagues and heads off back to Worlington before post-racing traffic snarls up the streets of Newmarket. It has been a day much like many others. A few more races captured, a few more photos closer to his second million, a few more satisfied customers.

Tomorrow he will be busy again and next week he will travel to France to undertake some work for a private client. Gill wants her husband to slow down and smell a few roses – and no doubt, in time, he will begin to reduce his commitments – but he is clearly still a happy snapper, a photoholic, who has yet to lose the thrill and satisfaction of photography.

It is about instincts again: the same instincts, acquired unconsciously over forty years that made him a photographer "head to toe, heart and soul". So although he appreciates the logic of reducing his demanding workload, there's also an instinct that keeps him clicking away, capturing attractive images that please the eye of both himself and his clients.

Warren Hill, another great photograph from Trevor Jones.

195

FOURTEEN

WINNING WAYS

"IT'S AN ADRENALIN BUZZ WHEN THEY ARE RACING INTO THAT
FINAL FURLONG AND YOU SEE YOU'VE GOT A CHANCE. YOU BEGIN
TO SHOUT AND YOU BEGIN TO HAVE A YELL … IF YOUR HORSE AND
ANOTHER ARE NECK AND NECK THEN YOU DO GIVE IT A BIT."

A GOOD WAY of describing Stan Singleton is to say he is an enthusiast. An enthusiast of real ale, rock music and quizzes. Above all an enthusiast and devotee of the sport of horseracing. Now sixty-four, he has gone racing for forty-four years. He has visited every racecourse in Great Britain at least once and the day that I shadowed him was the two hundred and fiftieth time he had visited either the Rowley Mile or the July Course at Newmarket. He has also introduced his children and their children into the racing way. As a result he is an ideal person to shine a light on the joys of race-going.

However, his enthusiasm is not blinkered. When asked what would be the most appropriate three words to describe him, his wife Pat, listening, was first to the punch. "Grumpy old man," she suggested, and her quip was not without a few grains of truth. Certainly he has an acid, though articulate, tongue on him and he is not shy of voicing an opinion.

And when it comes to horseracing those opinions really count, because in a sense Stan is the most important character in this book as well as being the least known. The rest of the racing community needs to please Stan because he actually puts his hand in his pocket and shells out some of his own hard-earned cash at racecourses across the country in admission fees, refreshments and gambling.

There are six million "Stans" who go racing each year, making it the second most popular spectator sport in Britain after football. Without their patronage the sport would be unable to hold its own in the highly competitive entertainment industry.

1.30pm, Saturday 4th August 2007. Stravinsky's Cafe, July Course, Newmarket Racecourse.

Stan Singleton sits at a small, circular table in Stravinsky's Cafe. He is balding, bearded and conservatively dressed in grey trousers and an open-necked blue shirt. A trendy striped jacket hangs over the chair next to him. Even on days as hot as this he likes to wear one as he moves around the racecourse.

He looks relaxed, studious and focused as befits the beginning of a happy hour of Zen-like research and contemplation. This is an investment of time intended to yield financial dividends throughout the afternoon. One hand intermittently turns the pages of the *Racing Post*. In the other he holds a small, lime green pen, courtesy of the Tote. Occasionally he scribbles guidance notes on the pages. Ahead of him is a plastic cup containing black coffee, two sugars, which he sips occasionally.

He explains: "For me the *Racing Post* is absolutely essential. I wouldn't dream of going racing without it. I like to get to a racecourse about an hour before the first race, sit down with a coffee and just pore over it. I might have had an earlier look at home but without any conviction – but that is when the business part of the day begins. I almost like that part of it more than the actual racing. It's so pleasurable. I go there with mates but during that hour we just don't talk to each other."

It is rare that Singleton goes to the racing alone. Now and then he enjoys family days out with his wife, Pat, and a selection of his three children and seven grandchildren. These are lighthearted picnics with the emphasis on family fun, followed by a meal on the way home.

More often, though, he meets up with his long-time "mates" for serious, adult race-going with the intention of giving the bookmakers a beating. They say you can tell a lot about a man by his friends, and one of his regular companions is Trevor, a retired Londoner, who is a pea from the same pod.

They were introduced thirty years ago at a party and found that they were kindred spirits when they discussed the merits of horseracing, real ale and a long catalogue of things in modern life that really got their goat. Trevor, like Singleton, is a prudent punter, who studies the *Racing Post* diligently before making informed choices. Indeed he keeps a record of every bet so that he knows the state of his gambling bank balance.

Bryan, another regular, is different. Bryan and Stan went to school together and have known each other for more than fifty years. He was a head teacher and, by all accounts, an outstanding one. Now, though, Singleton describes him as a "scurrilous character. His politics are even more right-wing than mine, in fact they are disgraceful. Bryan bets big. One day he will win £2,000, but even as he leaves the bookmakers they are smiling in anticipation. They know they will get it all back pretty soon."

Today, though, Pat, Trevor and Bryan are otherwise engaged – and the man sitting opposite is another lifelong friend, Harold, who is in his seventies. Harold sits opposite at the same table, and drinks red wine (Singleton is driving home) as he studies the form.

What all these mates have in common is that they are racing "enthusiasts", a label which is applied more precisely than might be immediately apparent. An offbeat, fascinating (and recommended) book on racegoers has been written by the anthropologist Kate Fox, and she categorised them into two broad types.

The first was described as "enthusiasts", racegoers with a genuine and serious interest in and understanding of the sport. Those

Ready for the off.
Stan Singleton prepares
for another day's racing
at his favourite track.

"enthusiasts", according to Fox, could be further broken down into:

Horseys – People like owner, Jan Harris, who love horseracing because they love horses.

Anoraks – "Train-spotters" who have an encyclopaedic knowledge of racing that they are keen to share with others.

Fans – Regular attendees who gain a genuine enjoyment from race meetings but are not obsessively interested in the sport's past or future. On race days they carry binoculars, the race card and the *Racing Post*.

Addicts – Compulsive and passionate devotees who suffer withdrawal symptoms if they have to miss an important meeting. They read the *Racing Post* each morning and watch *Morning Line* each Saturday. They will often analyse the field in the pre-parade ring as well as the parade ring and have only a grudging respect for less committed racegoers.

Horsey, anorak, fan or addict? The precise sub-category that best fits Singleton may be

The July Course turns on the style.

open to debate – but he is most definitely an enthusiast, just as his father and grandfather were before him. They were responsible for his initiation into the sport.

In the third form at school in 1957 "Singleton of the Third" would cycle to newsagents as a "runner" during milk breaks to place illicit, under-the-counter bets on behalf of more senior schoolmates. In those days high street betting shops did not exist (it was only in 1961 that they became legal) and so newsagents would take bets under the counter. He also began to have a punt himself. At that stage he liked gambling more than horseracing. Indeed he has never ridden a horse – and has no intention of starting now – though he did fall off a donkey in his youth. It is only over the years he has come to appreciate what he now calls "those gorgeous creatures". But he's no "horsey".

His first visit to a racecourse was to Newmarket's July Course as a nineteen-year-old in July 1963. He was with his wife-to-be Pat. They arrived by train, having been told by his father that they would be able to walk from station platform to racecourse. Unfortunately his father's visits had been to the Rowley Mile and being summer that day's racing was at the July Course, much further away. Until a journalist took pity on them and picked them up they were blissfully unaware. Their arrival was consequently delayed and they missed the first race. However, by races four and six on the card Stan was enjoying the adrenalin rush of backing winners and the bug of "being there" was beginning to bite. He was becoming a "fan".

Forty-four years later he has still got the bug and accepts that his enthusiasm has progressed him from fan into fully-fledged "addict". This is demonstrated by the statistics of his racecourse attendance, which also mark him down as a borderline "anorak". He keeps a meticulous list of all the racecourses he visits and their frequency. He maintains the ongoing total in his pocket diary, marks each new visit during the season and then transfers the details into next year's new diary.

At the time of writing, the diary states his total number of visits (United Kingdom and overseas) now numbers six hundred and sixty-seven. In the sixties and seventies, when his bank balance was more red than black and young children needed to be fed and watered, his visits were infrequent. Sometimes just four or five a year. Nowadays, as he nears retirement he is a far more regular racegoer. In 2006 his total was fifty. He aims for an average of forty visits in a normal season but by today, 4th August he has already chalked up forty-two visits during 2007.

The current standings are:

250 – Newmarket
64 – Huntingdon
62 – Yarmouth
29 – Goodwood
25 – Sandown
18 – Ascot
16 – Fakenham
14 – Bath, Lingfield and Epsom
11 – Kempton
9 – Newbury

8 – Windsor

7 – Brighton and Cheltenham

5 – Doncaster, Market Rasen, Salisbury, York, Folkestone and Fontwell

4 – Chepstow, Plumpton, Leicester and Towcester

3 – Perth, Ripon, Taunton, Thirsk, Uttoxeter and Wincanton

2 – Bangor-on-Dee, Hamilton, Hereford, Hexham, Musselburgh, Newcastle, Nottingham, Newton Abbott, Pontefract, Southwell, Stratford, Warwick, Wetherby, Beverley and Wolverhampton

1 – Aintree, Ayr, Carlisle, Cartmel, Catterick, Chester, Exeter, Haydock, Kelso, Ludlow, Redcar, Sedgefield and Worcester

In total he has visited all fifty-nine courses in Great Britain as well as courses in Australia, France, Kenya and South Africa. So no one could ever accuse Singleton of being an armchair critic. Along with the diaries his enthusiasm for "being there" is confirmed by two other sets of mementoes. On a hook on the bookshelf in the lounge ("along with the scissors that I use to trim my beard") there are membership badges accumulated down the years.

He has also kept his race cards from 1963 through to the early 1990s, when the price rose and he decided that the *Racing Post* provided more detailed information at a cheaper price.

Of the mass of statistics, the most pertinent is the number of visits to Newmarket. Although he likes Sandown and Ludlow ("a lovely place as well as a lovely racecourse") his primary affection is for the July Course and he breaks away from his analysis to explain why. "It's the olde worlde charm," he says. "The ambience, the people, the time of year that they race there, the friendliness, the excellent viewing and the position of the big screen."

He also explains that it holds happy memories from a brief but memorable involvement on the periphery of racehorse ownership in 1988. The tale begins with four of Singleton's friends, three women and a man, all with November birthdays. The prosperous partner of one of the women bought them a horse, which they named, appropriately, *Four Legged Friend*. They went as a group to study her progress in training at the stables and on the gallops and Singleton and his wife tagged along. They were there for the anticlimactic debut at Warwick where the filly refused to enter the stalls, failing to go under starter's orders, and when, second time out at Ripon, she came a more promising second.

Third time out she won at Goodwood and as a result was entered for a prestigious listed race at Newmarket, The Fairview New Homes Chesterfield Stakes. Even now Singleton has the discoloured one-shilling race card. It shows that the race was for two-year-olds, over a distance of five furlongs with prize money of £6,129 to the winner. It also shows that number one on the race card was a horse called *Superpower* with form of "1111111". Singleton's biro has marked that she was a 4-11 on favourite. *Four Legged Friend* was a comparative outsider at 14-1. The friends placed around £100 on its head, more in hope than expectation, Singleton's optimism amounting to £15.

"*Superpower* made all," he recalls, "and a furlong out looked as though he was running away with it – but jockey Ray Cochrane gave *Four Legged Friend* a backhander and she flew up the hill, leaving *Superpower* for dead. I remember screaming at the top of my voice. Along with Ipswich Town winning the FA Cup they are the two best days of my sporting life."

Little wonder, then, that the July Course has become a favourite. Indeed, Singleton says that his idea of racing heaven is "Here on a sunny Saturday when the place is not full and I'm here with my wife or friends, I've had a couple of winners and I can't go home out of pocket and I know that on the way home we're going to a pub and have a bloody good meal and three or four pints."

As if to celebrate the notable milestone of his two hundred and fiftieth visit conditions match his idea of racing heaven. By midday the thermometer is touching twenty-eight degrees Celsius, with an unbroken Mediterranean deep blue vista and a strong, warm breeze that provides relief from the humidity.

In these conditions the July Course looks particularly majestic. The newly cut lawns appear crisper and greener, the thoroughbreds even more athletic and aristocratic than normal and crowds can revel in the Pimm's and panama ambience of a blissful afternoon. This is also a day that flushes out the other main category of racegoer (other than the "enthusiast") defined by Kate Fox. They are "the socials", who primarily attend race meetings to establish and reinforce social relationships.

Normally "socials" make up around a third of racegoers, but that quota increases during the flat racing season, specifically at Royal Ascot, Glorious Goodwood and midsummer meetings on the July Course. "Socials", according to Fox's book, can be further broken down into:

Suits – usually found in private boxes, suites and hospitality enjoying corporate entertainment.

Pair-bonders – couples who use racegoing as part of their courtship.

Family day-outers – who enjoy the ice cream and chips as much as the racing.

Lads and Girls day outers – groups of similarly aged males and females who may, for instance, be attending hen and stag parties and

Be-seens – racegoers who take great care in their appearance and parade around in fashion finery.

Today is a perfect occasion for the "be-seens". They are here in numbers, a convention of human peacocks. The summer weather seems to have enticed the whole of East Anglia's young and female fraternity to doll up in their fashion finery. Vivid pinks, yellows and blues are on display; long legs and ample cleavage too, a point not lost on Singleton, whose admiration of fillies extends further than just the equine species. He remarks that at the previous meeting, a young lady had been walking down the steps of Stravinsky's Cafe and a breeze of similar strength to today had blown her dress above her hips, revealing shapely legs and pale blue knickers. He appears not unduly distressed by the memory.

However, like other "addicts", he's not always as forgiving of the "socials" and those who are less committed and knowledgeable than himself. "I know now that I'm a racing snob," he says. "Trevor and I say that there should be a rule in racing, that if you weren't here last week you shouldn't be here today. Go home. Go away."

Certainly he is happiest at lower-key dates in the racing calendar when crowds are smaller and the race card is tailored towards the connoisseurs. Although he is one of Newmarket's most reliable customers he usually gives the Guineas weekend a miss – and although he attends the Derby each year ("a pissy old day") you sense that the classics are not ringed in red on his racing calendar. He can take or leave them.

Certainly the yob element that he says can frequent racecourses bring out the "grumpy old man" in his character. "The coaches arrive, the lads get out of the bus: short-sleeved shirt, outside of the trousers," he gripes. "You know them a mile off. And they know it don't they? They give it large from the back of the stands and they think they're so f'ing funny – but they're not. They're so boring."

At 2.10pm Singleton folds up his *Racing Post* with a sense of finality. He has completed his initial research and is now armed with a well-thought-out plan of attack on the bookmakers, though it is subject to last-minute changes and flights of fancy. Viewing of the thoroughbreds in the parade ring, for example, can influence his thinking – and he moves there with Harold to watch the runners circling before the first, 2.25pm, race.

He explains: "It's quite handy to give them the once over in the parade ring before a race. Very often I won't have quite made up my mind until I go to the paddock. If there's a lot of form there's no problem. I'll probably have made my mind up early – but going to the paddock reinforces my thoughts. Y'know, 'He looks all right, he's walking well, got a nice shine on his coat' … And I'll also watch them in their slower paces going to post. In fact, thinking about it, this latter point can be quite influential. I don't think I'm a good gambler but I do like to think I have an eye for a horse."

In the first race his initial instincts to back a horse called *Cedar Mountain* do not change on viewing. The horse has, according to Singleton, "fewer question marks than the others", has "come back in distance" and is from the stable of John Gosden, whom he rates. Once he has left the parade ring, Singleton window-shops the rows of bookmakers, trying to pick out the best price. *Cedar Mountain* is generally available at 9-2 – but he spots that he has drifted out to 11-2 with bookmaker Paul Kay and, in the blink of an eye, places a £10 bet. Then it is back to his favoured viewing position and Harold to watch the drama unfold.

Alas there is little drama. *Cedar Mountain* is never in contention. One race complete, £10 down. Bookmakers ahead. Singleton accepts this minor loss without apparent distress and consoles himself with a crab sandwich from the seafood vendor in the concourse.

In the time up to, during and after the first race Singleton has followed the time-honoured racing cycle beloved by many racing enthusiasts. It is a cycle that he repeats through the afternoon. It begins in either the pre-parade ring or parade ring as he peruses the runners. Then, once the horses have been mounted and begin to canter down to the stalls, he places his bet with the bookmaker offering the best prices. There is a thrill in getting the best possible price, and beating the odds of the Tote is always something to which Singleton aspires. Then, of course, he watches the race unfold, usually from the same vantage point. After the race, any winnings are collected and it is time for brief refreshment and the odd conversation with associates before the cycle begins again.

For race two his eye is on a black, four-year-old colt, *Final Verse*, sixth in last year's 2000 Guineas. He gets warm in the paddock (as many do on such a scorching day) and drifts out to 4-1, then 9-2 in the betting. Singleton says that often the odds drift out then begin to shorten. The ideal time to back is just before the wholesale shortening. So when he sees William Hill shorten *Final Verse*'s odds back to 4-1 he is off again, virtually sprinting to the Ladbrokes stand to capture the available 9-2 and place another £10 bet.

This time his investment is sound. The pink and emerald colours of *Final Verse* cruise up on the outside and from a furlong out Singleton is confident. He watches him chalk up a comfortable victory and £55 in winnings. Within those few seconds it is clear to see why he goes racing time and time again. Singleton explains: "It's an adrenalin buzz when they are racing into that final furlong and you see you've got a chance. You begin to shout and you begin to have a yell. If I can see I'm going to win easily I don't shout but if your horse and another are neck and neck in the final furlong then you do give it a bit. There's no way the jockey's going to hear you because you are one voice in two hundred or three hundred who have backed one of the horses. But you've paid the admission money to have a yell really … it's a great stress reliever. I'm always looking to the next time I'm going racing."

Two races gone. Outlay: £20. Returns: £55. Profit: £35.

Those winnings supplement Singleton's "punting fund" – currently amounting to £300 – which he keeps in a bundle of tens and twenties in his pocket and which covers his gambling. Admission fees and refreshments are funded separately. The punting fund was created six years ago at a time when he used to travel to work by train. The trains were often late and he received some hefty compensation which allowed him to create a fund – and it has rarely needed to be topped up since. He says, "I reckon in forty years I've lost no more than a couple of grand in total. For entertainment that is amazingly cheap."

Singleton bets on most races when he's at the course, in amounts of ten, fifteen or twenty pounds. Normally he bets win only, though for longer priced shots (14-1, 16-1 and upwards) he may opt for an each-way bet. Typically he gambles around £110 at each race meeting and whether he is winning or losing he does not deviate from his game plan. He is the most disciplined of his friends; a dispassionate, considered and structured gambler who resists emotions or whims. He plays the averages. Nor does he gamble away from racecourses, on television racing or other sports.

He confirms: "In the last couple of years I reckon on losing very little betting on course. I put that down to never being greedy – I'm very happy to go home with the same amount of fund with which I set out. Don't chase your losses. And I have come to believe that I can pick a few winners and when you are in the midst of a barren run keep the faith – don't desert the thoughts that have brought you a winner or two only two weeks earlier."

Between races two and three he buys a chocolate bar and with Harold watches the Nassau Stakes from Goodwood on the big screen. Thereafter the two friends split for a while. Harold is presumed to have found an old friend or the bar, or possibly both.

The Goodwood race means that Singleton does not have time for a parade ring review before the 3.35pm race, which is the feature on the Newmarket card. Not that it matters. He is already quite taken with *Fidelias Dance*, trained by the in-form Mark Johnston. The filly is at decent odds too: 12-1. Singleton places £15 on the nose and moves to his normal vantage point, in the shadow of the main stand on a grassy incline that provides a raised position, a good view of the big screen, the last furlong of racetrack and protection from the mid-afternoon heat.

There are two other horses in similar colours – yellow and black – and Singleton takes care to log the differences in his mind. He says he dreads shouting home a perceived winner that does not turn out to be his horse. Alas, that is not a problem today. *Fidelias Dance* is only fleetingly involved in the run-in.

Three races. Outlay: £35. Return: £55. Profit: £20.

It is noticeable, though, that Singleton treats winners and losers with a remarkably even temper. No anguished swearing, gnashing of teeth or ripped-up betting slips tossed angrily into the air. That's probably a symptom of maturity and forty-four years of race-going, but it also supports his view that his gambling is a way of enhancing his enjoyment of the day rather than a dangerous addiction. If he has an addiction at all it is to race-going rather than gambling.

In race four, he backs *Sense of Joy*, another from the stable of John Gosden, this time ridden by Richard Hughes. Singleton likes Hughes and says that when choosing a horse he will "take the jockey into account although I am not so put off by an apprentice or inexperienced jockey as some of my racing colleagues". That said, Singleton does have a healthy regard for the top riders. His favourite was Joe Mercer and he pinpoints Lester Piggott as the jockey most likely to turn narrow defeat into a narrow victory.

"Piggott is without doubt the best jockey I've ever seen," he says. "No question of that. He was extremely dedicated at having winners – as AP (McCoy) is today in National Hunt – and he'd have no compunction in jocking one of his mates off a horse if he thought the thing could win. He was the best – he had strength, a sense of timing, rhythm, and the ability to get horses to run for him. He did things to a horse that you wouldn't be allowed to do today in racing culture when you're only allowed so many smacks with a whip. I've seen Piggott hit a horse five times in the last stride – when you think about how quick you've got to be do that – and he'd get it up by a short head. Amazing."

Although Singleton likes the connections of *Sense of Joy*, he puts on only £6 to win at 6-1. His only post-race frustration is that he did not trust his instincts more. Even the race commentator is predicting *Sense of Joy*'s victory two furlongs from home. This is a seriously impressive performance and, if need be, she could have won by a bigger distance. More profit for Singleton.

Four races. Outlay: £41. Return: £87. Profit: £46.

He has clearly got some skill when it comes to picking horses, so what is the Singleton strategy? He says his main focus is always on the formbook: "Form can cover so many aspects and the individual's own interpretation of what he/she reads. Sometimes the form is so rock-solid that you simply cannot escape a particular horse's chance in the race, but that's when you end up with a heavily odds-on favourite.

"When you have a race where the betting starts at 4-1 perhaps you will have many horses in the race with a chance. For me, I then usually follow 'hunches' – that is, a feel for a particular horse based on a number of things. Certainly its previous performances are important. I like to back a horse coming from a stable with good recent form, say, four or five winners in the last ten to fourteen days. However, these days horses can come out with a win after a long lay-off. And there are some trainers that are very adept at that. In the old days if an animal hadn't run for say nine months you could pretty well dispense with it in your considerations."

For the fifth race Singleton is undecided. He likes *Big Noise*, a colt, with Richard Hughes onboard again. But he receives inside information from a friend at the course that the Dettori-ridden *Classira* is likely to run well. During the afternoon Singleton bumps into around ten other "enthusiasts" that he has grown to know. Some are old friends, some are newer acquaintances; most have an opinion on upcoming races and are happy to share their insight.

In view of the tip-off Singleton opts for a small £2 (total outlay: £4) reverse forecast, which means that as long as *Big Noise* and *Classira* finish one-two, regardless of the order, he will win. If one finishes in the first two, but not the other then the money is lost. *Big Noise*, Singleton's first choice, finishes first and he cheers the colt home. *Classira*, however, fails to get in the frame. So much for the tip-off. It has caused money to be lost.

Five races. Outlay: £47. Return: £87. Profit: £40.

Singleton has no strong opinion on the likely winner of race six and is inclined not to bet at all. But buoyed by £40 profit on the day, he places a £6 win stake on a horse called *Crossbow Creek*. His thinking is influenced less by the qualities and form of the horse, more by the fortunes of his rider, Frankie Dettori. Dettori has ridden the favourite in the first, second, third, fourth and fifth races this afternoon.

However, any prospect of a repeat of Ascot and those seven winners in one afternoon was soon nipped in the bud and he has suffered a quite miserable afternoon. The only time he has made it into the top three was with the third-placed 6-4 shot, *Count Trevisio*, in the 3pm race. So Singleton – who says that he will occasionally deviate from his game plan and follow whims – backs Dettori and *Crossbow Creek* on the basis of the law of averages. He thinks Dettori must win soon.

Alas, he doesn't. He finishes all but last. And, in the last race of the day, Singleton's pick, *Abounding*, comes in third – not enough to provide any reward for a £10 bet to win.

So, in the final reckoning his total outlay has been a conservative £63 and his winnings £87, a £24 profit that can supplement his punting fund. And with that he leaves Newmarket, cash in hand. He might have been to Newmarket two hundred and fifty times but you know with an enthusiast like Singleton that it will not be his last. He summarises the day: "A pleasant afternoon at a racecourse that I really like. I spent it in the company of friends, sharing banter and information. Best of all I ended up coming out slightly on top which means, as far as I'm concerned, that next time I go for nothing."

FIFTEEN

THE SHERGAR CUP

"ALL YOU THINK ABOUT IN A RACE IS WHAT'S GOING WELL, ARE YOU IN THE RIGHT PLACE, ARE THEY GOING TOO QUICK, ARE THEY GOING TOO SLOW? YOU ARE CONSTANTLY THINKING – 'SHALL I GO, SHALL I WAIT? SHALL I SWITCH HIM BEHIND HIM 'COS HE'S GOING BETTER?' SO MANY THINGS TO THINK ABOUT, EXCEPT YOU'RE NOT REALLY AWARE OF THINKING AT ALL. YOU'RE JUDGING WHAT OTHERS ARE DOING. YOU CAN BE TOLD HOW TO RIDE A RACE BUT SOMETIMES YOU JUST CAN'T DO IT AND YOU HAVE TO ADAPT…"

Wednesday 8th August, 2007. Summertime. For the likes of Hayley Turner, who rode one hundred and twenty-six times on all-weather surfaces in the first two months of the year, the 2007 flat racing season has been ongoing for more than seven months – and August is peak season, the busiest time of the year. With the long days there are both afternoon and evening meetings and Turner, chasing rides and winners, may take in two in a day. When she does, she returns to her Newmarket base late and can be up at 5am the next morning to ride "work".

It's an undeniable challenge to body and mind and only grafters last the distance. But Turner, typically, takes a balanced, pragmatic view. If she's on a treadmill it's a treadmill that she enjoys. Even though she's ridden for nearly eight years she's still endearingly wide-eyed and pleased that racing is her profession.

"The first thing I do when I wake up is think where am I going today and what am I riding?" she explains. "It's nice. I like that I'm not in a routine. I go to different places every day. A lot of people get bored with their job and I don't think I ever would. It's such a good job. You have the travelling but I never wake up bored and thinking 'What am I going to do my life?' I'm always quite happy.

"It's nice when you have winners but when you look at the papers and you've got a load of horses with little chance it takes some motivating to get going. Still, at the end of the day, it's not all year round. We get a holiday. It's a lot easier in the winter on the all-weather and peak season you've just got to get your head down and get on with it. It's the same with everyone. Everyone works hard. Jamie

Spencer rides a lot of work in the morning as well, y'know. Everyone has to ride out and graft. This time of year it's really hard but as I say, there is light at the end of the tunnel. The evening meetings will stop soon so that will help. Everyone is tired but it's August. If you're not busy in August then you need to start worrying."

Statistics illustrate the full extent of this feat of endurance. So far this year Turner has ridden four hundred and nine times on thirty-three different racetracks. The majority of those rides have been on the all-weather: seventy-six at Southwell, sixty at Lingfield and Wolverhampton and thirty-five at Kempton. Of the turf venues, she's most frequently ridden at Yarmouth and Bath (twenty-three) and Nottingham and Windsor (fourteen).

These are generally regarded as modest, bread-and-butter racetracks and she's generally ridden modest, bread-and-butter racehorses in front of comparatively small crowds. She's been less visible at the A-list venues and at none of them has she chalked up a winner. However, so far in 2007 Turner has twenty-six wins to her credit, only ten fewer than in the whole of 2006 and has re-set her personal target at forty.

So far in the jockeys' championship (contested between 31st March and 10th November) two hundred and nineteen jockeys have won one race or more. Of those Turner sits in forty-seventh place with a strike rate that averages around one win in seventeen rides. In comparison the main contestants for the title, Jamie Spencer and Seb Sanders, win around one in five rides. They have both just passed one hundred winners and are tireless in their search for more.

The sporting media tends to shine its light most readily on moments of controversy, skill and drama. That's what creates headlines. As a result what can get overlooked is the perseverance, graft and consistency of combatants like Spencer and Sanders. Inside the various sports, however, it rarely goes unnoticed. Dedication to duty and commitment to cause are what gives sport its nobility of spirit every bit as much as flashes of inspiration.

Like Spencer and Sanders, Turner has long since earned the respect of her colleagues in the weighing room. They know she's a grafter, can race-ride, has "bottle" – and, as a result, is the outstanding female jockey in Britain by a country mile. Of course there are also material benefits that accompany this achievement. She earns a prosperous living, receiving £125.74 a ride as well as a proportion of prize money; is about to move into a new property in Newmarket and at twenty-four has her prime years ahead of her. Most jockeys peak in their thirties. Whether she can break into the top echelon of race-riders remains to be seen. It is certainly the next hurdle to be cleared and something to which she aspires.

Today, though, she's limited to riding a series of long shots beside the seaside at

Can't win them all. Hayley Turner returns to the weighing room.

Hayley Turner The Jockey

Yarmouth. She notches two second places, but fails to add to her tally of winners. Despite this 8th August proves to be a good day, potentially a very good one, as she is put on tentative standby for the prestigious Shergar Cup which features some of the most outstanding jockeys from around the world and will be contested at Ascot in three days' time.

One of her season's ambitions is to repeat what she dubbed "the highlight of her career so far" when she represented the England and Ireland team that contested the cup against the Rest of the World in 2006. Turner acquitted herself with distinction and was only beaten in the last race by a short head. She is understandably keen to have the opportunity to compete again.

Thursday 9th August.
An even better day than Wednesday. At precisely 11.25am the call is received. It's confirmed that Seb Sanders, who was due to be riding in the Great Britain team, has been suspended for a riding offence and will not be able to take part at Ascot. Turner is formally invited to take his place.

During the afternoon she rides five more unsuccessful long shots at Brighton but her mood is upbeat. Last year's Shergar Cup was fun and she knows that the event will be high profile with terrestrial television and national newspaper coverage in front of a large crowd at an elite racecourse. A great way to raise her profile and showcase her talents to watching owners and trainers.

Saturday 11th August.
The alarm goes off at 5am. Today there is excitement in the air and Turner is immediately alert. However, she never struggles to get out of bed and, at least on race days, never wakes up to a hangover. This is because she is disciplined enough to make sure that she's fiddle fit.

She says, "I just can't go out and get drunk and ride the next day". She notes, though, that others are less inhibited. "Some people can't control themselves in Newmarket. It's the nightlife. There's so many racing people, it's easy for a lot of young lads and apprentices – and this is where a lot of them go wrong – to go out Thursday, Friday, Saturday, Sunday. There are always friends out and you'll always have a good time. But that's where you have to be disciplined and just let your mates go out… Besides it's such a small town and there's so much gossip that you know that if you were out and drunk, it would get back to the trainer."

Turner recognises that this frugal lifestyle is one of the sacrifices she chooses to make. Another is holidays. Every year the whole Turner family goes to Center Parcs for four days. Hayley also attends but has to leave each morning, ride and then travel back.

She takes few days off because she's concerned at turning away rides. She says that trainers get annoyed if you miss a day and if someone takes her place and rides well then she may not get the ride again. That said she recognises that switching happens anyway: "Racing can be very up and down.

You can win on a horse and next time they'll put someone else on it. And it can get you down very easily but you have to just keep positive and let it go over your head. 'Cos that happens to everyone. Even the best jockeys get switched."

This morning Turner drives from her Newmarket home, with her dogs in the back, stopping at the local petrol station, as she does every morning, to pick up a copy of the *Racing Post*. Today there are several pages promoting the build-up to the Shergar Cup. By 5.30am she has arrived at the Newmarket stables of trainer John Ryan where she "works" a colt called *Baytown Blaze*.

Nowadays Turner often visits a trainer's yard specifically to work a horse that she will race-ride in the future. It's helpful preparation. She undertakes this groundwork on the heath amongst the trainer's stable lads and lasses and work riders. Turner is different. "I've always been ambitious," she says. "I wouldn't be happy just riding out each day. I'd get so fidgety." Like many others, though, she does recognise the appeal of the dawn gallops: "It's so unique; when you're riding out in the morning you look around and how many places in the world are like Newmarket? I like the sense of history."

Having finished with *Baytown Blaze*, she takes an opportunity to take her dogs for a walk on the heath. Sometimes she sprints up Warren Hill with them, building up her stamina and fitness. But in midsummer, by which time she's become entirely race fit, there's little time, energy or need for additional exercise.

She then works a two-year-old for Michael Bell, for whom she often rides out on a Wednesday and Saturday. By 11am, showered and changed, Turner has been driven to Frankie Dettori's house in Stetchworth three miles out of Newmarket and together they fly to Ascot in the Dettori helicopter. Turner gets on well with Dettori, admires his talent, verve and achievements, and is grateful for the travel assistance.

Several of the top jockeys hire or own helicopters and Turner also gets lifts from Daryll Holland and Jamie Spencer. But more often she travels by car.

Sometimes she drives herself but because Newmarket is the home for so many jockeys they often travel together. So costs and cars are shared and Hayley can sit in the back seat and relax. Sometimes that involves catching up with her sleep but more often she is on the mobile.

She admits, "My phone bill is terrible. I'm always ringing my sisters, Connie and Gemma. They get so annoyed with me. They say 'What do you want?' and I say 'I'm just ringing for a chat'. We talk about rubbish and have a laugh." Turner is also often in touch with her agent who arranges her rides for her and keeps the peace with trainers.

No matter how she tries to make good use of the time, travelling remains one of the bugbears of a jockey's existence. It's also one of the reasons why they enjoy a changing-room kinship more usually found in teams.

The second reason is the sheer peril that

Hayley Turner The Jockey

accompanies the profession. Every time Turner gets on board a thoroughbred, danger and risk rides with her. So far, though, so good. "Touch wood," she says, "I've been so lucky. I've fallen off a lot but never had a serious injury. I've always landed well when I've fallen." But she knows the law of averages is against her: "I know at some stage in my career I'll get an injury. If you fall off in a flat race the impact is so much greater than

Hayley Turner in action.

jump racing because you're going so much quicker. But overall jump racing is even more dangerous – they're so brave."

The third reason becomes visibly apparent after the helicopter lands as Turner and Dettori enter the weighing room and set eyes on the snacks and energy drinks that are laid on at Ascot to allow jockeys to cope with the worst of hunger pangs between races.

Turner says racecourses vary in the culinary delights on offer, some of which are

not recommended for "wasting" jockeys. "It's hard because of the hours we work," she says. "You pick all day at the racecourse. Matt, who does the food at Newmarket and Ascot has crabsticks and prawns, but at the all-weather racing there's chips and stuff."

It is about now – 11.10am – that Turner has her first food of the day. She recognises that nutritionists may not recommend skipping breakfast but says that she just doesn't feel hungry in the mornings. She's fortunate. Most jockeys have to maintain an unnatural and unhealthy weight and an athlete's fitness and strength on a minimal diet. Their career hangs in the balance every time they register on the weighing room scales. Owners and trainers soon jettison jockeys who carry excess pounds. So, put simply, most have to starve.

Fortunately, for Turner, it is not the need to "waste" that dictates her refuelling patterns. She does not live in a dietary straightjacket and can eat take-aways if she feels the urge. "I'm lucky," she says again. "The lads get there early to sit in the sauna which must drain them a little bit. I'm naturally about eight stones, so usually I don't have to worry about my weight. I eat what I want really. It's such a big advantage compared to the lads who don't eat and then get in the sauna. They say that girls aren't as strong as blokes – but once they've sat in the sauna and not eaten you've equalled it out."

She laughs, "Besides, after that first experience in the sauna I've never been in there since. Never will, ever again. The lads still laugh about it. If I have a light ride I'll be careful what I eat the day before. But I won't starve myself."

It is now 1pm – Turner is in the female changing room at Ascot (virtually all racecourses in Great Britain have separate facilities for women riders) donning her red Great Britain waterproof before undertaking some promotional work with the other jockeys, signing autographs and chatting with spectators. At first her family – particularly her sisters – found this "celebrity" amusing but she is unfazed by the attention. Nor is she unnerved by the planet's top jockeys. Not by one of the most famous men in Japan, Yutaka Take. Not by the Australia legend, Darren Beadman. Not even by her travelling companion, the most famous face in horseracing, Frankie Dettori. There's no sense of awe here. Why would there be when she considers herself the equal of most?

"I'm not Frankie Dettori or Kieren Fallon," she admits. "But I think I'm as good as anyone barring a few of the best. Without blowing my own trumpet, a lot of people would say that you wouldn't be able to pick me out in a finish among the lads. It's making sure you're in the right position in the race at the right time, and getting a tune out of the horse. It's not all about strength. It's the horses who are the athletes. They're doing the running. We're just on top, guiding them."

Once the promotional work is complete Turner dons red and white silks for the first race on the card.

Hayley Turner The Jockey

The 2007 Shergar Cup will be contested by four teams (Great Britain, Ireland, Europe and the Rest of the World), each with three riders. There will be six races, with ten horses due to run in each race. Two jockeys sit out each race. Horses have been allocated to jockeys by ballot. Points will be awarded to the top five finishing jockeys in each race and these contribute to the overall team prize and the Silver Saddle, which is the jockeys' prize.

Turner's first ride is a strapping two-year-old, *Relative Order*, who has never won, is 33-1 in the betting and the outsider of a field of ten. It is her least promising ride of the day and appears to give her little chance of breaking her Ascot duck. However, a glimmer of hope appears as the pace quickens. *Relative Order*, drawn on the outside, has stayed in the pack and, as others fall back, is staying on. "About two furlongs out I knew I had a chance," Turner says later. "She was one of the first ones off the bridle and she was hanging into them – but she stayed on quite well at the end."

Despite hanging to the left, horse and rider are still in with a chance coming into the final stages. She says, "I get excited in the last furlong. You're concentrating on basically anything you can do to get the horse going forward as best you can. Good jockeys need the strength to hold a horse back or drive him forward, as well as experience, a split-second sense of timing and of course a high standard of horsemanship, to win races. I certainly enjoy it more if my horse has got a chance."

Not only does *Relative Order* have a chance but Turner drives her through a powerful final furlong challenge to secure her maiden Ascot victory. In addition the horse smashes the course record for a two-year-old over seven furlongs. The prize money of £17,000 dwarfs previous wins – and it's been achieved in front of a television audience of millions and an Ascot crowd of more than twenty-seven thousand. Publicity like this can't be bought and it represents the pinnacle of her career so far.

It had been a cause of regret to her that so far her career tally of winners didn't contain a real headline maker. She has already committed in her mind that when the "big winner" comes along then the appropriate photo will have prominence on the wall in her Newmarket flat. Perhaps *Relative Order*'s win will not quite fit the bill because of the modest quality of the race, but the long-term significance for her profile is undoubted.

Dettori is first to ride up and congratulate Turner. "We were flying down and he noticed that I hadn't had any winners at Ascot," she says, "so he came and gave me a pat on the back which was nice." Behind the dark goggles that jockeys wear during races it's hard to pick up on any emotion but, ultimately, the reason that jockeys cope with the demands of their profession is for that indescribable thrill of booting home a winner. It's no different to the footballer scoring a goal and certainly it's a thrill that Turner never tires of. She says, "It's great – it just makes your day so much better if you have a winner. Anything bad just goes away. It's the best thing about racing. You never get bored with winning."

Cameras follow her as she enters the parade ring, dismounts, and is interviewed live by Clare Balding. In winning she has collected fifteen points for both the Great Britain team and herself and it settles her for the rest of the meeting. "After that I relaxed into it," she says later. "Once I had a winner I didn't feel like I had to prove anything."

Thirty minutes later she has an excellent opportunity to extend her lead in the silver saddle. She is riding *Dark Missile*, the joint favourite, in a six-furlong race.

And, after cruising through the first half of the contest and looking good to secure an Ascot double, Turner becomes engaged in an on-the-line battle against Jimmy Fortune.

Turner needs to employ all the attributes of a race-rider that she had previously outlined: "It's not just strength, you've got to be good at talking to the owners, you've got to connect with your horse and be in the right place at the right time, keep your balance and you've got to be strong in the finish. I think I'm just as strong as the lads. You've got to be ruthless and courageous; you've got to be sharp."

Sometimes it's just not enough and Turner is just pipped on the line. For *Relative Order*'s shock win the horse had the bottom weight. *Dark Missile* carries more pounds and this proves crucial. She reflects: "The filly had quite a lot of weight. It was close but I think she got beaten by a better handicapped horse, which was a shame."

Nevertheless ten more points retains Turner's lead in the Silver Saddle, three points ahead of Fortune. It does not last long. The lead is swallowed up in the third race. Turner rides a long shot called *Everymanforhimself* who finishes last. Turner and Fortune share the lead on twenty-five points at the halfway mark.

The fourth race is better. Turner rides *Colloquial*, an 8-1 shot, in a manner that gives her quiet professional satisfaction. "Ran really well. Everything went to plan," she says later. *Colloquial*'s yellow blinkers are prominent through the first mile and a half of the two-mile race, settling comfortably on the bridle in third place, poised to attack. As the field takes the uphill climb to begin Ascot's home straight Turner's brain is focused. Her thinking is cool, clear and bright, displaying a tactical nous that has always been part of the make-up of top jockeys. They all think well.

Later, she explained her thought process: "All you think about in a race is what's going well, are you in the right place, are they going too quick, are they going too slow? You are constantly thinking – 'Shall I go, shall I wait? Shall I switch him behind him cos he's going better?' So many things to think about, except you're not really aware of thinking at all. You're judging what others are doing. You can be told how to ride a race but sometimes you just can't do it and you have to adapt to the circumstances."

Hayley Turner The Jockey

With three furlongs to go the pace increases. Turner, pushing her mount forward with every ounce of vigour, briefly hits the front but is challenged by Frankie Dettori before Yutaka Take drives his mount, *Leg Spinner*, from last to first in a furlong to snatch the race. Turner finishes third after an energy-sapping three and a half minutes. She has ridden the perfect tactical race, free from pilot-error, but has been beaten by the better horse.

Nevertheless she has established her abilities with a new trainer, Henry Candy. She talks to him in the parade ring after the race, explaining what happened, building the relationship and trust. She says, "I had media training. From the moment you walk out of the car to the weighing room, you're constantly seeing owners and trainers and you need to say hello and bye – and put you in their minds for the next ride. It's important to be able to communicate with them after a race, talk them through what's happened; what your horse needs – whether it's a longer trip, dropping back, softer ground or riding differently."

The seven points that Turner gains for third place takes her points tally to thirty-two and she leads the fight for the Silver Saddle. If she wins the fifth race she takes the title. Her father comes down from the family box to offers some encouragement: "C'mon, you need to get close and get some points in this."

This is typical of her family. They have been strongly supportive through her career and most have managed to attend in the flesh today despite Hayley's last-minute call-up. Her sisters were unable to get out of their obligations but her mother managed to postpone her scheduled riding lessons. Many of those customers have been sending congratulatory texts through the afternoon. Clearly they've spent their unexpectedly free time watching the Shergar Cup unfold on BBC television.

Hayley's mother, father and grandmother have each compiled scrapbooks to chronicle her achievements, of which the grandmother's are the most organised and up-to-date. She pastes in each new press cutting immediately, details each new ride in a notebook and texts the rest of the family when her granddaughter posts a win. "Nana" is arguably her biggest armchair fan and, like the rest, emotionally "rides" every race with her.

In addition her father has created a DVD collection that features all Hayley's televised races. He always attends if his daughter rides at Nottingham. If the venue is her native Southwell then mother and nana are bound to be there, often armed with sustenance. Turner laughs, "When Southwell racing is on Nana comes all the time and often brings me shepherd's pie or cottage pie, plum pie and a flask of hot soup."

Turner's mother also likes to cook but time is limited as she spends so much time looking after a family of animals. At the last count there were ducks, goats, sheep, horses, dogs, cats, chickens and a budgie. Once Noah and his Ark turn up then she'll be ready to set sail – though the fact that her home is in Southwell, deep in the Midlands, may limit their adventures.

Back at Ascot the whole family would like nothing better than for young Hayley to win the fifth race but her mount, *Bandama*, becomes boxed in during the run-in, never threatens and finishes out of the points. Nevertheless she retains her seven-point lead going into the last – though the rules dictate that it is one that she has to miss. She later says, "It was a shame I had to sit out the last race and I wasn't hopeful at that stage because there were a few who could could have beaten me on points."

However, between the fifth and sixth races she gets the benefit of some free publicity. The British Broadcasting Corporation are not supposed to "advertise" but for twelve minutes the rules seem to be breached, and she is the chief beneficiary as Clare Balding and Willie Carson discuss the merits of women jockeys, and, specifically, a certain Hayley Turner.

Turner laughed later: "I must have got more publicity than Dubai Duty Free (the sponsors)! It was really good for me to have so much publicity, especially from the BBC and it's helped a lot. Something like that really does help my career."

During the discussion Carson says, "Most of the owners and trainers don't think girls are as a good as boys when it comes to the strength needed to win races... But she is the best girl we have in this country. She's as good as most jockeys in this country but she's a one-off. She rides well."

They analyse her style, watching video footage, commenting that "she gets back and behind the horse" and "you can't tell that she's a girl looking at that". They also explain that she rides the American way, knees bent, balanced on the balls of her feet. As this style becomes more fashionable they feel that women jockeys may emulate their counterparts in America and become more successful.

Carson, a sixteen-time classic winner, sums up: "Today, she's shown that's she's a good jockey. But it doesn't tell me that all the girls riding out at home are good jockeys. But she's good. She'll be riding group one races before long and one day there will be a girl champion jockey in this country. But not in the near future."

With that they interview Turner, now showered after completing her rides for the day. She's asked if there are some horses that she is less equipped to ride than males. The subtle implication is that a woman's skills may be suited to certain horses but when it comes to the heavily physical side of race-riding – controlling a headstrong juvenile or a stick-up, head-down, arms pumping, full-on run into the line – then this may be work better suited for men.

Her answer is emphatic: "I think I could ride any horse around any course. Girls get on better in the US because it's more about timing and balance and that's why they get more opportunities. But give me a backward three-year-old colt at Epsom and I'll ride him just like anyone else."

Later she develops the theme away from the cameras: "The hardest part of getting on as a jockey is getting on the horses with the ability. For the Shergar Cup, our horses are picked out of a hat for us, which meant I got on some of those better horses, and I think I proved I can ride them. Half the reason that girls don't get on in Britain is because they don't get the opportunities, so it was nice to get the opportunity to come here today. Give me the right horses and I can ride them.

"Anyway, it's not actually riding the horse that's the hard part. That's the easy bit, just riding round the track. It's finding the owners and trainers with the courage to put a girl on a horse. People can be prejudiced here. Some owners won't put girls up on horses; some people wouldn't back a horse with a girl riding. I do my best whatever. I don't feel that I have to work harder or do better than the others because I'm a girl. Maybe at the start but not now.

"I'm on twenty-eight winners now and I had thirty-six last year so I'm well on target for beating last year. I want to get to forty really. I'm not going to be ridiculous, and so, realistically, I'm not going to be champion jockey but I'll have forty, fifty winners a year and plenty of rides. I'm also not expecting to be on the favourite for the next classic, but I would like a few chances in the slightly better races, the listed and group events, which hopefully will happen in time.

"Realistically I'd like to be the female jockey that's broken a few barriers; someone for younger girls to look up to you and say 'it can be done'."

She certainly will have some new admirers after her performance at Ascot. Hugh Bowman pips her to the Silver Saddle (and secures the team prize for the Rest of the World) by winning the last race. However, in many ways Turner has achieved all that she could have wanted: a first win on the course and free, prime-time publicity.

She seeks out her family, accepts their congratulations and has a couple of celebratory glasses. Soon, though, she's on her way back to Newmarket, this time by car with Jason Weaver and his wife. These return journeys, with the day's work complete, are often filled with laughter. And when you've had a good day the laughs are longer and the clock hands move more quickly. Tomorrow Turner is back on the "modest, bread-and-butter" treadmill. She smiles: "Back to reality."

SIXTEEN

THE POST MAN

"On certain occasions you'll go and watch a horse work
– maybe an unknown – and they're sat on the bridle
and you're thinking 'aye, aye, here we go'."

I ARRIVED FOR THE first meeting with Tony Elves precisely one minute before the agreed time. The front door was opened by one of his teenage daughters who clearly suspected a double-glazing salesman. I smiled. "Hi, I'm John Carter, here to see Tony Elves." She looked none the wiser but his response from halfway up the stairs was more animated: "Oh shit ... Bollocks ... Bollocks."

Elves, draped in only a small towel, was about to enter the bath. He explained that he had been fishing all day, was back late and had forgotten my visit. He desperately needed a bath, he said, as he was "a bit fishy". I sat in the lounge with two of his daughters and watched Neighbours *for the first time in ten years. They texted friends continuously. Presumably something like "we r hvn dble glzn". Upstairs I could hear Tony splashing around and rock music pumping at high volume. Occasionally he sang a few words.*

It was a memorable if inauspicious start. However, I grew to appreciate that his minor oversight was not due to any lack of respect. He just fills up each day so full of activity that there is bound to be the odd spillage.

Tony is a sociable, open and generous northerner; with a vim and vigour that belies his birth certificate, honest to the point of blunt and free of airs and graces. So he tells it exactly as he sees it, in words spoken with an accent undiluted by twenty years down south. He also knows horseracing inside out and what I liked best about him was that every time he shared a tip with me it romped home to victory...

Saturday 22nd September, 5.50am, Ashley, near Newmarket.

Tony Elves was in bed and asleep by ten o'clock last night. Eight hours is ample for a man with unusual reserves of energy and he's as "fresh as paint" and wide awake ten minutes before his 6am alarm call.

Half an hour later he has washed, dressed and undertaken the three-mile journey from his home in the village of Ashley to Newmarket's dawn gallops to begin his working day. For him, it's a well-used road, one he's travelled for nigh on twenty years since he first moved to the town, though in the first few months there he couldn't drive and so pedalled around by bicycle.

During those two decades – a twenty-three month intermission apart – he has been Newmarket Correspondent, firstly for the *Sporting Life* and more recently for the *Racing Post*.

And "work-watching" at gallops most mornings helps him to undertake a skilled and varied role that needs a bottomless knowledge of horses, horseracing and the town itself.

Today provides a good example of what's required. He will watch the gallops for a couple of hours before returning home to produce around six hundred words of copy on what he has seen and heard. He will also provide tips for races at Plumpton and Hamilton. Then, this afternoon, he will travel to the Rowley Mile to produce an analysis of a six-race card (around two hundred words a race) and a five hundred word report containing quotes from winning trainers supplemented by his own informed opinion. In all, he will work a twelve-hour, two thousand word shift – just like he did the day before.

And, of course, if anything likely to "hold the front page" should bubble up in the town then Elves will be expected to get the inside track on the story. So his presence here on the heath this morning is critical to help him research and evaluate horses, and keep his journalistic ear to the ground by speaking to trainers, stable lads and other "connections".

Indeed this need to keep his ear to the ground explains why he chose to live in Ashley when he first moved to East Anglia. It was, he says, "Because the pub, The Old Plough, was the place where all the jockeys and trainers used to eat and drink. So I thought, well, I might as well be there and then I'm within walking distance of a pub where I'll be socialising and finding out bits and pieces."

Elves is adept at the acquisition of "bits and pieces" and he loves talking about horseracing. Indeed that's what gets him out of bed for the early morning shift, along with the fresh air (like many racing folk Elves has that hale and hearty ruddiness to his complexion that suggests frequent exposure to the elements) and the opportunity to watch top-quality thoroughbreds being put through their paces.

He elaborates: "It's a way of life really. Sometimes you wish you were an accountant getting a hell of a lot more money – but then the bonuses are that I'm healthy and I get to see the best racehorses in the world at the best venues. You get nice perks like going to Dubai and you get to meet a lot of nice people... Racing has got us by the balls. We're so infected by it we can't let go. I suppose it's fortunate and unfortunate."

So imagine his distress when he suffered that "twenty-three month intermission". It occurred when the *Racing Post* took over the *Sporting Life*, and became the only daily newspaper devoted to horseracing. Elves was made redundant, a memory that still jars. "That was a bad time. I was struggling to survive. Eighteen months before the closure I split up with my wife, so I'd started getting over that and then the mat's been pulled out from under me again. I had three kids and my greatest fear was that I would lose them. During that time I applied for well over one hundred and fifty jobs: *FHM*, music magazines,

Tony Elves interviews Frankie Dettori.

football magazines. I also applied for a job at Middlesbrough Football Club as their press officer because I wouldn't have minded going back up north. But most of them didn't even reply, even though I was a journalist and had plenty of experience."

But in May 2000, Tom Goff, who had been the *Racing Post* incumbent, left to become a bloodstock agent, and Elves was offered the equivalent of the job he had undertaken at *Sporting Life*. Since then, he's been back on the gallops most mornings, come rain or shine; low in profile, binoculars in hand; watching the horses, chatting to their connections.

This morning, as usual, he is with his regular companions, David Milnes (who works for *Racing Post*'s sister publication, the *Weekender*) and Jean Bucknell. "I couldn't do the job I do without my good friend and colleague David," says Elves. "He's got a great eye for a horse. He also covers me when I go racing at all the major meetings like Goodwood, Ascot, Chester and York or when I go on holiday."

This morning they stand under grey, leaden skies. It's still, mild and misty so that the equine athletes ghost into view, growing more vivid in colour as they ease past, before turning milky pale again as they move off into the middle distance.

The ongoing transition from late summer to autumn is evident in the heavy dew but although Elves wears waterproof boots he has no need, as yet, of thermal underwear, heavy duty clothing and woolly hats. They'll come out of the winter wardrobe when the frosts arrive and East Anglian winds blow across the heath, making his fingers so numb with cold that it will be difficult to grip his binoculars or pen hieroglyphics into his notebook. The compensation, though, is that by then the yearlings will have been introduced onto the gallops, bringing fresh viewing to excite the eyes.

Not that Elves ever struggles to find a horse to follow. They're every-where. Nowadays the town contains more than three thousand thoroughbreds (just after the Second World War there were less than a thousand) and there are fifty-seven miles of training grounds. So he has to be selective, clever and canny, so that he's on the right gallop at the right time to cast his educated eye over the strings he most wants to see. It is a skill that comes with experience and contacts. This morning, for instance, he begins at the Al Bahathri Polytrack where he watches the strings of John Gosden, Jeremy Noseda, Ed Vaughan and Henry Cecil. Then he moves to the Limekilns gallops to watch his prime target, *Authorized*.

The colt usually works on Tuesdays and Fridays. However, yesterday he had just a couple of canters and overnight rain suggested to Elves that trainer Peter Chapple-Hyam would probably utilise the turf at the Limekilns rather than the all-weather track. His prediction – typically – is accurate and so he is in prime position to assess the Derby winner's exertions and then obtain quotes from Chapple-Hyam.

Their conversation is relaxed and the pair have a rapport that Elves tries to replicate with all the Newmarket trainers. However, it can be tough. Down the years, some trainers have distrusted "work-watchers" and been economical with their information. Whilst Elves, a miner's son from the north, bridles against what he considers the elitism of some of the rich and powerful within the town – those rich and powerful, of course, include some trainers in their number. Racing might have him "by the balls" but he is not awestruck by Newmarket's four hundred years of history and its status as racing HQ.

"There are a lot of characters in Newmar-ket," he says, "and you can have a lot of fun, but it's a strange sort of town. I'm from the north – Sunderland – and people in the north are a lot warmer. In Newmarket there's a bit of a them and us mentality as well.

"I've been here for twenty years and been invited for drinks by three or four trainers out of fifty odd because I'm not part of the upper class or a public schoolboy. There's a lot of wealthy people in town and there's a lot of people with nothing and I think in an industry where there's so much money it could be shared out a bit better. There's a lot of backstabbing within the town, between those people who have a certain amount of power. It's a bit false. The people in the north of England are certainly more genuine."

This morning, though, in addition to Chapple-Hyam, he will have amiable chats with several trainers including his personal favourite, Henry Cecil. Elves says, "Henry Cecil I adore. Since I've been in the town he's done nothing but help me. Luca Cumani, John Gosden, Jeremy Noseda. All the same. I've been around quite a long time now so that they trust me a lot more than they did."

And that trust can translate into helpful snippets of information. Of course, as he explains, you have to pick your moments: "You've got to think from someone's body language, is this a good time to approach them? One Monday I wanted to talk to Sir Michael Stoute about a news story and the people around him told me it wasn't the right time. But I said, 'Well, I really need to speak to him about something' and I interrupted. Well, who was standing five yards away from him but a little old lady in a mac. It was the Queen and I didn't even look at her. I was looking at Stoutey over there and wanted to speak to him and then I copped the Queen and said 'Oh sorry' and thought I'd better leave it for now."

Elves's admiration for Stoute is immense, though tinged with regret. "I think Sir Michael Stoute is an absolute genius. He's great with

his staff. But he's not particularly good with journalists – he doesn't like us knowing too much about his horses. I've got a lot of respect for him, but every journalist in the country would like to have a better relationship with him."

Talking of high achievers, Elves is pleased to see the good form of *Authorized* as he goes through his paces this morning. Later he will write for the *Racing Post* under the headline "*Authorized* takes Limekilns gallop in his stride" that:

"*Authorized* continued his preparation towards the Prix de l'Arc de Triomphe at Longchamp on October 7 in a work-out on the Limekilns round gallop yesterday.

"The Vodafone Derby Winner, a best priced 13-8 shot with Betfred for Longchamp, has been building up steadily on the Al Bahathri Polytrack in Newmarket and the millimetre of rain allowed trainer Peter Chapple-Hyam to get him back on the grass."

Elves will go on to explain that he had "no problems with conditions", that he "looked full of running" and was watched by both his trainer and the racing manager of his owners. He ends the two-hundred-word article with quotes from the work-rider ("He was pulling out my arms at the end") and Chapple-Hyam ("I'm delighted with that").

Elves remembers when he first saw the horse in action: "Frankie Dettori was riding him on the Racecourse side and he came up the gallops and I thought 'Aye, aye. Here

225

Tony Elves's "beat". The gallops at dawn.

we go. Pay day!'. But that happens, if you're lucky, half a dozen times a season. I said to my colleague David Milnes, 'Wherever he runs that will win'. I happened to be on holiday in Miami when he ran in a group one race. I've got more balls than David and I stick my neck out. He tends to play a bit safer. So I backed him, he won at 25-1 and it paid for my holiday."

That's the way of "work-watching". Often it's mundane then, just occasionally, it happens: that wonderful moment when a horse is spotted with the x-factor. Elves explains, eyes sparkling: "I'm looking for a sign of class. It might be the way that they move, the way they hold themselves together. A lot of it on the gallops is like a sixth sense. On certain occasions you'll go and watch a horse work – maybe an unknown – and they're sat on the bridle and you're thinking 'Aye, aye, here we go.'" He rubs his hands as though counting money.

When that "sixth sense" leads to successful tipping of a long shot then Elves enjoys a sense of achievement. "Being right in your judgement – even now that's what gives me the satisfaction. If you see a horse and form an opinion of that horse and your opinion is right then it gives you a buzz. I have to give my opinion in the papers every day…"

The reason he rubs his hands when describing that x-factor moment is that, as with *Authorized*, he usually puts his own money where his words have gone. "As a tipster it's my duty," he says. "If I'm telling people to back horses I think I should be backing them myself."

Of course, there are many factors that contribute to that judgement: the going, the length of the race, the form, the draw, the trainer and the jockey. All have a weighting that Elves computes in his head. The going, for instance, is influential, as is the choice of jockey if one of the legends is on board.

Elves explains, "I think Kieren Fallon's an incredible jockey. I hope to God we don't lose him 'cos I think he's fantastic. Frankie obviously. It's hard to split them. If Frankie gets hold of one – Jesus! They'll be the main ones. And there'll never be another like Piggott. With the likes of Piggott, Dettori, Fallon, and Pat Eddery – they won races they shouldn't have won. Now a lot of the time it's down to the horse, the best horse wins. But on certain occasions the jockey will make that much difference and that's what Lester had."

Generally, though, he says that tipping is formulaic. "A lot of times it's bread and butter," he advises. "You study the formbook. It's like Sir Michael Stoute has said: 'You get more from the formbook than you do from the gallops.' But the thing with Newmarket is that you've got the formbook, you've got what you see on the gallops with your own eyes and you've got your contacts. Some are worth their weight in gold; some will have you in the poorhouse. I'd rather rely on my own judgement and be judged on that."

This ability as a tipster becomes more apparent once he has left the gallops – having stayed for two hours and watched the "first lot", visited the local supermarket and returned home to enjoy a breakfast of toast, fruit and black coffee. His tiny, box office – filled with form books, a desk and the all-important laptop – contains photographs illustrating two occasions when he "stuck it up the bookmakers".

The first one features a horse called *Commander in Chief* which did not run as a two-year-old then won the 1993 Epsom Derby at odds of 15-2. Elves says, "That's my first claim to fame because at the time *Tenby* was odds on to win the Derby and I tipped *Commander in Chief* to win and he won. I've got a photo that was signed 'To the man who tipped him from the man who rode him – Mick Kinane'. That was one of my ante-post coups. I put £100 on it at 20-1."

Thirteen years later his support for *George Washington* was more profitable still. At different times during the preceding year Elves had backed the horse to win the 2006 running of the 2000 Guineas. He made bets at 50-1, 33-1 and 25-1. By race day George Washington was 6-4 favourite and he waltzed home in fine style.

Elves recalls: "We had some fun – in that example it was inside information. I backed it a year in advance. The intention was to lay some of it off and then I thought 'Bollocks, stick with it'. As they say, I've got balls of steel. Afterwards we had a massive party with a house full of people and I took the girls to Capri and Miami with the winnings."

"We had a massive party" is a phrase that ends many of his anecdotes with the regularity that children's stories conclude with "and they lived happily ever after". And when Elves describes it as a "party" then rest assured that it would have been a corker. It becomes increasingly apparent that despite the fact that he is grey-haired and fifty years of age he has the enthusiasm, energy and sheer joie de vivre of a teenager. He is never happier than when merrymaking and it motivates some of his gambles. He smiles. "With the lifestyle I've got, I've got to win. I like going out. I like travelling. I go out most nights during the week. I love a party. Restaurants, dancing, partying: it all has to be funded!"

Yet despite the occasional life-changing pay-day Elves is keen to state that not every gamble yields an income and that he is by no means addicted. He says, "I've always had a passion for gambling, though I'm not compulsive. In fact I don't bet that much now. I put more on and bet less."

It is all about knowing horses and horseracing, playing the averages and recognising and seizing the opportunities when they arise; skills he had to learn the hard way. Like many others Elves served a long apprenticeship that enabled him to perform his role for the *Racing Post*, both as tipster and scribe.

Of course, it helps if racing is in the blood and he was born one hundred and fifty yards from a grandmother who encouraged the young boy to go to the local bookmakers and place bets on her behalf. Elves remembers that the tannoy system in the bookmakers blared out distorted commentary from racetracks around the country. In addition his father, a miner, took him to Redcar racecourse to watch the Vaux Gold Tankard, which for a while was one of the most valuable handicap races in Europe. And he remembers watching the Derby on black and white television at the age of fourteen.

He was a bright lad who gained nine O levels and three A levels and decided to go to York University, a choice that reflected his growing enthusiasm for the sport as there are thirteen racecourses in the county of Yorkshire. It was at university that the enthusiasm snowballed into a passion. He took – and passed – a degree in social sciences but was just as interested in his role as chairman of the University "Turf Club".

He shared this role with Dominic Burke, now something big in the business world of insurance brokers and a lifelong friend. Together they organised visits to racecourses and dinners with guest speakers. Elves decided that he would like to pursue a career in the sport despite advice that said "Don't waste your time; in horseracing it's who you know, not what you know."

His interest, though, was fuelled by a brief flirtation with racehorse ownership. He recalls, "*Celtic Breeze* was the first and last horse I ever owned. Six of us left university and vowed we'd buy a horse and so there was this field full of horses and there was this thing in the corner, caked in shit, and the seller said to us 'There's your horse'." Nevertheless *Celtic Breeze* gave him one of his best sporting moments when it won a novice hurdle at Ayr by twenty lengths.

After university, Elves's first job was at *Timeform*, which produces a daily race card providing detailed runner-by-runner analysis of every race at every meeting and rates the chances of each horse according to its own ratings. It was interesting, educational work but there were downsides: the university graduate had to relocate from the family home to a tiny flat in Halifax and start his career earning £2,800 per annum, which even in 1979 was a meagre amount.

Nevertheless he stayed at *Timeform* for three and a half years, building up knowledge and gaining friends such as the now Channel Four commentator, Jim McGrath against whom he regularly played squash. Socially, too, it was fun. He recalls, "We used to have a good time at a place called Maggie McFly's. They used to have a happy hour and a half so I used to drag everybody from the editorial department to Maggie McFly's and then onto other places and get everyone in trouble."

But from a career perspective Elves eventually grew frustrated. He wanted to write, not undertake statistical analysis, and moved to the *Racing Calendar*, based in Wellingborough. It brought him nearer London and introduced him to Elaine, who worked in horse insurance and was to become his wife. Yet, professionally, he grew frustrated once again. Nine-to-fivers in the office had little interest in racing. There was no spark and before long itchy feet walked to the *Sporting Life*, which had been the principal daily racing newspaper since 1859.

"The editor at the time was one of the brightest guys I've worked with, Neil Cook," he says. "He was a young lad but very, very sharp and he produced a good product. At the time he employed me, Mike Cattermole and Simon Holt who both work for Channel Four. We've remained friends throughout."

Elves commuted into the *Sporting Life* offices in Holborn from Wellingborough working double shifts on Sundays, Mondays and Tuesdays, leading up to a weekly publication on a Wednesday. The rest of the week he was racing; building contacts, acquiring knowledge, as well as undertaking some casual work for the *Guardian*. And his industrious nature paid dividends when he was offered promotion to become Newmarket correspondent.

By now he was married to Elaine, the first full day of matrimony spent at Cheltenham – standing together next to footballer Emlyn Hughes – watching *Dawn Run* win the 1986 Gold Cup amidst the most emotional scenes that Elves has ever seen at a racecourse. He and Elaine produced a daughter and another was on the way. Once a house in nearby Ashley was secured, the whole family relocated – and Elves has lived there ever since.

You suspect the family home has been a lively location, full of activity, both work and social in nature. Elves has written thousands of words from his office at the front of the house (he only goes to the *Racing Post* headquarters in London if his computer or car needs to be repaired), there have been the numerous parties, filled with music and laughter – and maybe the odd moment of discord. Several years ago Elves parted company with his wife, and – admirably – he has brought up three daughters himself, all of whom are now in their teens.

The noise of his daughters moving around the house forms a domestic background this Saturday morning as Elves focuses on writing his copy. In addition to the *Authorized* story, he sends another four hundred words from the gallops headed "Kotsi shows up well in her workout with Dettori". He features information on all the strings that he witnessed. He also sends in his tips for tomorrow – and by ten minutes past midday he is finished. He then sends it through the wires, showers and changes clothes. He is off to Newmarket's Rowley Mile for the afternoon shift.

At 1pm Elves enters the press box, now wearing a blue pin-striped suit, white shirt and light blue floral tie. He carries a leather holdall containing his tools of the trade: a laptop, mobile, notebook and numerous pens.

The Rowley Mile press box is based in the Millennium Grandstand in an elevated position. At one end large picture windows offer an unbroken view of the racetrack. Inside there are around fifty workstations. Most have plaques that indicate who should sit where. These range from national dailies such as the *Daily Telegraph*, *Daily Mail* and *Independent* to the *Newmarket Journal* and the

Cambridge Evening News. The *Racing Post*, being the only dedicated racing newspaper, has five privileged positions, next to the door, allowing easy access to view the action.

In addition to the journalists there are also workstations for photographers and radio – and on Guineas weekend, for instance, they will all be taken and the rooms will be packed. Today, though, there are only fifteen others. These include Jonathan Powell from the *Mail on Sunday* and Sue Montgomery from the *Independent* who are here to provide "colour" pieces on Lester Piggott because today's meeting is being held in his honour. Certainly the bread-and-butter quality of the racing itself would not normally warrant their attendance.

In the room there are six televisions, with muted sound. One shows action from Rugby's World Cup, another from the women's football World Cup. However, as time passes most channels become tuned to racing; three on Newmarket (one with a video so that the race can be watched, re-run and watched again), others on the action from Ayr and Haydock.

Elves greets his colleagues, sits down, sets up his computer and rings the office to ensure that this morning's copy has been safely received. The work of a journalist has been simplified by email. In the olden days copy had to be dictated down a telephone line. Nowadays, Newmarket, like most racecourses, has wi-fi, which aids easy online working. Only the smaller provincial tracks like Fakenham, Leicester, Yarmouth and Huntingdon are yet to house this technology.

Computer operational, Elves collects a plate of lasagne (provided at no cost by the racecourse), a bottle of spring water and eats lunch chatting with his old friend Mike Cattermole. Cattermole is one who enjoys Elves's respect but, overall, Elves is, shall we say, sparing in his praise for others in the horseracing media.

Who does he respect amongst journalists? "Amongst journalists? That's a difficult one. God! Do I have to answer that one (laughing)? I suppose there are certain people I respect. People like Mike Cattermole and Simon Holt, Alastair Down, Jim McGrath, David Yates – people like that I've got time for. But I think a lot of them have an easy job. Ideally I'd like fifty grand a year working on a tabloid and writing six paragraphs a day. Money for old rope that. I'm not a workaholic but I don't mind hard work…

"Some of them don't know tuppence. One thing that does particularly gall me about these people is that they're out there offering their advice to people – back this horse, back that horse, but they may only have put £5 on themselves. They're on fat salaries telling some guy who might be putting on £200 thinking he knows, sort of thing. They don't know what it's like to hurt when you lose."

Would other journalists respect him? "Don't know. Don't give a toss to be honest."

He is even less enamoured with those who work in television: "I've done a bit of TV work but it's not for me. It doesn't really appeal. To be honest most of them just massage their egos."

Despite Elves's reservations there is a convivial atmosphere within the pressroom. Most of the attendees are die-hards and as with the jockeys and the stable lads there is a tangible kinship. Throughout the afternoon they help each other, and interpretations of the ebb and flow of the races are a result of collective analysis. In the first race, for instance, a jockey drops his whip and hinders his mount's chances. One of the journalists spots this – and could have kept it to himself – but it is useful information for everyone and is shared.

Although there are quiet periods they are spiced by quick-witted banter with just a tinge of sarcasm and cynicism. However, fascination with horseracing – indeed all sports action – seems genuine enough. It seems to have them all "by the balls".

By 2.10pm the pressroom is further depleted. Photographers have gone onto the course, journalists such as Powell and Montgomery have moved outside in search of the flavour of the day and Cattermole, who is performing on-course commentary, has assumed his position at the microphone.

Elves, though, stays rooted to his seat as the horses enter the stalls for the first race. His eyes are on the TV, pen poised. Throughout the afternoon he never goes outside to watch a race "live". As the stalls open he is stern and focused, entering a bubble of professional concentration that he does not leave until he has completed the analysis and report of the race. During this period his normal ebullience is suppressed. As a result he explains, "I like to go racing socially when I've got a day off just so that I can find the time to talk to people. When I'm working people know I've got analysis to do, reports to write. It's like anyone – if you're in your office then it's time to work. The racecourse is my office."

Throughout the race he makes hasty notes ("held-up", "stand-side") on the racecard printed in the *Racing Post*. Then once the race finishes he rushes down to the winners' enclosure, notebook and pen in hand. He is there when the day's first winner returns to glean a few words from the successful trainer, Luca Cumani. That done he rushes back up the escalators and stairs at speed to write up the race, beginning with the "analysis".

"There was barely a millimetre of rain," he writes, "and the ground was riding as forecast. The race may not have amounted to much but it provided CANDY MOUNTAIN with a valuable first success that will enhance claims when she goes to the paddock. She was always travelling smoothly off the pace and was brought with a well-timed challenge to lead over a furlong out and held on well under a rhythmical drive from her young apprentice."

He continues with an overview of the fortunes of the horses placed in second, third, fourth and fifth places. The language is littered with racing-isms – "capable of scoring", "held-up", "did little wrong" and "making his ground" – in a written shorthand that regular readers will expect and understand. Shakespeare it ain't – but the words contain informed opinion and are written at an astonishing speed with few supporting notes.

This is a task that could only be executed by those who possess a deep reservoir of racing knowledge – and there is no time for writer's block. Nor should the ability to string sentences together fluently be overlooked. "That's the part of the job that I take the most pride in," says Elves. "I always used to enjoy writing. At college I was the one writing the most letters."

As he types Elves unconsciously mouths the words to himself like a child who has just learned to read aloud and is now trying to read silently to himself. If it looks strange it is also prudent journalistic practice as it helps the writer ensure that sentences flow and are free from repetition.

Once the analysis is complete and sent to the "office" he turns to the race day report, typing:

"Luca Cumani may not have been responsible for the ballot in the European Association of Racing Schools Apprentice Handicap but he would probably have chosen Italian compatriot Concetto Santangelo for *Candy Mountain* if given the choice – and the pre-race instructions worked out to the letter.

"The 5-1 shot was held up off the pace set by *Recalcitrant* and the 20-year-old jockey, who has ridden nine winners in Italy, brought his mount through to lead over a furlong out and held on by a head.

"Cumani said: 'Two wops together – what more could you ask for? I was asked this morning if she would win and said 'I don't know but at least the jockey will understand my instructions'. He rode the filly to absolute perfection and I'm delighted she has won.'"

Once Elves has added in subsequent races the report will amount to six hundred words. This cycle will be repeated throughout the six-race card: watch the race on television, making notes as it happens; rush down and get quotes from the winning trainer, return to the press box, write "analysis" and continue to add to the report.

For a prestigious meeting at, say, Cheltenham or Aintree there may be a contingent from the *Racing Post* sharing this workload. But more often than not, Elves works solo. He can, though, always call upon the help of other journalists from other publications. And because his analysis of the third race takes longer to write (there is a big field) he asks a colleague to get the quotes from the winners' enclosure for the fourth race.

It also allows him the luxury of a last-minute decision to back the 5-2 favourite in the race. It is not his first gamble of the day. Earlier in the afternoon he had received a tip from a trusted friend for the 2.50 at Ayr. So he nipped out to place £20 each way "just for a bit of fun". It finished second and he collected £76.

Now there is a momentary panic as his

mobile refuses to locate a signal but after being loaned a line from another journalist he places £200 on the nose. He is in no mood to remain impartial as the horse, held up at the back of the field, accelerates up the rising ground to victory. Elves punches the air, whoops with delight and writes up the analysis of the fourth race with a heightened degree of enjoyment; his words interrupted by the beep, beep of regular texts from bookmakers informing him that the winners' odds for the upcoming "Cambridgeshire" (at Newmarket in two weeks' time) have plummeted.

By the end of the fifth race (at 4.30) Elves has broken the back of his work. The analyses have been sent through after each race and the overall report, largely containing quotes from winning trainers, is ready to go. His deadline on a Saturday is 5pm and so he will only add minimal information about the sixth and seventh races if requested later. He is proud that he has never missed a deadline and only

the unexpected causes anxiety; an accident to a horse or jockey, perhaps, or a steward's enquiry. These complicate life because there may be a last-minute additional story to pen.

By 6pm Elves has turned off his laptop and leaves Newmarket. He has grafted today, contributing four separate articles in addition to some tips. He is grateful that the meeting is in his hometown. Travelling to and from, say, Goodwood or Ascot, makes for a much longer shift.

So days off like tomorrow are to be savoured. He will cook a roast Sunday lunch for eight friends and family, drink red wine, socialise, and watch the big televised match between Manchester United and Chelsea. Tonight, though, he is off into Newmarket "to get hammered". Elves is a man who plays as hard as he works, living life at a speed that even the thoroughbreds that he follows would struggle to match.

SEVENTEEN

END OF TERM

I APPROACHED CHAMPIONS' DAY – Saturday 20th October 2007 – with a mixture of anticipation and sadness. A day at the races is always something to look forward to, especially one that showcases some of the most outstanding equine talent on the planet. However, the visit would also mark the end of my formal involvement with the horseracing fraternity.

Newmarket's last race meeting of the season takes place on the 3rd November, the jockeys' championship runs until 10th November and all-weather tracks mean that flat racing takes place throughout the calendar year. Nevertheless, Champions' Day is the last major meeting of the season in Britain. With seven races of unquestionable magnitude it is contested on the Rowley Mile with autumn and an end of term feel in the air. Meanwhile, during October the biggest yearling sale in Europe takes place a mile away at Tattersalls. So there is a definite sense of renewal, of one season ending, just as the purchase of fresh talent provides hopes of future glories.

I used Champions' Day to revisit a few of the locations that make Newmarket special – the dawn gallops, Tattersalls, the Museum and the Rowley Mile racecourse – and this chapter details the chronology, albeit pausing regularly and at length for a progress update on how the season panned out for the subjects featured in the previous pages.

At the start of the year most had high hopes, and that is the nature of horseracing. If you cannot be optimistic at the start then when can you be? However, reality cannot always match the expectation and during the summer most rode the rollercoaster of highs and lows that are part and parcel of the sport.

No one, for instance, could have been more filled with jubilation and relief than Frankie Dettori when he achieved his childhood ambition of winning the Derby Stakes. Conversely it is difficult to comprehend the full extent of the frustration that trainer, Jeremy Noseda, must have felt when his star three-year-old filly had to be withdrawn on the morning of the 1000 Guineas.

In each case, though, the season did not end there – and, in addition to telling the story of Champions' Day, the next few pages document what happened next; for Dettori, for Noseda and the others whose fortunes have been followed in this book.

A last visit for the season to the heart and soul of Newmarket: the gallops. It is 6.50am and first light at Warren Hill reveals autumn's first dusting of frost on the heathland. Headlights shine bright from the cars that trundle through the town and the rider-outers aboard the thoroughbreds wear day-glo jackets over their waterproofs, for warmth as well as visibility. These include Frankie Dettori, who rides out for Sir Michael

Champions' Day

Stoute on his Breeders' Cup prospect, *Jeremy*, then hurries to a television studio in the Rowley Mile's Millennium Grandstand to contribute to Channel Four's live *Morning Line* programme.

It is two degrees Celsius with a zing in the air; cold enough to tingle the ears and moisten the eyes. Horse and rider silhouettes gallop up Long Hill and when they return dragon-smoke puffs out from the flared nostrils of the thoroughbreds. Certainly observers can sense winter's imminent arrival. Not until eight o'clock does the sun peep above the top of the trees overlooking Warren Hill and illuminate the old town. By then the first lot have undertaken their "work" and long, loose-limbed legs have loped back to the stables.

As the days pass there is a noticeable wind-down of the action on the gallops. For some of the thoroughbreds the season is over. It is now, for instance, over a week since Danni Deverson and *Dutch Art* have been seen on the heathland.

It was a demanding campaign for the colt: six races, five at group one standard, contested against the highest achievers in the class of 2007. Of course the season had started in April with a warm-up race at Newbury, followed by May's 2000 Guineas where he came third, winning his race on the far side of the track, blissfully unaware that he had been pipped by *Cockney Rebel*, the winner, and *Vital Equine* on the stands side.

Dutch Art exacted revenge on *Cockney Rebel* six weeks later at Royal Ascot, but finished fourth in a tight finish on unsuitably firm ground. Similar frustration came on the next outing in the July Cup at Newmarket. Spot on for the race, the colt was not so much baulked as assaulted in the early stages. He finished torpedo-fast, sparks flying from his hooves, but second behind *Sakhee's Secret*.

August was Deauville and another second place, despite a spirited run on a firmer than ideal surface. Then at Longchamp in October the benefits of ideal ground were neutralised by a debilitating draw in the stalls. He finished sixth.

Three seconds, a third, a fourth and a sixth: outstanding consistency considering the quality of the opposition – but no visits to the winners' enclosure. Of course, Danni Deverson was "Dutchy's" companion through it all, riding him out most mornings, chaperoning him on his travels.

How did she view the season? "A little disappointing," she admits. "He's been very unlucky with the ground, though each time he ran his heart out and tried his best. It's a shame that he hasn't been able to win one this year because he should have done. Still, to be placed in so many group one races is quite an achievement."

True enough, yet it is not Dutchy's past that is on her mind at present. It is his future. He has not just finished his racing for the season. He is finished for good. Fourteen days ago Deverson "rode out" the colt for the last time and two days after that he left St Gatien Stables to make the two-mile journey to Cheveley Park Stud to take up residence as a stallion.

"I was absolutely gutted," says Deverson.

There is a zing in the air on the early morning gallops as the year draws to a close.

"Mortified. In floods of tears all day. A complete mess. I was hoping they would keep him next year, and he'd have strengthened up over the winter and would have had a good chance of picking up a couple of group one races. But they wanted to retire him to stud and start earning some money there.

"He's gone to Cheveley Park where his Dad (*Medicean*) is, and they let me take him up there. They showed me around and it's really nice. He's got a lovely big box and a lovely paddock to be turned out in. He'll have the life of Riley but it was still heartbreaking. They've said I can visit at any time, which is a relief."

Cheveley Park enlisted the services of Trevor Jones to capture the arrival of their new star stallion. As Jones snapped, Deverson snivelled and she is mildly concerned that the photos will show a tear-stained red-eyed figure in the background. Nevertheless she smiles when she says, "At least we'll be able to put up all the other photos we've got of Dutchy (the superstition which dictates that it is bad luck to hang up photos of racehorses during their racing career is not to be ignored). We're getting them framed at the moment."

Dutch Art's young life tells us much about how top-flight, big-money horseracing works. He was conceived on a stud farm; bought and sold for profit as a foal and a yearling; initiated into racing as a two-year-old; contested classics and group ones during his three-year-old prime time – and now he has been put out to stud to help begin the cycle again. His racing career was high-speed, and over in the blink of an eye – just like the races in which he competed. It spanned ten contests and two seasons (yielding nearly half a million pounds in prize money) and even though he will not become a fully developed physical specimen until the age of five, he will race no more.

Still, at least he had two full seasons of competition. Precisely one year ago a couple of peers contested an epic Dewhurst Stakes and established themselves, along with *Dutch Art*, as ante-post favourites for the 2000 Guineas. Yet neither made it to that race or any thereafter. *Holy Roman Emperor* replaced the misfiring *George Washington* at stud even before the 2007 season began – and *Teofilo*, the potential wonder horse, never recovered from the knee injury that forced his withdrawal from the Guineas. He will also stand at stud in Ireland. Even the winner of that race, *Cockney Rebel*, subsequently suffered an injury that led to his retirement and residence at the National Stud in Newmarket.

It is sad they raced so little, but thoroughbreds are deceptively fragile and, besides, that is just the way of horseracing on the flat. The wheel is always turning – and it turns at dizzying speed. As if to illustrate the point, on the very same day that Deverson said her tearful goodbyes to "Dutchy" she received better news.

In the next few weeks there will be a new addition to Peter Chapple-Hyam's line-up at St Gatien and Deverson has been assigned as rider-outer to a yearling filly who is *Dutch Art*'s half-sister. Deverson says she was "high as a kite" after her appointment and it will certainly help to fill the void left by Dutchy's departure.

The filly was acquired on the first day of Tattersalls' October yearling sales by bloodstock agent Tom Goff on behalf of a client who is establishing a new breeding operation. She cost just short of half a million guineas and the intention is that she will become a foundation mare once her racing career is over.

Goff, of course, also purchased *Dutch Art* – albeit at a fraction of the cost – and noticed similarities between the siblings. "Although she was a bay, she had the same head as *Dutch Art* and the same genuine attitude," he says. "She's very racy and not backward so hopefully she'll be a good two-year-old as well as a decent three-year-old."

9.45am – Tattersalls, Newmarket.
Goff and Blandford Bloodstock have been active and successful throughout the October Yearling sale, which, so far, has spanned nine days, spread over two weeks. Today, a four-hour morning session will complete book three, leaving one "book" to go.

Outside the sales ring the horses circle, stickers on their backsides to denote their number in the catalogue, awaiting their turn to go under the hammer. Up close the equine beauty parade is eye-pleasing and one thought is irresistible: that these are supremely noble and athletic animals. Put simply, the best thing about horseracing is the horses.

As a result you sense that some of the small crowd of around twenty who eye them up this morning may surprise themselves by parting with rather more money than they expect in the sales ring. If you love horses then Tattersalls is a seriously dangerous place to visit. Nearly one hundred million guineas have been spent here on yearlings over the past two weeks, including one purchase of two and a half million guineas.

Owner Jan Harris was not responsible for that particular purchase. However, four days ago she visited Tattersalls with her husband Colin and trainer Paul D'Arcy and made additions to her portfolio. "We went to the sales and saw two that we liked", she says. "It's quite difficult not to buy anything when you're there! You get caught up in it, caught in the moment – and we thought it worth taking a chance on a couple. They were our choices and Paul (D'Arcy) OK'd them for us."

The couple, a colt and filly, cost twenty-three thousand and sixteen thousand guineas respectively. Have they bagged a couple of bargains? "We think we paid a pretty good price," she says, "but you never know till they start running. It's too early to tell."

Both are expected to be prominent as two-year-olds, which gives the Harrises the same "buy, race and sell" option that they may follow with *Kylayne*, the filly they ran at Royal Ascot. *Kylayne* contested ten races in 2007, notching two wins and earning £14,000 in prize money. She is entered in the upcoming sales at Tattersalls and Harris explains, "If we get a price for her we sell, if not we'll take her back and resume racing." *Kylayne*'s half-sister recently sold for 45,000 guineas and a similar figure would be well received.

A tearful Danni Deverson says goodbye to *Dutch Art* as he goes to stud.

Also due to be sold – if the price is right – are two more of their fillies, both in foal. One, *Ti Adora*, is the first horse that Jan Harris ever purchased. Her departure may tug at the heartstrings.

In 2007, Harris has watched her charges competing all around the country: Ascot, Ayr, Chester, Epsom, Haydock, Kempton, Leicester, Lingfield, Newmarket, Redcar, Salisbury, Southwell, Warwick, Windsor, Wolverhampton and Yarmouth. Regardless of location the buzz of ownership remains. "All in all, I have enjoyed this year", she says. "We have been so close to having super success. It just goes to show that you can have the right horse on the right day but if you get blocked in or hampered or any of the other things that can happen during the race – you lose!"

In all she has tasted the champagne of victory in five races out of thirty, two courtesy of a horse called *Sir Duke* who will go "over the sticks" next season. Harris explains, "*Sir Duke* did not turn out to be like his dad (*Danehill*) but he can gallop for miles and miles so we will be trying him over some hurdles soon and that will be something new."

And that is one of the many attractions of racehorse ownership. There is always something to look forward to. Stan Singleton knows that feeling. He has become another moth attracted to the flame of ownership, albeit at a fraction of Jan Harris's outlay. Singleton, along with his wife, is a member of The Racegoers Club, and a couple of years ago they joined a syndicate that owned the two-year-old *Diamond Tycoon*.

The colt's activity that season was restricted to an encouraging second place on the Rowley Mile. Then, as a three-year-old, he won a mile maiden at Newbury. Singleton recalls with some relish that "Jamie Spencer pinged him from the gate and after five furlongs had the entire field rowing away in earnest. He won by a hard-held six lengths. Watching him surge clear with Spencer patting him on the neck one hundred yards from the line was so exciting. I travelled on the day with my usual colleague, Trevor, and we were both pleased with the return starting price of 8-1!

"*Diamond Tycoon* then ran in the 2000 Guineas," he continues, "but ran a lacklustre race to trail back in midfield. Very soon after it was discovered that he was suffering from chipped bones on two of his knee-joints. But we're hopeful that he will return to the racecourse for the 2008 season – and that we will again be invited to join the syndicate."

Now, though, it is time to leave the sales, before a half-involuntary twitch leads to an unexpected purchase and the necessity of a second mortgage.

1 0.25am – National Horseracing Museum, Newmarket High Street.

From Tattersalls it is no more than a five-minute stroll to the National Horseracing Museum. It just requires a walk down the hill from the Sales Ring, a left turn into The Avenue and a right turn into the high street. Past the bookmakers, the post office, and the offices of the Jockey Club – and there, opposite "thing-me-bobs", is the narrow entrance to the museum.

Champions' Day

Enter its shop and you can browse a range of products and memorabilia, including the Frankie Dettori range for men, with eau de toilette and hair gel. Stop for a coffee and snack in the café and you can enjoy the murals of Jacquie Jones, "artist in residence", that adorn the walls. All racing's main characters are featured: Frankie Dettori, Lester Piggott, John McCririck, Peter O'Sullevan and Dick Francis to name just a few.

Within the museum itself, curator Graham Snelling is working this Saturday morning. He moves around, low-key, mug of coffee in hand, overseeing operations. The main exhibition this year features seventy paintings, oil studies and sketchbooks by the equine artist, Sir Alfred Munnings. Snelling has been delighted with the public response. "It's gone tremendously well," he says. "We're twenty-eight per cent up on last year's figures and this is largely down to the exhibition. We've had people travel from America just to see it. It's been a clear winner. All in all I'd say we've had a successful season."

There is also cause for hope that the Museum will soon move into much-needed larger premises. Progress has been snail-slow but progress there has most definitely been. "We are about to make a lottery application and the feelers are going out to private donations and fund-raising for the project," Snelling says. "Nothing in concrete yet, nothing guaranteed, but looking very positive. We have had plans drawn up and allocated space and we're down to the finer details on finances."

11am, Rowley Mile, Newmarket.

A short drive and the scene changes from the Museum to the Rowley Mile racecourse. It is still three hours before the racing begins yet Lisa Hancock, managing director of Newmarket Racecourses, is on-site and on the move. She has begun her "management by walkabout", walkie-talkie in hand. Like a good party host she is ticking off a checklist in her head, making sure all is in place. She wants it to go well, perhaps even more than usual, because it is her big-race-day swansong in the public eye before she leaves to devote herself to her young family.

How does she feel? "Today it's incredible," she says. "The weather is magical and I'm just really buzzing. I was buzzing yesterday and that was a standard day. I'm really excited but I think that probably tells the story that underneath I'm thinking to myself 'This is the big one.'"

Her successor will be Stephen Wallis, who worked as managing director at Epsom Downs and was involved in fourteen runnings of the Derby. He has been learning the ropes with Hancock over the final weeks of the season.

As she approaches the finishing line after a seven-year tenure does she feel any regrets at relinquishing her prestigious post? "No. I've been so focused on today," she replies "When that's over then I'll focus on the rest of my life!"

And did the development on the July Course continue to be well received? "Yes, it has been met with unanimous approval and that is something of a miracle. It has worked extremely well."

As she walks around the racecourse grounds, currently bereft of spectators, she is bathed in warm sunlight and she should be grateful for that. It is not always so benign at this time of year. Twenty years ago, for instance, the storms of October 1987 forced the morning postponement of racing. Marquees were strewn across Newmarket Heath and the roof of the grandstand was ripped out and hung dangerously over the members' enclosure for a while.

Today, though, there is not a breath of wind and the only complication caused by the elements is the deluge that drenched the course during midweek. This is of some concern to Hancock and certainly the cause of a few headaches to her friend and colleague, Michael Prosser. There is not the slightest chance of a postponement, but the aim is always for ideal racing ground and the rain – though not unexpected – has not helped.

As Hancock moves towards the parade ring, Prosser, her clerk of the course, is at the four-furlong marker, criss-crossing down the Rowley Mile. He is walking the racetrack for the second time today and intermittently jabbing his stick into the turf to gauge its softness. Despite a series of dry days the ground has not fully recovered from the midweek dousing. Prosser's official going will be "good to soft, soft in places."

"We had a light frost on the ground this morning with temperatures dipping to one degree Celsius," he says with typical precision of phrase. "The mist cleared by 9am. The ground on the stands side is in fantastic shape. Though I say it myself I doubt you will find a better strip of racing ground anywhere in the country at this time of year."

Prosser always enjoys course walking and this clean, crisp morning is particularly invigorating. The emerald landscape stretches in all directions, the white Millennium Grandstand is on the horizon, and an unblemished blue sky above. It is a pity his mobile rings every other minute to interrupt his reverie, but that goes with the territory on big race days.

The efforts of people such as Lisa Hancock and Michael Prosser have set up an afternoon of top-quality sport. Champions' Day has six group races including two group ones, the Totesport Cesarewitch Handicap and a million pounds in prize money. It is the highest-class race day in the British flat racing calendar and boasts a real international flavour. It will be interesting to see if the foreign contingent take the spoils. Either way, though, the community at HQ has enjoyed a successful 2007, having strong connections, for instance, with four of the five classic winners.

● Newmarket-based Geoff Huffer trained the 2000 Guineas winner, *Cockney Rebel*.

● The flags were flying over Warren Place again for Henry Cecil after his rejuvenating Oaks victory with *Light Shift*.

● Newmarket-based *Authorized*, Frankie

Celebrations after the indefatigable *Soldier's Tale* wins the 2007 Golden Jubilee Stakes at Royal Ascot.

Dettori and Peter Chapple-Hyam in the Derby provided the racing story of the season.

● And John Gosden, another Newmarket trainer, enjoyed success with *Lucarno* in the St Leger.

Newmarket. Newmarket. Newmarket. Only the Irish-trained and ridden *Finsceal Beo* broke the stranglehold when winning the 1000 Guineas.

2pm – Rowley Mile.

By now all is in place. Fifteen thousand spectators are at the Rowley Mile, many more in front of their TV sets; the runners for the first race are cantering down to the starting stalls; Tony Elves sits in the press box, laptop and pen at the ready and Trevor Jones is down by the finishing line to capture the essential images.

It is time for the racing to begin and the main combatants to take centre stage, including

Jeremy Noseda and jockeys Frankie Dettori and Hayley Turner.

This afternoon Noseda's involvement is low-key and brief. He has just two runners in that first race and he oversees their preparations in the pre-parade and parade ring in what has become familiar fashion: grey-haired, blue-suited, dapper, businesslike and focused.

Neither of his runners are placed and once they have returned and the debrief with their jockeys is complete, Noseda leaves the course and makes the short journey back to his office at his Shalfleet Stables to attend to day to day business.

It is there that he keeps a handwritten list detailing what he thinks is achievable for his horses if each one stays sound and accomplishes all that it is capable of. This is the list created every March and returned to at the end of the season to reflect on how the season actually panned out. The reason no one else sees it is because Noseda recognises horseracing is a game of chance and circumstance, fate and fortune and the list might raise unrealistic expectations in others. However, when Noseda does review the list in the next few weeks you can be sure that the most glaring gap between aspiration and accomplishment will be *Sander Camillo*, the filly lovingly ridden out through the winter by Noseda's wife, Sally, in preparation for the 1000 Guineas.

Having scored impressive victories as a two-year-old, "Sander" became the race's ante-post favourite, the pin-up of the stable and Noseda's main hope for a second English classic. Yet, of course, she had to be withdrawn from the race because she was in season and suffering – and she never recovered from that false start. *Sander Camillo* ran three more times, finishing last in the latest two – and in December, she will be sold by owner Sir Robert Ogden at Tattersalls. Perhaps she will race as a four-year-old and rediscover her earlier promise. More likely she will be used as a broodmare.

Noseda confirms, "*Sander Camillo* was the disappointment of the year. Promised the world and did not deliver. She was sound and well and had the talent but things went wrong and we could never get her back on track."

Fortunately, in amongst the Sanders is the odd Soldier. *Soldier's Tale*, to be precise. Noseda admires the six-year-old's fighting spirit and grittiness. His physique may be fragile but his heart is gargantuan and he mounted a thunderous late challenge to pip *Takeover Target* on the line in the group one Golden Jubilee Stakes at Royal Ascot in June.

"This is most probably the most rewarding day I've had as a trainer," said an emotional Noseda at the time. "For a horse to come back from all his problems and win a race like this is huge and personally it is very satisfying. It is great for the horse – he deserves it." Four months on the glow remains and Noseda adds, "*Soldier's Tale* is a result that will live in my memory for a long, long time and that was great." It is clear that there is one horse that can melt the trainer's English cool.

Leaving aside the unexpected elation of *Soldier's Tale* and the equally unexpected demise of *Sander Camillo*, how would Noseda summarise his season? "More than happy," he says. "A good, solid, satisfactory season. Results were good and we had seven group wins. We just missed having a star three-year-old colt or filly to carry us through the season."

The statistics support his diagnosis. Compared with 2006 he has enjoyed more winners and a better strike rate (only Sir Michael Stoute and Saeed bin Suroor can better his proportion of wins per races) but is down on prize money, leapfrogged in the rankings of English-based trainers by John Gosden and Peter Chapple-Hyam who benefited from big pay-day, classic wins.

He knows – and the stats again underpin his view – that to make a quantum leap he needs a bigger stable. Of those above him in the rankings only Chapple-Hyam had fewer runners. He has yet to find a suitable location, which may irk this most ambitious of men. Yet, if he is frustrated he hides it well and his tones are philosophical when he says, "We'll stay the same and we'll keep laying down the foundations for the future. We learn to live with it, stay on the plan and keep making sure you put a good solid year behind you, year after year."

Either way he looks forward to 2008 with the kind of optimism that is essential for sanity retention for those who work in the industry. "Next year is going to be something we're going to find out over the first two months of the season," he says. "I'll approach it with my biggest ever team of three-year-olds and only the racetrack will reveal how good they

are. What I know is that I've got a lot of untapped talent and unraced ammunition. It's interesting and something to look forward to when you know that you've got a good team of horses that could emerge into the picture. So I'm very positive."

As he speaks there remains the possibility of "finishing the year with a bang". In two days' *Simply Perfect* and *Strike the Deal* will undertake fourteen hours of travelling from Stansted Airport to stables in America to race at the Breeders' Cup next weekend.

Once there *Strike the Deal* will be ridden by one of Noseda's preferred jockeys, Frankie Dettori. However, before then the Italian has a busy Champions' Day ahead of him with six rides. In the opening race he was unplaced but in the next two – the afternoon's two big-money feature races – he has cause for optimism. He will ride in the royal blue of trainer Saaed bin Suroor and Godolphin on fancied runners.

2.40pm, Rowley Mile, Darley Dewhurst Stakes.

Firstly, Frankie Dettori teams up with *Rio de la Plata* in the Darley Dewhurst Stakes, a contest that features many of Europe's best two-year-old colts. They come fourth, a creditable showing considering that the horse was nearly withdrawn due to the softness of the ground. The spoils, though, go to Ireland. In 2006 Irish trainer Jim Bolger's *Teofilo* beat *Holy Roman Emperor* in a closely fought finish. This year it is another Bolger horse, *New Approach*, who establishes his credentials as the next potential "wonder-horse" wit h a hard-earned victory over *Fast Company* and *Raven's Pass*.

New Approach seems to have it all: a sprinter's acceleration that will hold him in good stead come next spring's 2000 Guineas, and the kind of stamina that encourages high hopes for the Derby. However, the tale of *Teofilo* has underlined that potential is not always fulfilled. The mighty colt, named in honour of the great heavyweight Olympic gold medallist Teofilo Stevenson, also looked to have it all. Yet injury terminated his career as a three-year-old before it had begun.

Either way it is sobering to think that even if he stays fit there is every chance that *New Approach*, this autumn's two-year-old deemed most likely to succeed, might be all but retired and put to stud in twelve months' time.

3.15pm – Rowley Mile, Emirates Airline Champion Stakes.

Dettori's second opportunity to add another line to his already lengthy CV comes in the centrepiece of the afternoon. He rides *Creachadoir*, another who prefers firm ground. Nevertheless Dettori mounts a genuine threat as the field thunders into the last furlong. Alas, *Creachadoir's* suspect stamina is found out and it is Ireland's *Eagle Mountain* and the French-based *Literato* who go head to head in a thrilling finish, culminating in a short-head victory for *Literato*.

Indeed Dettori fails to notch a winner in any of his six rides on Champions' Day, so denying the crowd around the winners' enclosure the flying dismount that accompanies his group

standard successes. However, it is just one barren day in a vintage summer. This season his ratio of wins per rides (twenty-one per cent) is unmatched by any other jockey, and he has amassed over three million pounds in prize money and fifteen group wins.

These include *Ramonti's* success in the Queen Elizabeth II Stakes and Queen Anne Stakes at Royal Ascot and Sussex Stakes at Goodwood; *Lawman's* victory in the Prix du Jockey Club (French Derby) at Chantilly; and who can forget *Authorized* in the International Stakes at York and, of course, the Derby Stakes on that blistering midsummer afternoon on Epsom Downs.

The only reason that Dettori does not rank higher than ninth in the jockeys' championship is that, as at today, he has had just three hundred and sixty-seven rides compared, say, to Seb Sanders who has notched up nine hundred and eighty-four in his exhausting quest for the title. The Italian's role as Godolphin's stable jockey and his pre-eminence in the sport means that he concentrates on quality rather than quantity, on group races and the classics – and, of course, the 2007 flat racing season and the name of Frankie Dettori will be forever entwined because of his win in the season's blue riband event.

Authorized's victory filled the cavity in his career. One of the most charismatic and successful figures that the sport of horseracing has ever seen will continue to ride, simply because he still loves his job. However, now, the shadow no longer hangs over him. He has achieved all he ever wanted to achieve

The appropriately named *Last Post* is the last horse to go to post in the last race on Champions' Day as dusk begins to fall.

Champions' Day

and whenever he chooses to retire it will be with a comprehensive record of achievement. No gaps. No ifs, buts or maybes. No regrets. Frankie Dettori will always remember 2007 with pride and pleasure.

3.55pm – Rowley Mile, £2.5 million totescoop6 Cesarewitch (Heritage Handicap).

One day, perhaps, a woman will ride the winner in the Derby – and, maybe, it will be Hayley Turner. So far, though, only one woman has ever ridden in the historic race and, for now, the very fact that Turner is plying her trade here at Champions' Day on the Rowley Mile rather than the all-weather at Wolverhampton says much about her progression.

Originally she had targeted a repeat of her thirty-six winners in 2006. At the Shergar Cup she adjusted her aim to forty. Now, with forty-three already in the bag, a repeat of the fifty-three winners she achieved when she became champion apprentice in 2005 looks distinctly possible. She is currently ranked a lofty forty-second in the jockeys' championship, but statistics alone do not convey the way she has continued to advance.

In September, for instance, she enjoyed her first winner, at the thirty-ninth attempt, on the Rowley Mile. Then she took up a last-minute invitation to ride in a group two race at Ascot on a filly called *Dark Missile* (benefiting from the good impression she had created when riding her in the Shergar Cup) and was beaten only by a short head after a storming race at 25-1.

Now, in October, she has ridden in the first part of Newmarket's autumn double in the Cambridgeshire, where she rode a 33-1 outsider into fourth place in a field of thirty-four.

Today she rides in the second half of the double, in the historic Cesarewitch handicap, the fourth race on the card. These are the calibre of contests when trainers and owners only employ jockeys who enjoy their complete trust and confidence. So when a trainer of the stature of David Elsworth wants you to ride one of the more fancied runners then that alone is a feather in the cap.

The race is a unique test in modern racing. It spans two miles and two furlongs, which makes it the longest contest in the Newmarket calendar. So long that it begins in Cambridgeshire and ends in Suffolk, examining the stamina of both horse and jockey.

Turner rides her mount *Sunley Peace* in the middle of the thirty-three horse field for much of the race. When the pace begins to quicken, her mount is outpaced but under Turner's persuasion plugs on to finish a most creditable seventh. So this time there is no headline-making victory. However, you feel that one day it will come. She continues to strike blows for girl power in a male-dominated industry with ability, valour and fortitude. It might not be the Derby. It might not be the Jockeys' Championship. However, you just sense that one fine day the name of Hayley Turner will really be in lights. And you sense that, deep down, she is quietly confident too.

Today, though, the Cesarewitch winner's cheque of just shy of one hundred thousand pounds goes to Ireland and *Leg Spinner*, trained by Tony Martin and ridden by Johnny Murtagh.

The fifth race goes to Ireland, the sixth to France. So it has been an afternoon when the best of the European "raiders" have struck back. Only in the seventh and last race does Godolphin's *Greek Renaissance* achieve some consolation for Newmarket.

By the time the colt reaches the winners' enclosure and the welcoming pats of his connections, some of the crowd have already slipped away through the exits, trying to dodge the worst of the traffic. Many more are about to follow. The evening sunshine is also on its way, softening as it drops – as inexorably as the flat racing season itself – towards the horizon.

6 pm – One man who feels the imminent end of the season more acutely than most is not at Newmarket today. Currently Mark O'Reilly is just returning to the town having dropped off his two young daughters and wife at Stansted Airport. They are flying out to spend the October half-term week in Ireland with family.

The nature of his job as a stable lad at Peter Chapple-Hyam's yard means that he is generally on duty at first light, if not before. "What you've got now is the full picture," he reflects. "Last winter it was dark and gloomy. In the summer we had the highs and now we're back to the dark and gloomy. We're winding down. Horses are going to the sales. All we've got to look forward to is cold and windy and wet. But overall it's been a good season. One of the best."

O'Reilly will certainly miss the peaks and troughs of competition. As recently as a fortnight ago, for instance, he was in Longchamp to look after the promising two-year-old, *Declaration of War*. He says that the colt ran a "fantastic race, his best performance of the season" to finish second in a group one race.

Later that same afternoon it would have capped a memorable year for O'Reilly – and all at the stable of Peter Chapple-Hyam – if *Authorized* and Dettori had cleaned up on foreign soil in the Prix de l'Arc de Triomphe. Just as at Epsom in June, O'Reilly was called into duty to walk the colt around at the starting stalls. Yet there the similarities ended. As horse and rider entered the home straight Dettori again asked for that trademark injection of acceleration. This time, though, *Authorized* could not respond. There was no petrol left in the tank after a long season. He finished in the pack. It was to be the last race of a short but glittering career. Two days later he left the yard to become a stallion at stud.

Two weeks on, O'Reilly is philosophical: "It just didn't happen for *Authorized* at Longchamp," he says. "Horses get over the top, but they can't talk and tell you. That's the way it goes. In some ways it was sad to see the old boy go to stud. I've been round a lot of good horses, but he's probably one of the best I've ever been around."

After all that excitement it is little wonder

Champions' Day

that O'Reilly does not want the season to end. "At least," he says, "the boxing is always on the go and that keeps me going." He is now a divisional coach for Suffolk and having those twin sporting pursuits will help his winter speed past. It also reminds us that although flat racing is nearly at an end for 2007, sport goes on.

Today, for instance, a National Hunt race meeting at Cheltenham moves their season up a gear – and other sports are claiming the limelight. In just four hours' the England Rugby Union team will contest the World Cup Final against South Africa (they lost, valiantly). Tomorrow Lewis Hamilton will drive in the race that will decide the Formula One Drivers' Championship (he lost by a point).

Time then for the flat racing folk to slip into the shadows for the winter; to reflect, ruminate and rest awhile, then to dream and begin to prepare for next year's action. That is what keeps them all going. Memories of the past, optimism for the future. They are all hooked and mercifully soon it will be spring again in Newmarket and a new season will turn from a tasty prospect into a splendid reality.

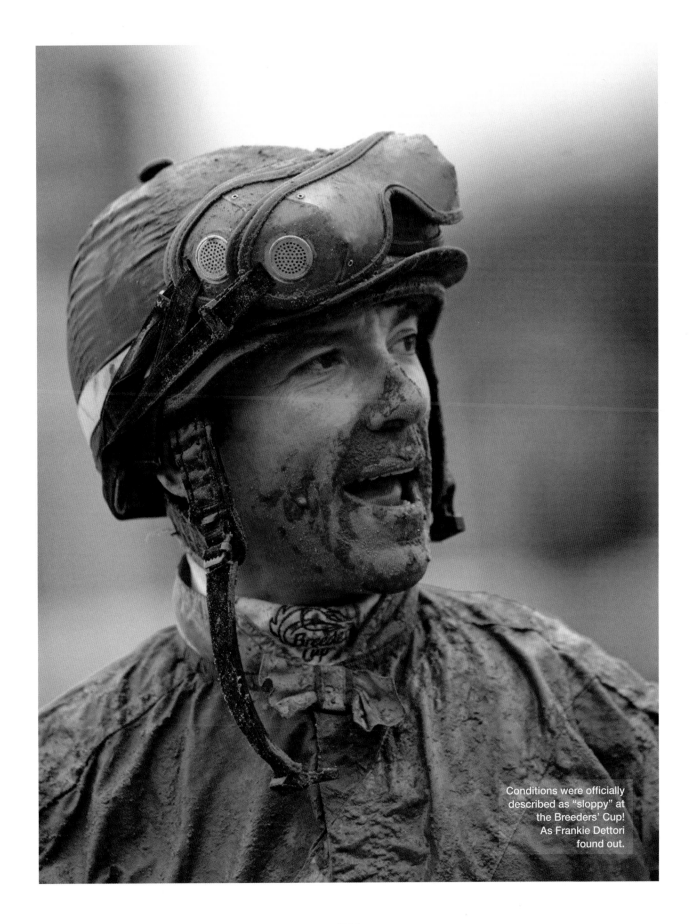

Conditions were officially described as "sloppy" at the Breeders' Cup! As Frankie Dettori found out.

BIBLIOGRAPHY

An arm and four legs – a journey into racehorse ownership – Stan Hey, Yellow Jersey Press, 1998

A concise history of British horse racing – Hilary Bracegirdle, English Life Publications – 1999. (created for the national horse racing museum)

A Sportswriters Year – Simon Barnes – William Heinemann, 1989

Classic Horse Races – Anne Holland, Macdonald and Co, 1989

Complete a-z of horseracing – Sean Magee, Channel 4 books, 2001

Frankie, the autobiography of Frankie Dettori – Collins Willow, 2004

Front Runners – Brough Scott – Victor Gollanz Ltd, 1991

Horsesweat and Tears – Simon Barnes – Heinemann Kingswood, 1988

Horse Sense – Bert Sugar with Cornell Richardson – John Wiley and Sons inc, 2003

Newmarket – From James I to the Present Day – Laura Thompson, Virgin, 2000

The Racing Tribe – watching the horsewatchers – Kate Fox – Metro Publishing, 2005,

221, Peter Scudamore's Record Season – Dudley Doust – Hodder and Stoughton, 1989

Websites

www.bbc.co.uk

www.blandfordbloodstock.com

www.britishhorse racing.com

www.nhrm.co.uk

www.newmarketracecourses.co.uk

www.jeremynoseda.co.uk

www.racingpost.co.uk

www.tattersalls.com

www.thoroughbredphoto.com

www.sportinglife.co.uk

www.wikipedia.org